My Life Today

DAILY DEVOTIONAL BOOKS
FROM THE WRITINGS OF ELLEN G. WHITE

Christ Triumphant
Conflict and Courage
The Faith I Live By
God's Amazing Grace
In Heavenly Places
Lift Him Up
Maranatha—The Lord Is Coming
My Life Today
Our High Calling
Reflecting Christ
Sons and Daughters of God
That I May Know Him
This Day With God
The Upward Look
Ye Shall Receive Power

To order, call **1-800-765-6955.**

Visit us at *www.rhpa.org* for more information on Review and Herald products.

My Life Today

*Every act of obedience to Christ, every
act of self-denial for His sake, every trial
well endured, every victory gained over
temptation, is a step in the march to
the glory of final victory.*
—Mount of Blessing, *p. 201.*

REVIEW AND HERALD® PUBLISHING ASSOCIATION
HAGERSTOWN, MD 21740

Cover design copyright © 2000 by
Review and Herald® Publishing Association
Cover designed by Madelyn Ruiz
Cover photo by PhotoDisc

ISBN 0-8280-1517-1

FOREWORD

The choice devotional readings appearing in this volume, selected to accompany an appropriate text for each day, have been drawn from the voluminous writings of Ellen G. White, who through seventy years ministered to the spiritual needs of those about her. The principles of Christian living were to her not merely the subject of writing or public address, but they were exemplified in her own life as a teen-age girl, a young woman, a mother, a helpful neighbor, a prominent figure in her community, and a world traveler. A feature of this volume that will be appreciated especially is the appearance of many select statements from Ellen White's pen which heretofore have not been available in her current published works, for the content of this book has been drawn very largely from the thousands of E. G. White articles published originally in such weekly and monthly journals as the *Youth's Instructor, Review and Herald, Signs of the Times,* et cetera, and from her manuscript files.

Because the reading of each day is limited to just one printed page, much excellent material on many of the subjects could not be included, and often omissions had to be made within a given statement. All omissions are recognized in the usual way. In some cases the reading for the day consists of several choice utterances grouped together as one composite statement. At the close of the volume the individual source credits will be found.

Some of the words of admonition contained in this little volume were addressed originally to the family as a whole, others to parents or children or youth. Many of the statements are of a more general nature. In every case the message is one that speaks clearly to the heart of the reader regardless of age, position, or vocation.

My Life Today was compiled under the direction of the Board of Trustees of the Ellen G. White Publications, who carry the responsibility of the care and publication of the E. G. White writings. The work has been done in full harmony with Mrs. White's instruction to these trustees providing for the printing of compilations from her writings.

That the brief day-by-day messages concerning your life today may serve as a guide and an encouragement on the Christian way is the sincere wish of the publishers and

THE TRUSTEES OF THE ELLEN G. WHITE PUBLICATIONS.

MONTHLY TOPICS

January
A Consecrated Life

February
A Spirit-filled Life

March
A Challenging Life

April
A Progressive Life

May
A Healthful Life

June
A Happy Life

July
A Social Life

August
A Life of Service

September
A Sanctified Life

October
A Reverent Life

November
A Victorious Life

December
An Eternal Life

A CONSECRATED LIFE

THE WAY OF RIGHTEOUSNESS IS LIFE

In the way of righteousness is life; and in the pathway thereof there is no death.

Another year now opens its fair unwritten pages before you. The recording angel stands ready to write. Your course of action will determine what shall be traced by him. You may make your future life good or evil; and this will determine for you whether the year upon which you have just entered will be to you a happy new year. It is in your power to make it such for yourself and for those around you.[1]

Let patience, long-suffering, kindness, and love become a part of your very being; then whatsoever things are pure and lovely and of good report will mature in your experience.[2]

Angels of God are waiting to show you the path of life. . . . Decide now, at the commencement of the new year, that you will choose the path of righteousness, that you will be earnest and true-hearted, and that life with you shall not prove a mistake. Go forward, guided by the heavenly angels; be courageous; be enterprising; let your light shine; and may the words of inspiration be applicable to you—"I write unto you, young men, because you are strong and have overcome the wicked one."[3]

If you have . . . given yourself to Christ, you are a member of the family of God, and everything in the Father's house is for you. All the treasures of God are open to you, both the world that now is and that which is to come. The ministry of angels, the gift of His Spirit, the labors of His servants—all are for you. The world, with everything in it, is yours so far as it can do you good. Even the enmity of the wicked will prove a blessing, by disciplining you for heaven. If "ye are Christ's" "all things are yours."[4]

I CONSECRATE MY ALL

I beseech you therefore, brethren, by the mercies of God, that ye present your bodies a living sacrifice, holy, acceptable unto God, which is your reasonable service.

God calls for whole-souled consecration to His ways. Our highest powers are to be carefully cultivated. Our talents are lent us by God for use, not to be perverted or abused. They are to be improved by use, that they may do the work of God.[5]

We are to give ourselves to the service of God, and we should seek to make the offering as nearly perfect as possible. God will not be pleased with anything less than the best we can offer. Those who love Him with all the heart will desire to give Him the best service of the life, and they will be constantly seeking to bring every power of their being into harmony with the laws that will promote their ability to do His will.[6]

Personal consecration is necessary, and we cannot have this unless heart holiness is cultivated and cherished.[7]

Let your prayer be, "Take me, O Lord, as wholly Thine. I lay all my plans at Thy feet. Use me today in Thy service. Abide with me, and let all my work be wrought in Thee." This is a daily matter.[8]

The surrender of all our powers to God greatly simplifies the problem of life. It weakens and cuts short a thousand struggles with the passions of the natural heart. Religion is as a golden cord that binds the souls of both youth and aged to Christ. Through it the willing and obedient are brought safely through dark and intricate paths to the city of God. . . .

How many times have the deep things of God been unfolded before us, and how highly should we prize these precious privileges. . . . The bright beams of Heaven's light are shining upon your pathway. . . . Receive and cherish every Heaven-sent ray, and your path will grow brighter and brighter unto the perfect day.[9]

I GIVE MY HEART

My son, give me thine heart, and let thine eyes observe my ways.

The Lord says to every one of you, "My son, give Me thine heart." He sees your disorders. He knows that your soul is diseased with sin, and He desires to say to you, "Thy sins are forgiven." The Great Physician has a remedy for every ill. He understands your case. Whatever may have been your errors, He knows how to deal with them. Will you not trust yourself to Him? [10]

The blessing of God will rest upon every soul that makes a full consecration to Him. When we seek for God with all the heart, we shall find Him. God is in earnest with us, and He wants us to make thorough work for eternity. He has poured out all heaven in one gift, and there is no reason why we should doubt His love. Look to Calvary. . . .

God asks you to give Him your heart. Your powers, your talents, your affections, should all be surrendered to Him, that He may work in you to will and to do of His good pleasure, and fit you for eternal life. [11]

When Christ dwells in the heart, the soul will be so filled with His love, with the joy of communion with Him, that it will cleave to Him; and in the contemplation of Him, self will be forgotten. Love to Christ will be the spring of action. Those who feel the constraining love of God, do not ask how little may be given to meet the requirements of God; they do not ask for the lowest standard, but aim at perfect conformity to the will of their Redeemer. With earnest desire they yield all, and manifest an interest proportionate to the value of the object which they seek. [12]

It is the submissive, teachable spirit that God wants. That which gives to prayer its excellence is the fact that it is breathed from a loving, obedient heart. [13]

ASK IN FAITH

Let him ask in faith, nothing wavering. For he that wavereth is like a wave of the sea driven with the wind and tossed.

It is our privilege, our duty, to receive light from heaven, that we may perceive the wiles of Satan, and obtain strength to resist his power. Provision has been made for us to come into close connection with Christ and to enjoy the constant protection of the angels of God. Our faith must reach within the veil, where Jesus has entered for us. We must lay hold with firmer grasp on the unfailing promises of God. We must have faith that will not be denied, faith that will take hold of the unseen, faith that is steadfast, immovable. Such faith will bring the blessing of heaven to our souls. The light of the glory of God that shines in the face of Christ may shine upon us, and be reflected upon all around, so that it can be truly said of us, "Ye are the light of the world." And it is this connection of the soul with Christ, and this alone, that can bring light to the world. Were it not for this connection, the earth would be left in utter darkness. . . . The deeper the surrounding gloom, the brighter should shine out the light of Christian faith and Christian example.

The fact that unbelief prevails, that iniquity is increasing all around us, should not cause our faith to grow dim or our courage to waver. . . . If we will but seek God with all our hearts, if we will work with that same determined zeal, and believe with that unyielding faith, the light of heaven will shine upon us, even as it shone upon the devoted Enoch.[14]

Oh that I could impress upon all the importance of exercising faith moment by moment, and hour by hour! We are to live the life of faith; for "without faith it is impossible to please God." Our spiritual strength depends upon our faith.[15]

ALL THINGS ARE POSSIBLE

All things are possible to him that believeth.

It is faith that connects us with heaven, and brings us strength for coping with the powers of darkness. In Christ, God has provided means for subduing every evil trait, and resisting every temptation, however strong.[16]

The righteous have ever obtained help from above. How often have the enemies of God united their strength and wisdom to destroy the character and influence of a few simple persons who trusted in God. But because the Lord was for them, none could prevail against them. . . . Let them be separated from their idols and from the world, and the world will not separate them from God. Christ is our present, all-sufficient Saviour. In Him all fullness dwells. It is the privilege of Christians to know indeed that Christ is in them of a truth. "This is the victory that overcometh the world, even our faith." All things are possible to him that believeth; and whatsoever things we desire when we pray, if we believe that we receive them we shall have them. This faith will penetrate the darkest cloud and bring rays of light and hope to the drooping, desponding soul. It is the absence of this faith and trust which brings perplexity, distressing fears, and surmisings of evil. God will do great things for His people when they put their entire trust in Him.[17]

Through faith God's children have "subdued kingdoms, wrought righteousness, obtained promises, stopped the mouths of lions, quenched the violence of fire, escaped the edge of the sword, out of weakness were made strong, waxed valiant in fight, turned to flight the armies of the aliens." And through faith we today are to reach the heights of God's purpose for us.[18]

HAVE FAITH IN GOD

Trust ye in the Lord for ever: for in the Lord Jehovah is ever-lasting strength.

His is the greatness, the power, the glory, the victory and the majesty. Let us not limit the Holy One of Israel. . . .

What a source to which we can look in all times of trouble; the heart can have no misgivings! Man is erring, stubborn, rebellious, and defiant even against God; but the Lord is kind and patient and of tender compassion. He has heaven and earth at His command, and He knows just what we need even before we present our necessities and desires before Him.

We can see only a little way before us; "but all things are naked and opened unto the eyes of Him with whom we have to do." He never becomes confused. He sits above the confusion and distractions of the earth, and all things are opened to His divine survey; and from His great and calm eternity He can order that which His providence sees is best.

If we were left to ourselves to plan, we should make mistakes. Our prejudices, our weaknesses, our self-deceptions, and our ignorances would be manifest in many ways. But the work is the Lord's, the cause is His; He never leaves His workmen without divine directions. . . .

Whatever burdens lay heavily, cast them on the Lord. He that keepeth Israel neither slumbers nor sleeps. Repose in God. He is kept in perfect peace whose mind is stayed on God. At times it will seem that you cannot take another step. Well, wait and know that "I am God." "Be strong and of a good courage; be not afraid, neither be thou dismayed: for the Lord thy God is with thee whithersoever thou goest.". . . We need to cherish faith.[19]

◆ ◆ ◆

You must learn the simple art of taking God at His word; then you have solid ground beneath your feet.[20]

ONE WITH GOD THROUGH FAITH

That they all may be one; as thou, Father, art in me, and I in thee, that they also may be one in us.

"I am the vine, ye are the branches." Can we conceive of a more intimate relation to Christ than this? The fibers of the branch are almost identical with those of the vine. The communication of life, strength, and fruitfulness from the trunk to the branches is unobstructed and constant. The root sends its nourishment through the branch. Such is the true believer's relation to Christ. He abides in Christ, and draws his nourishment from Him.

This spiritual relation can be established only by the exercise of personal faith. This faith must express on our part supreme preference, perfect reliance, entire consecration. Our will must be wholly yielded to the divine will; our feelings, desires, interests, and honor, identified with the prosperity of Christ's kingdom and the honor of His cause, we constantly receiving grace from Him, and Christ accepting gratitude from us.

When this intimacy of connection and communion is formed, our sins are laid upon Christ, His righteousness is imputed to us. He was made sin for us, that we might be made the righteousness of God in Him. We have access to God through Him; we are accepted through the Beloved. Whoever by word or deed injures a believer, thereby wounds Jesus. Whoever gives a cup of cold water to a disciple because he is a child of God, will be regarded by Christ as giving to Himself.

It was when Christ was about to take leave of His disciples that He gave them the beautiful emblem of His relation to believers. . . . A union with Christ by living faith is enduring; every other union must perish. . . . The true believer chooses Christ as first and last, and best in everything.[21]

11

DOUBTING NOTHING

O thou of little faith, wherefore didst thou doubt?

Life is not all made up of pleasant pastures and cooling streams. Trial and disappointment overtake us; privation comes; we are brought into trying places. Conscience-stricken, we reason that we must have walked far away from God, that if we had walked with Him, we should not have suffered so. Doubt and despondency crowd into our hearts, and we say, The Lord has failed us, and we are ill-used. Why does He permit us to suffer thus? He cannot love us; if He did He would remove the difficulties from our path. . . .

He does not always bring us to pleasant places. If He did, in our self-sufficiency we should forget that He is our helper. He longs to manifest Himself to us, and to reveal the abundant supplies at our disposal, and He permits trial and disappointment to come to us that we may realize our helplessness, and learn to call upon Him for aid. He can cause cooling streams to flow from the flinty rock.

We shall never know until we are face to face with God, when we shall see as we are seen and know as we are known, how many burdens He has borne for us, and how many burdens He would have been glad to bear, if with childlike faith we had brought them to Him. . . .

God's love is revealed in all His dealings with His people; and with clear, unclouded eyes, in adversity, in sickness, in disappointment, and in trial we are to behold the light of His glory in the face of Christ and trust to His guiding hand. But too often we grieve His heart by our unbelief. . . .

God loves His children, and He longs to see them overcoming the discouragement with which Satan would overpower them. Do not give way to unbelief. Do not magnify your difficulties. Remember the love and power that God has shown in times past.[22]

THE TOUCH OF FAITH

For she said within herself, If I may but touch his garment, I shall be whole. But Jesus turned him about, and when he saw her, he said, Daughter, be of good comfort; thy faith hath made thee whole. And the woman was made whole from that hour.

To talk of religious things in a casual way, to pray for spiritual blessings without real soul hunger and living faith, avails little. The wondering crowd that pressed close about Christ realized no vital power from the contact. But when the poor, suffering woman, in her great need, put forth her hand and touched the hem of Jesus' garment, she felt the healing virtue. Hers was the touch of faith. Christ recognized that touch, and He determined there to give a lesson for all His followers to the close of time. He knew that virtue had gone out of Him, and turning about in the throng He said, "Who touched My clothes?" Surprised at such a question, His disciples answered, "Thou seest the multitude thronging Thee, and sayest Thou, Who touched Me?"

Jesus fixed His eyes upon her who had done this. She was filled with fear. Great joy was hers; but had she overstepped her duty? Knowing what was done in her, she came trembling, and fell at His feet, and told Him all the truth. Christ did not reproach her. He gently said, "Go in peace, and be whole of thy plague."

Here was distinguished the casual contact from the touch of faith. Prayer and preaching, without the exercise of living faith in God, will be in vain. But the touch of faith opens to us the divine treasure house of power and wisdom; and thus, through instruments of clay, God accomplishes the wonders of His grace.

This living faith is our great need today. We must know that Jesus is indeed ours; that His Spirit is purifying and refining our hearts. If the followers of Christ had genuine faith, with meekness and love, what a work they might accomplish! What fruit would be seen to the glory of God![23]

13

GOD SHALL SUPPLY MY NEED

My God shall supply all your need according to his riches in glory by Christ Jesus.

It is difficult to exercise living faith when we are in darkness and discouragement. But this of all others is the very time when we should exercise faith. "But," says one, "I do not feel at such times like praying in faith." Well, then, will you allow Satan to gain the victory, simply because you do not *feel* like resisting him? When he sees that you have the greatest need of divine aid, he will try the hardest to beat you back from God. If he can keep you away from the Source of strength, he knows that you will walk in darkness and sin. There is no sin greater than unbelief. And when there is unbelief in the heart, there is danger that it will be expressed. The lips should be kept in as with bit and bridle, lest by giving expression to this unbelief you not only exert an injurious influence over others, but place yourselves upon the enemy's ground.

If we believe in God, we are armed with the righteousness of Christ; we have taken hold of His strength. . . . We want to talk with our Saviour as though He were right by our side. . . .

It is our privilege to carry with us the credentials of our faith— love, joy, and peace. When we do this, we shall be able to present the mighty arguments of the cross of Christ. When we learn to walk by faith and not by feeling, we shall have help from God just when we need it, and His peace will come into our hearts. It was this simple life of obedience and trust that Enoch lived. If we learn this lesson of simple trust, ours may be the testimony that he received, that he pleased God.[24]

If we commit the keeping of our souls to God in the exercise of living faith, His promises will not fail us; for they have no limit but our faith.[25]

14

PRAY IN THE MORNING

My voice shalt thou hear in the morning, O Lord; in the morning will I direct my prayer unto thee, and will look up.

The very first outbreathing of the soul in the morning should be for the presence of Jesus. "Without Me," He says, "ye can do nothing." It is Jesus that we need; His light, His life, His spirit, must be ours continually. We need Him every hour. And we should pray in the morning that as the sun illuminates the landscape, and fills the world with light, so the Sun of Righteousness may shine into the chambers of mind and heart, and make us all light in the Lord. We cannot do without His presence one moment. The enemy knows when we undertake to do without our Lord, and he is there, ready to fill our minds with his evil suggestions that we may fall from our steadfastness; but it is the desire of the Lord that from moment to moment we should abide in Him, and thus be complete in Him. . . .

God designs that every one of us shall be perfect in Him, so that we may represent to the world the perfection of His character. He wants us to be set free from sin, that we may not disappoint Heaven, that we may not grieve our divine Redeemer. He does not desire us to profess Christianity, and yet not avail ourselves of that grace which is able to make us perfect, that we may be found wanting in nothing.[26]

Prayer and faith will do what no power on earth can accomplish. We are seldom, in all respects, placed in the same position twice. We continually have new scenes and new trials to pass through, where past experience cannot be a sufficient guide. We must have the continual light that comes from God. Christ is ever sending messages to those who listen for His voice.[27]

❧ ❧ ❧

It is a part of God's plan to grant us, in answer to the prayer of faith, that which He would not bestow did we not thus ask.[28]

PRAYER NEVER OUT OF PLACE

Continue in prayer, and watch in the same with thanksgiving.

There is no time or place in which it is inappropriate to offer up a petition to God. There is nothing that can prevent us from lifting up our hearts in the spirit of earnest prayer. In the crowds of the street, in the midst of a business engagement, we may send up a petition to God, and plead for divine guidance.[29]

We may speak with Jesus as we walk by the way, and He says, I am at thy right hand. We may commune with God in our hearts; we may walk in companionship with Christ. When engaged in our daily labor, we may breathe out our heart's desire, inaudible to any human ear; but that word cannot die away into silence, nor can it be lost. Nothing can drown the soul's desire. It rises above the din of the street, above the noise of machinery. It is God to whom we are speaking, and our prayer is heard.[30]

Every earnest petition for grace and strength will be answered. . . . Ask God to do for you those things that you cannot do for yourselves. Tell Jesus everything. Lay open before Him the secrets of your heart; for His eye searches the inmost recesses of the soul, and He reads your thoughts as an open book. When you have asked for the things that are necessary for your soul's good, believe that you receive them, and you shall have them. Accept His gifts with your whole heart; for Jesus has died that you might have the precious things of heaven as your own, and at last find a home with the heavenly angels in the kingdom of God.[31]

ॐ ॐ ॐ

If you will find voice and time to pray, God will find time and voice to answer.[32]

PRAY ALWAYS

Watch ye therefore, and pray always, that ye may be accounted worthy to escape all these things that shall come to pass, and to stand before the Son of man.

Remember that He was often in prayer, and His life was constantly sustained by fresh inspirations of the Holy Spirit. Let your thoughts, your inner life, be such that you will not be ashamed to meet its record in the day of God.

Heaven is not closed against the fervent prayers of the righteous. Elijah was a man subject to like passions as we are, yet the Lord heard, and in a most striking manner answered his petitions. The only reason for our lack of power with God is to be found in ourselves. If the inner life of many who profess the truth were presented before them, they would not claim to be Christians. They are not growing in grace. A hurried prayer is offered now and then, but there is no real communion with God.

We must be much in prayer if we would make progress in the divine life. When the message of truth was first proclaimed, how much we prayed. How often was the voice of intercession heard in the chamber, in the barn, in the orchard, or the grove. Frequently we spent hours in earnest prayer, two or three together claiming the promise; often the sound of weeping was heard and then the voice of thanksgiving and the song of praise. Now the day of God is nearer than when we first believed, and we should be more earnest, more zealous, and fervent than in those early days. Our perils are greater now than then. Souls are more hardened. We need now to be imbued with the Spirit of Christ, and we should not rest until we receive it.[33]

Cultivate the habit of talking with the Saviour. . . . Let the heart be continually uplifted in silent petition for help, for light, for strength, for knowledge. Let every breath be a prayer.[34]

POWER IN PRAYER

And whatsoever ye shall ask in my name, that will I do.

The petitions of a humble heart and contrite spirit he will not despise. The opening of our hearts to our heavenly Father, the acknowledgment of our entire dependence, the expression of our wants, the homage of grateful love—this is true prayer.[35]

Angels record every prayer that is earnest and sincere. We should rather dispense with selfish gratifications than neglect communion with God. The deepest poverty, the greatest self-denial, with His approval, is better than riches, honors, ease, and friendship without it. We must take time to pray. If we allow our minds to be absorbed by worldly interests, the Lord may give us time by removing from us our idols of gold, of houses, or of fertile lands.

The young would not be seduced into sin if they would refuse to enter any path save that upon which they could ask God's blessing. If the messengers who bear the last solemn warning to the world would pray for the blessing of God, not in a cold, listless, lazy manner, but fervently and in faith, as did Jacob, they would find many places where they could say, "I have seen God face to face, and my life is preserved." They would be accounted of heaven as princes, having power to prevail with God and with men.[36]

True prayer, offered in faith, is a power to the petitioner. Prayer, whether offered in the public assembly, at the family altar, or in secret, places man directly in the presence of God. By constant prayer the youth may obtain principles so firm that the most powerful temptations will not draw them from their allegiance to God.[37]

The greatest victories to the church of Christ or to the individual Christian . . . are those victories that are gained in the audience chamber with God, when earnest, agonizing faith lays hold upon the mighty arm of power.[38]

FIND GOD THROUGH PRAYER

*Then shall ye call upon me, and ye shall go and pray unto me,
and I will hearken unto you. And ye shall seek me, and find me,
when ye shall search for me with all your heart.*

There are two kinds of prayer—the prayer of form and the
prayer of faith. The repetition of set, customary phrases when the
heart feels no need of God, is formal prayer. . . . We should be ex-
tremely careful in all our prayers to speak the wants of the heart and
to say only what we mean. All the flowery words at our command
are not equivalent to one holy desire. The most eloquent prayers are
but vain repetitions if they do not express the true sentiments of the
heart. But the prayer that comes from an earnest heart, when the
simple wants of the soul are expressed just as we would ask an
earthly friend for a favor, expecting that it would be granted—this is
the prayer of faith. The publican who went up to the temple to pray
is a good example of a sincere, devoted worshiper. He felt that he
was a sinner, and his great need led to an outburst of passionate desire, "God be merciful to me a sinner." . . .

After we have offered our petitions, we are to answer them ourselves as far as possible, and not wait for God to do for us what we
can do for ourselves. The help of God is held in reserve for all who
demand it. Divine help is to be combined with human effort, aspiration, and energy. But we cannot reach the battlements of heaven
without climbing for ourselves. We cannot be borne up by the
prayers of others when we ourselves neglect to pray; for God has
made no such provision for us. . . . The unlovely traits in our characters are not removed, and replaced by traits that are pure and
lovely, without some effort on our part. . . .

In our efforts to follow the copy set us by our Lord, we shall
make crooked lines. . . . Yet let us not cease our efforts. . . .
Temporary failure should make us lean more heavily on Christ.[39]

EXAMPLES OF PRAYER LIFE

If ye abide in me, and my words abide in you, ye shall ask what ye will, and it shall be done unto you.

The patriarchs were men of prayer, and God did great things for them. When Jacob left his father's house for a strange land, he prayed in humble contrition, and in the night season the Lord answered him through vision. . . . The Lord comforted the lonely wanderer with precious promises; and protecting angels were represented as stationed on each side of his path. . . .

Joseph prayed, and he was preserved from sin amid influences that were calculated to lead him away from God. When tempted to leave the path of purity and uprightness, he rejected the suggestion with, "How can I do this great wickedness, and sin against God?"

Moses, who was much in prayer, was known as the meekest man on the face of the earth. . . . While he was leading the children of Israel through the wilderness, again and again it seemed that they must be exterminated on account of their murmuring and rebellion. But Moses went to the true Source of power; he laid the case before the Lord. . . . And the Lord said, "I have pardoned according to thy word." . . .

Daniel was a man of prayer, and God gave him wisdom and firmness to resist every influence that conspired to draw him into the snare of intemperance. Even in his youth he was a moral giant in the strength of the Mighty One. . . .

In the prison at Philippi, while suffering from the cruel stripes they had received, their feet fast in the stocks, Paul and Silas prayed and sang praise to God; and angels were sent from heaven to deliver them. The earth shook under the tread of these heavenly messengers, and the prison doors flew open, setting the prisoners free.[40]

❧ ❧ ❧

Prayer takes hold upon Omnipotence, and gains us the victory.[41]

20

MOTHER'S PRAYERS

For I will contend with him that contendeth with thee, and I will save thy children.

Those who keep the law of God look upon their children with indefinable feelings of hope and fear, wondering what part they will act in the great conflict that is just before them. The anxious mother questions, "What stand will they take? What can I do to prepare them to act well their part, so that they will be the recipients of eternal glory?"

Great responsibilities rest upon you, mothers. . . . You may aid them to develop characters that will not be swayed or influenced to do evil, but will sway and influence others to do right. By your fervent prayers of faith you can move the arm that moves the world. . . .

The prayers of Christian mothers are not disregarded by the Father of all. . . . He will not turn away your petitions, and leave you and yours to the buffetings of Satan in the great day of final conflict. It is for you to work with simplicity and faithfulness, and God will establish the work of your hands.[42]

The lifework performed on earth is acknowledged in the heavenly courts as a work well done. With joy unutterable, parents see the crown, the robe, the harp, given to their children. . . . The seed sown with tears and prayers may have seemed to be sown in vain, but their harvest is reaped with joy at last. Their children have been redeemed.[43]

When the "well done" of the great judge is pronounced, and the crown of immortal glory is placed upon the brow of the victor, many will raise their crowns in sight of the assembled universe and, pointing to their mothers, say, "She made me all I am through the grace of God. Her instruction, her prayers, have been blessed to my eternal salvation.[44]

SEARCH THE SCRIPTURES

O the depth of the riches both of the wisdom and knowledge of God! how unsearchable are his judgments and his ways past finding out.

In the Scriptures thousands of gems of truth lie hidden from the surface seeker. The mine of truth is never exhausted. The more you search the Scriptures with humble hearts, the greater will be your interest, and the more you will feel like exclaiming with Paul: "O the depth of the riches both of the wisdom and knowledge of God! . . ."

Every day you should learn something new from the Scriptures. Search them as for hid treasures, for they contain the words of eternal life. Pray for wisdom and understanding to comprehend these holy writings. If you would do this, you would find new glories in the Word of God; you would feel that you had received new and precious light on subjects connected with the truth, and the Scriptures would be constantly receiving a new value in your estimation.[45]

The great truths necessary for salvation are made as clear as noonday. . . . A single text has proved in the past, and will prove in the future, to be a savor of life unto life to many a soul. As men diligently search, the Bible opens new treasures of truth, which are as bright jewels to the mind.[46]

You must dig deep in the mine of truth if you would find its richest treasures. Comparing scripture with scripture, you may find the true meaning of the text; but if you do not make the sacred teachings of God's Word the rule and guide of your life, the truth will be nothing to you. . . . If any part of God's Word condemns any habit you have cherished, any feeling you have indulged, any spirit you have manifested, turn not from the Word of God; but turn away from the evil of your doings, and let Jesus cleanse and sanctify your heart.[47]

THE BIBLE STANDS WITHOUT A PEER

Call unto me, and I will answer thee, and shew thee great and mighty things, which thou knowest not.

No other study will so ennoble every thought, feeling, and aspiration as the study of the Scriptures. No other book can satisfy the questionings of the mind and the craving of the heart. By obtaining a knowledge of God's Word, and giving heed thereto, men may rise from the lowest depths of ignorance and degradation to become the sons of God, the associates of sinless angels. . . .

As an educating power, the Bible is without a rival. Nothing will so impart vigor to all the faculties as an effort to grasp the stupendous truths of revelation. The mind gradually adapts itself to the subjects upon which it is allowed to dwell. If occupied with commonplace matters only, it will become dwarfed and enfeebled. . . .

In its wide range of style and subjects the Bible has something to interest every mind and appeal to every heart. . . . In it the most simply stated truths are involved—principles that are as high as heaven and that encompass eternity.[48]

There is no position in life, no phase of human experience, for which the Bible does not contain valuable instruction. Ruler and subject, master and servant, buyer and seller, borrower and lender, parent and child, teacher and student—all may here find lessons of priceless worth.

But above all else, the Word of God sets forth the plan of salvation: shows how sinful man may be reconciled to God, lays down the great principles of truth and duty which should govern our lives, and promises us divine aid in their observance. It reaches beyond this fleeting life, beyond the brief and troubled history of our race. It opens to our view the long vista of eternal ages—ages undarkened by sin, undimmed by sorrow.[49]

THE BIBLE BEGETS NEW LIFE

Being born again . . . by the word of God, which liveth and abideth for ever.

In the Bible the will of God is revealed. The truths of the Word of God are the utterances of the Most High. He who makes these truths a part of his life becomes in every sense a new creature. He is not given new mental powers, but the darkness that through ignorance and sin has clouded the understanding is removed. The words, "A new heart also will I give you," mean, "A new mind will I give you." A change of heart is always attended by a clear conviction of Christian duty, an understanding of truth. He who gives the Scriptures close, prayerful attention will gain clear comprehension and sound judgment, as if in turning to God he had reached a higher plane of intelligence.

The Bible contains the principles that lie at the foundation of all true greatness, all true prosperity, whether for the individual or for the nation. The nation that gives free room for the circulation of the Scriptures opens the way for the minds of the people to develop and expand. The reading of the Scriptures causes light to shine into the darkness. As the Word of God is searched, life-giving truths are found. In the lives of those who heed its teachings there will be an undercurrent of happiness that will bless all with whom they are brought in contact.[50]

Thousands have drawn water from these wells of life, yet there is no diminishing of the supply. Thousands have set the Lord before them, and by beholding have been changed into the same image. Their spirit burns within them as they speak of His character, telling what Christ is to them and what they are to Christ. . . . Thousands more may engage in the work of searching out the mysteries of salvation. . . . Each fresh search will reveal something more deeply interesting than has yet been unfolded.[51]

MY COUNSELOR AND GUIDE

Thou shall guide me with thy counsel, and afterward receive me to glory.

The Christian evidence that we need, is found not in the experience of men, but in our Bibles. The Word of God is the man of our counsel; for it brings us down from age to age, bearing its testimony to the unchangeableness of the truth. Not one of the ancient defenses of the word of God, appropriate for special times, has become worn out. No part of the Bible has died from old age. All the past history of the people of God is to be studied by us today, that we may benefit by the experiences recorded.[52]

Men break their word, and prove themselves untrustworthy, but God changes not. His word will abide the same forever.[53]

Give the Word its honored position as a guide in the home. Let it be regarded as the Counselor in every difficulty, the standard of every practice. . . . There can never be true prosperity to any soul in the family circle unless the truth of God, the wisdom of righteousness, presides.[54]

We all need a guide through the many straight places of life, as much as the sailor needs a pilot over the sandy bar or up the rocky river. . . .

The sailor who has in his possession chart and compass, and yet neglects to use them, is responsible for placing the lives of those on board his vessel in peril. The vessel may be lost by his neglect. We have a Guidebook, the Word of God, and we are inexcusable if we miss the way to heaven, for plain directions have been given us.[55]

The Bible presents a perfect standard of character; it is an infallible guide under all circumstances, even to the end of the journey of life.[56]

25

FOOD FOR MY SOUL

Thy words were found, and I did eat them, and thy word was unto me the joy and rejoicing of mine heart.

It is impossible for any human mind to exhaust one truth or promise of the Bible. One catches the glory from one point of view, another from another point; yet we can discern only gleamings. The full radiance is beyond our vision. As we contemplate the great things of God's Word, we look into a fountain that broadens and deepens beneath our gaze. Its breadth and depth pass our knowledge. As we gaze, the vision widens; stretched out before us, we behold a boundless, shoreless sea. Such study has vivifying power. The mind and heart acquire new strength, new life.

This experience is the highest evidence of the divine authorship of the Bible. We receive God's Word as food for the soul through the same evidence by which we receive bread as food for the body. Bread supplies the need of our nature; we know by experience that it produces blood, bone, and brain. Apply the same test to the Bible; when its principles have actually become the elements of character, what has been the result? what changes have been made in the life?—"Old things are passed away; behold, all things are become new." In its power men and women have broken the chains of sinful habit. They have renounced selfishness. The profane have become reverent, the drunken sober, the profligate pure. Souls that have borne the likeness of Satan have been transformed into the image of God. The change is itself the miracle of miracles. A change wrought by the Word, it is one of the deepest mysteries of the Word. We cannot understand it; we can only believe, that, as declared by the Scriptures, it is "Christ in you, the hope of glory." A knowledge of this mystery furnishes a key to every other. It opens to the soul the treasures of the universe, the possibilities of infinite development.[57]

MY LIGHT

The entrance of thy words giveth light; it giveth understanding unto the simple.

It [the Word of God] is a light shining in a dark place. As we search its pages, light enters the heart, illuminating the mind. By this light we see what we ought to be.

We see in the Word, warnings and promises, with God behind them all. We are invited to search this Word for aid when brought into difficult places. If we do not consult the Guidebook at every step, inquiring, Is this the way of the Lord? our words and acts will be tainted by selfishness. We shall forget God, and walk in paths that He has not chosen for us.

God's Word is full of precious promises and helpful counsel. It is infallible; for God cannot err. It has help for every circumstance and condition of life, and God looks on with sadness when His children turn from it to human aid.

He who through the Scriptures holds communion with God will be ennobled and sanctified. As he reads the inspired record of the Saviour's love, his heart will melt in tenderness and contrition. He will be filled with a desire to be like his Master, to live a life of loving service. . . . By a miracle of His power He has preserved His Written Word through the ages.[58]

This book is God's great director. . . . It flashes its light ahead, that we may see the path by which we are traveling; and its rays are thrown back on past history, showing the most perfect harmony in that which, to the mind in darkness, appears like error and discord. In that which seems to the worldling an inexplicable mystery, God's children see light and beauty.[59]

Happy is the man who has discovered for himself that the Word of God is a light to his feet and a lamp to his path—a light shining in a dark place. It is heaven's directory for men.[60]

A TREASURE IN MY HEART

Receive, I pray thee, the law from his mouth, and lay up his words in thine heart.

It is of the greatest importance that you continually search the Scriptures, storing the mind with the truths of God. You may be separated from the companionship of Christians and placed where you will not have the privilege of meeting with the children of God. You need the treasures of God's Word hidden in your heart.[61]

All over the field of revelation are scattered grains of gold—the sayings of the wisdom of God. If you are wise, you will gather up these precious grains of truth. Make the promises of God your own. Then when test and trial come, these promises will be to you glad springs of heavenly comfort.[62]

Temptations often appear irresistible because, through neglect of prayer and the study of the Bible, the tempted one cannot readily remember God's promises and meet Satan with the Scripture weapons. But angels are round about those who are willing to be taught in divine things; and in the time of great necessity they will bring to their remembrance the very truths which are needed. Thus "when the enemy shall come in like a flood, the Spirit of the Lord shall lift up a standard against him."[63]

The heart that is stored with the precious truths of God's Word is fortified against the temptation of Satan, against impure thoughts and unholy actions.[64]

Keep close to the Scriptures. The more you search and explain the Word, the more your mind and heart will be fortified with the blessed words of encouragement and promise.[65]

Let us commit its precious promises to memory, so that, when we are deprived of our Bibles, we may still be in possession of the Word of God.[66]

MORNING AND EVENING WORSHIP

O come, let us worship and bow down: let us kneel before the Lord our maker.

The Lord has a special interest in the families of His children here below. Angels offer the smoke of the fragrant incense for the praying saints. Then in every family let prayer ascend to heaven both at morning and at the cool sunset hour, in our behalf presenting before God the Saviour's merits. Morning and evening the heavenly universe takes notice of every praying household.[67]

Come in humility with a heart full of tenderness and with a sense of the temptations and dangers before yourselves and your children; by faith bind them upon the altar, entreating for them the care of the Lord. Ministering angels will guard children who are thus dedicated to God.[68]

Family worship should not be governed by circumstances. You are not to pray occasionally, and when you have a large day's work, neglect it. In thus doing you lead your children to look upon prayer as of no special consequence. Prayer means very much to the children of God, and thank offerings should come up before God morning and evening. Says the Psalmist, "O come, let us sing unto the Lord: let us make a joyful noise to the rock of our salvation."[69]

It should be a pleasure to worship the Lord. . . . He desires that those who come to worship Him shall carry away with them precious thoughts of His care and love, that they may be cheered in all the employments of daily life, that they may have grace to deal honestly and faithfully in all things.[70]

In the home it is possible to have a little church which will honor and glorify the Redeemer.[71]

ॐ ॐ ॐ

When we have good home religion we will have excellent meeting religion.[72]

TEACH THEM DILIGENTLY

And these words, which I command thee this day, shall be in thine heart: and thou shalt teach them diligently unto thy children.

In his childhood, Joseph had been taught the love and fear of God. Often in his father's tent, under the Syrian stars, he had been told the story of the night vision at Bethel, of the ladder from heaven to earth, and the descending and ascending angels, and of Him who from the throne above revealed Himself to Jacob. He had been told the story of the conflict beside the Jabbok, when, renouncing cherished sins, Jacob stood conqueror, and received the title of a prince with God.

A shepherd boy, tending his father's flocks, Joseph's pure and simple life had favored the development of both physical and mental power. By communion with God through nature and the study of the great truths handed down as a sacred trust from father to son, he had gained strength of mind and firmness of principle.[73]

Younger than Joseph or Daniel was Moses when removed from the sheltering care of his childhood's home; yet already the same agencies that shaped their lives had molded his. Only twelve years did he spend with his Hebrew kindred; but during these years was laid the foundation of his greatness; it was laid by the hand of one little known to fame. . . .

Through no other woman, save Mary of Nazareth, has the world received greater blessing. Knowing that her child must soon pass beyond her care, . . . she sought to implant in his heart love and loyalty to God. And faithfully was the work accomplished.[74]

In arousing and strengthening a love for Bible study, much depends on the use of the hour of worship. The hours of morning and evening worship should be the sweetest and most helpful in the day. Let it be understood that into these hours no troubled, unkind thoughts are to intrude; that parents and children assemble to meet with Jesus and to invite into the home the presence of holy angels.[75]

BOW BEFORE GOD

Humble yourselves in the sight of the Lord, and he shall lift you up.

If ever there was a time when every house should be a house of prayer, it is now. Infidelity and skepticism prevail. Iniquity abounds. Corruption flows in the vital currents of the soul, and rebellion against God breaks out in the life. Enslaved by sin, the moral powers are under the tyranny of Satan. The soul is made the sport of his temptation; and unless some mighty arm is stretched out to rescue him, man goes where the arch rebel leads the way.

And yet in this time of fearful peril some who profess to be Christians have no family prayer. . . .

The idea that prayer is not essential is one of Satan's most successful devices to ruin souls. Prayer is communion with God, the fountain of wisdom, the source of strength and peace and happiness. Jesus prayed to the Father "with strong crying and tears." . . . "Pray one for another," James says; "the effectual fervent prayer of a righteous man availeth much."

By sincere, earnest prayer parents should make a hedge about their children. They should pray with full faith that God will abide with them, and that holy angels will guard them and their children from Satan's cruel power. . . .

How appropriate it is for parents to gather their children about them before the fast is broken and point them to the heavenly Father, who so liberally gives them the bounties of His providence! How fitting for them to thank Him for His protection during the night and to ask for His help and grace and the watchcare of His angels during the day! How fitting, also, when evening comes, to gather once more before Him and praise Him for the mercies and blessings of the day that is past![76]

CONFESS YOUR FAULTS ONE TO ANOTHER

Confess your faults one to another, and pray one for another, that ye may be healed. The effectual fervent prayer of a righteous man availeth much.

I am instructed to urge upon our people most earnestly the necessity of religion in the home. Among the members of the household there is ever to be a kind, thoughtful consideration. Morning and evening let all hearts be united in reverent worship. At the season of evening worship let every member of the family search well his own heart. Let every wrong that has been committed be made right. If during the day, one has wronged another or spoken unkindly, let the transgressor seek pardon of the one he has injured. Often grievances are cherished in the mind, and misunderstandings and heartaches are created that need not be. If the one who is suspected of wrong be given an opportunity, he might be able to make explanations that would bring relief to other members of the family.

"Confess your faults one to another, and pray one for another," that ye may be healed of all spiritual infirmities, that sinful dispositions may be changed. Make diligent work for eternity. Pray most earnestly to the Lord and hold fast to the faith. Trust not in the arm of flesh, but trust implicitly in the Lord's guidance. Let each one now say, "As for me, I will come out, and be separate from the world. I will serve the Lord with full purpose of heart.". . .

The Lord will show His loving favor to those who will keep His commandments. The Word, the living Word, received and obeyed, will be a savor of life unto life. The reception of the truth will regenerate and cleanse the sinful heart.

This work of individual purification of character cannot be safely delayed. . . . With confession and prayer, take your stand to be wholly the Lord's henceforth and forever. . . . We cannot afford to delay this work of confession and humbling of soul, that our offerings may be acceptable unto God. Fullness of joy is to be found in an entire surrender to God.[77]

WORSHIP GOD AND BE AT PEACE

And all thy children shall be taught of the Lord, and great shall be the peace of thy children.

Your home is a little world of itself. . . . You are the ones who must decide whether your children shall choose the service of God or the service of mammon, eternal life or eternal death. . . .

Like the patriarchs of old, those who profess to love God should erect an altar to Him wherever they pitch their tent. . . . Let the father, as priest of the household, lay upon the altar of God the morning and evening sacrifice, while the wife and children unite in prayer and praise. In such a household Jesus will love to abide.

From every Christian home a holy light should shine forth. Love should be revealed in every act. It should flow out in all home intercourse, showing itself in thoughtful kindness, in gentle, unselfish courtesy. There are homes where this principle is carried out— homes where God is worshiped and truest love reigns. From these homes morning and evening prayer ascends to God as sweet incense, and His mercies and blessings descend upon the suppliants like morning dew.[78]

Let us raise our eyes to the open door of the sanctuary above, where the light of the glory of God shines in the face of Christ, who "is able also to save them to the uttermost that come unto God by Him." . . .

The soul may ascend nearer heaven on the wings of praise. God is worshiped with song and music in the courts above, and as we express our gratitude, we are approximating to the worship of the heavenly hosts. "Whoso offereth praise glorifieth" God. Let us with reverent joy come before our Creator, with "thanksgiving, and the voice of melody."[79]

TIMOTHY'S LIFE A RESULT OF FAMILY RELIGION

Continue thou in the things which thou hast learned and hast been assured of, knowing of whom thou hast learned them; and that from a child thou hast known the holy scriptures, which are able to make thee wise unto salvation through faith which is in Christ Jesus.

Those who profess the name of Christ should not neglect to establish the family altar, where they can seek God daily with all the earnestness with which they would seek Him in a religious assembly.[80]

We may learn precious lessons in this respect from the life and character of Timothy. From a child Timothy had known the Scriptures. Religion was the atmosphere of his home. The piety of his home life was . . . pure, sensible, and uncorrupted by false sentiments. . . . The Word of God was the rule which guided Timothy. He received his instruction, line upon line, precept upon precept, here a little, and there a little. And the spiritual power of these lessons kept him pure in speech and free from all corrupting sentiments. His home instructors cooperated with God in educating this young man to bear the burdens that were to come upon him at an early age. . . .

The lessons of the Bible have a moral and a religious influence upon the character as they are wrought into the practical life. Timothy learned and practiced these lessons. He had no specially wonderful talents, but his work was valuable because he used his God-given abilities as consecrated gifts in the service of God. His intelligent knowledge of the truth and of experimental piety gave him distinction and influence. The Holy Spirit found in Timothy a mind that could be molded and fashioned to become a temple for the indwelling of the Holy Spirit. . . .

The youth should place themselves under the teaching of the Holy Scriptures and weave them into their daily thoughts and practical life. Then they will possess the attributes classed as highest in the heavenly courts. They will hide themselves in God, and their lives will tell to His glory.[81]

ABRAHAM BUILT AN ALTAR WHEREVER HE WENT

And the Lord appeared unto Abram, and said, Unto thy seed will I give this land: and there builded he an altar unto the Lord, who appeared unto him. And he removed from thence unto a mountain on the east of Bethel, and pitched his tent, . . . and there he builded an altar unto the Lord, and called upon the name of the Lord.

The life of Abraham, the friend of God, was a life of prayer. Wherever he pitched his tent, close beside it was built an altar, upon which was offered the morning and evening sacrifice. When his tent was removed, the altar remained. And the roving Canaanite, as he came to that altar, knew who had been there; and when he had pitched his tent, he repaired the altar and worshiped the living God.

So the homes of Christians should be lights in the world. . . . Fathers and mothers, each morning and evening gather your children round you, and in humble supplication lift your hearts to God for help. Your dear ones are exposed to temptation and trial. Daily annoyances beset the path of young and old. Those who would live patient, loving, cheerful lives must pray. Victory can be gained only by resolute and unwavering purpose, constant watchfulness, and continual help from God.

Parents, each morning consecrate yourselves and your family to God for that day. Make no calculation for months or years; these are not yours. One brief day is given you. As if it were your last on earth, work during its hours for the Master. Lay all your plans before God, to be carried out or given up as His providence shall indicate. Accept His plans instead of your own, even though their acceptance requires the abandonment of cherished projects. Thus the life will be molded more and more after the divine Example.[82]

Eternity alone will reveal the good results with which such seasons of worship are fraught.[83]

A SPIRIT-FILLED LIFE

February 1   *Gifts of the Holy Spirit*   *John 14:16, 17*

GOD'S GIFT OF THE SPIRIT

And I will pray the Father, and he shall give you another Comforter, that he may abide with you for ever; even the Spirit of truth; whom the world cannot receive, because it seeth him not, neither knoweth him: but ye know him, for he dwelleth with you, and shall be in you.

During the Jewish economy the influence of God's Spirit had been seen in a marked manner, but not in full. For ages prayers had been offered for the fulfillment of God's promise to impart His Spirit, and not one of these earnest supplications had been forgotten.

Christ determined that when He ascended from this earth He would bestow a gift on those who had believed on Him and those who should believe on Him. What gift could He bestow rich enough to signalize and grace His ascension to the mediatorial throne? It must be worthy of His greatness and His royalty. He determined to give His representative, the third person of the Godhead. This gift could not be excelled. He would give all gifts in one, and therefore the divine Spirit, that converting, enlightening, and sanctifying power, would be His donation. . . . It came with a fullness and power, as if for ages it had been restrained, but was now being poured forth upon the church. . . .

Believers were reconverted. Sinners united with Christians seeking the pearl of great price. . . . Every Christian saw in his brother the divine similitude of benevolence and love. One interest prevailed. One object swallowed up all others. Every pulse beat in healthy concert. The only ambition of the believers was to see who could reveal most perfectly the likeness of Christ's character, who could do the most for the enlargement of His kingdom.[1]

ɕ ɕ ɕ

The Holy Spirit was sent as the most priceless treasure man could receive.[2]

TO EVERY ONE IS GIVEN A GIFT

Unto every one of us is given grace according to the measure of the gift of Christ.

The talents that Christ entrusts to His church represent especially the gifts and blessings imparted by the Holy Spirit. "To one is given by the Spirit the word of wisdom; to another the word of knowledge by the same Spirit; to another faith by the same Spirit; to another the gifts of healing by the same Spirit; to another the working of miracles; to another prophecy; to another discerning of spirits; to another divers kinds of tongues; to another the interpretation of tongues: but all these worketh that one and the selfsame Spirit, dividing to every man severally as He will." All men do not receive the same gifts, but to every servant of the Master some gift of the Spirit is promised.

Before He left His disciples, Christ "breathed on them, and saith unto them, Receive ye the Holy Ghost." Again he said, "Behold, I send the promise of My Father upon you." . . . "Unto every one of us is given grace, according to the measure of the gift of Christ," the Spirit "dividing to every man severally as He will." The gifts are already ours in Christ, but their actual possession depends upon our reception of the Spirit of God.[3]

God does not ask us to do in our own strength the work before us. He has provided divine assistance for all the emergencies to which our human resources are unequal. He gives the Holy Spirit to help in every strait, to strengthen our hope and assurance, to illuminate our minds and purify our hearts. . . . There is no limit to the usefulness of the one who, putting self aside, makes room for the working of the Holy Spirit upon his heart and lives a life wholly consecrated to God. . . . Christ declared that the divine influence of the Spirit was to be with His followers unto the end.[4]

FOR THE PERFECTING OF THE SAINTS

And he gave some, apostles; and some, prophets; and some, evangelists; and some, pastors and teachers; for the perfecting of the saints, for the work of the ministry, for the edifying of the body of Christ: till we all come in the unity of the faith, and of the knowledge of the Son of God, unto a perfect man, unto the measure of the stature of the fulness of Christ.

All these gifts are to be in exercise. Every faithful worker will minister for the perfecting of the saints. . . . There is something for everyone to do. Every soul that believes the truth is to stand in his lot and place, saying: "Here am I; send me." . . . Give each one something to do for others. Help all to see that as receivers of the grace of Christ they are under obligation to work for Him. And let all be taught how to work. Especially should those who are newly come to the faith be educated to become laborers together with God. If set to work, the despondent will soon forget their despondency; the weak will become strong, the ignorant intelligent, and all will be prepared to present the truth as it is in Jesus. They will find an unfailing helper in Him who has promised to save all that come unto Him.[5]

The influence of the Holy Spirit is needed that the work may be properly balanced and that it may move forward solidly, in every line.[6]

The truth for this time embraces the whole gospel. Rightly presented, it will work in man the very changes that will make evident the power of God's grace upon the heart. It will do a complete work and develop a complete man.[7]

He [God] tells us to be perfect as He is—in the same manner. We are to be centers of light and blessing to our little circle, even as He is to the universe. We have nothing of ourselves, but the light of His love shines upon us, and we are to reflect its brightness. . . . We may be perfect in our sphere, even as God is perfect in His.[8]

FOR THE UNITY OF THE SAINTS

I . . . beseech you that ye walk worthy of the vocation wherewith ye are called with all lowliness and meekness, with longsuffering, forbearing one another in love; endeavoring to keep the unity of the Spirit in the bond of peace.

The stars of heaven are all under law, each influencing the other to do the will of God, yielding their common obedience to the law that controls their action. And, in order that the Lord's work may advance healthfully and solidly, His people must draw together.

The spasmodic, fitful movements of some who claim to be Christians are well represented by the work of strong but untrained horses. When one pulls forward, another pulls back, and at the voice of their master, one plunges ahead, and the other stands immovable. If men will not move in concert in the great and grand work for this time, there will be confusion. . . . If men wear the yoke of Christ, they cannot pull apart; they will draw with Christ. . . .

To the prophet, the wheel within a wheel, the appearance of living creatures connected with them, all seemed intricate and unexplainable. But the hand of infinite wisdom is seen among the wheels, and perfect order is the result of its work. Every wheel, directed by the hand of God, works in perfect harmony with every other wheel.[9]

By the influence of the Spirit, the most discordant may be brought into harmony. Unselfishness is to bind God's people together with firm, tender bonds. There is a vast power in the church when the energies of the members are under the control of the Spirit, gathering good from every source, educating, training, and disciplining self. Thus is presented to God a powerful organization, through which He can work for the conversion of sinners. Thus heaven and earth are connected, and all divine agencies cooperate with human instrumentalities.[10]

TRUTH REVEALED BY GOD'S PROPHETS

Surely the Lord God will do nothing, but he revealeth his secret unto his servants the prophets.

Before the entrance of sin, Adam enjoyed open communion with his Maker; but since man separated himself from God by transgression, the human race has been cut off from this high privilege. By the plan of redemption, however, a way has been opened whereby the inhabitants of the earth may still have connection with heaven. God has communicated with men by His Spirit, and divine light has been imparted to the world by revelations to His chosen servants. "Holy men of God spake as they were moved by the Holy Ghost." 2 Peter 1:21. . . .

The Infinite One by His Holy Spirit has shed light into the minds and hearts of His servants. He has given dreams and visions, symbols and figures; and those to whom the truth was thus revealed, have themselves embodied the thought in human language.[11]

"Surely the Lord God will do nothing, but He revealeth His secret unto His servants the prophets." Amos 3:7.

In His providence the Lord has seen fit to teach and warn His people in various ways. By direct command, by the sacred writings, and by the spirit of prophecy has He made known unto them His will.[12]

In ancient times God spoke to men by the mouth of prophets and apostles. In these days He speaks to them by the Testimonies of His Spirit. There was never a time when God instructed His people more earnestly than He instructs them now concerning His will and the course that He would have them pursue.[13]

Of special value to God's church on earth today—the keepers of His vineyard—are the messages of counsel and admonition given through the prophets who have made plain His eternal purpose in behalf of mankind. In the teachings of the prophets His love for the lost race and His plan for their salvation are clearly revealed.[14]

THE SPIRIT OF PROPHECY—A GIFT FOR ME

The testimony of Jesus is the spirit of prophecy.

God has been pleased to communicate His truth to the world by human agencies, and He Himself, by His Holy Spirit, qualified men and enabled them to do this work. He guided the mind in the selection of what to speak and what to write. The treasure was entrusted to earthen vessels, yet it is, nonetheless, from Heaven. The testimony is conveyed through the imperfect expression of human language, yet it is the testimony of God; and the obedient, believing child of God beholds in it the glory of a divine power, full of grace and truth.

In His Word God has committed to men the knowledge necessary for salvation. The Holy Scriptures are to be accepted as an authoritative, infallible revelation of His will.[15] . . .

As presented through different individuals, the truth is brought out in its varied aspects. One writer is more strongly impressed with one phase of the subject; he grasps those points that harmonize with his experience or with his power of perception and appreciation; another seizes upon a different phase; and each, under the guidance of the Holy Spirit, presents what is most forcibly impressed upon his own mind—a different aspect of the truth in each, but a perfect harmony through all. And the truths thus revealed unite to form a perfect whole, adapted to meet the wants of men in all the circumstances and experiences of life. . . .

Yet the fact that God has revealed His will to men through His Word has not rendered needless the continued presence and guiding of the Holy Spirit. On the contrary, the Spirit was promised by our Saviour, to open the Word to His servants, to illuminate and apply its teachings. And since it was the Spirit of God that inspired the Bible, it is impossible that the teaching of the Spirit should ever be contrary to that of the Word.[16]

BELIEVE AND PROSPER

Believe in the Lord your God, so shall ye be established; believe his prophets, so shall ye prosper.

The light of prophecy still burns for the guidance of souls, saying, "This is the way, walk ye in it." It shines on the pathway of the just to commend, and on the way of the unjust to lead to repentance and conversion. Through its agency sin will be rebuked and iniquity unmasked. It is progressive in the performance of its duty to reflect light on the past, the present, and the future.[17]

If those who have received the light will appreciate and respect the testimonies of the Lord, they will see the religious life in a new light. They will be convicted. They will see the key that unlocks the mysteries that they have never understood. They will lay hold of the precious things that God has given them to profit withal and will be translated from the kingdom of darkness into God's marvelous light.[18]

Those who despise the warning will be left in blindness to become self-deceived. But those who heed it, and zealously go about the work of separating their sins from them in order to have the needed graces, will be opening the door of their hearts that the dear Saviour may come in and dwell with them.[19]

He [God] has made provision that all may be holy and happy if they choose. Sufficient light has been given to this generation, that we may learn what our duties and privileges are and enjoy the precious and solemn truths in their simplicity and power.

We are accountable only for the light that shines upon us. The commandments of God and the testimony of Jesus are testing us. If we are faithful and obedient, God will delight in us, and bless us as His own chosen, peculiar people. When perfect faith and perfect love and obedience abound, working in the hearts of those who are Christ's followers, they will have a powerful influence.[20]

TO CONVICT ME OF SIN

And when he is come, he will reprove the world of sin, and of righteousness, and of judgment: of sin, because they believe not on me.

The office of the Holy Spirit is distinctly specified in the words of Christ: "When He is come, He will reprove the world of sin, and of righteousness, and of judgment." It is the Holy Spirit that convicts of sin. If the sinner responds to the quickening influence of the Spirit, he will be brought to repentance, and aroused to the importance of obeying the divine requirements.[21]

As Saul yielded himself fully to the convicting power of the Holy Spirit, he saw the mistakes of his life, and recognized the far-reaching claims of the law of God. He who had been a proud Pharisee, confident that he was justified by his good works, now bowed before God with the humility and simplicity of a little child, confessing his own unworthiness and pleading the merits of a crucified and risen Saviour. Saul longed to come into full harmony and communion with the Father and the Son; and in the intensity of his desire for pardon and acceptance, he offered up fervent supplications to the throne of grace.

The prayers of the penitent Pharisee were not in vain. The inmost thoughts and emotions of his heart were transformed by divine grace, and his nobler faculties were brought into harmony with the eternal purposes of God. Christ and His righteousness became to Saul more than the whole world. The conversion of Saul is a striking evidence of the miraculous power of the Holy Spirit to convict men of sin.[22]

It is through the mighty agency of the Holy Spirit that the government of Satan is to be subdued and subjected. It is the Holy Spirit that convinces of sin and expels it from the soul by the consent of the human agent. . . . Through the merits of Christ man may be able to exercise the noblest powers of his being and expel sin from his soul.[23]

TO ENLIGHTEN MY UNDERSTANDING

The God of our Lord Jesus Christ, the Father of glory, may give unto you the spirit of wisdom and revelation in the knowledge of him: the eyes of your understanding being enlightened; that ye may know what is the hope of his calling, and what the riches of the glory of his inheritance in the saints.

For the mind renewed by the Holy Spirit, divine beauty and celestial light shine from the sacred page. That which is to the earthly mind a desolate wilderness, to the spiritual mind becomes a land of living streams.[24]

The Holy Spirit alone can cause us to feel the importance of those things easy to be understood, or prevent us from wresting truths difficult of comprehension. It is the office of heavenly angels to prepare the heart so to comprehend God's Word that we shall be charmed with its beauty, admonished by its warnings, or animated and strengthened by its promises. We should make the psalmist's petition our own, "Open Thou mine eyes, that I may behold wondrous things out of Thy law."[25]

God's holy, educating Spirit is in His Word. A light, a new and precious light, shines forth from every page. Truth is there revealed, and words and sentences are made bright and appropriate for the occasion, as the voice of God speaking to them.

We need to recognize the Holy Spirit as our enlightener. That Spirit loves to address the children, and discover to them the treasures and beauties of the Word. The promises spoken by our Great Teacher will captivate the senses and animate the soul of the child with a spiritual power that is divine. There will grow in the receptive mind a familiarity with divine things which will be as a barricade against the temptations of the enemy. . . . The sparks of heavenly love will fall upon the hearts of the children as an inspiration.[26]

TO BRING ALL THINGS TO MY REMEMBRANCE

The Comforter, which is the Holy Ghost, whom the Father will send in my name, he shall teach you all things, and bring all things to your remembrance, whatsoever I have said unto you.

Christ has risen from the dead, proclaiming over the rent sepulcher, "I am the resurrection and the life." He has sent His Spirit into our world to bring all things to our remembrance. By a miracle of His power He has preserved His Written Word through the ages. Shall we not, then, make this Word our constant study, learning from it God's purpose for us.[27]

The servants of Christ were to prepare no set speech to present when brought to trial. Their preparation was to be made day by day in treasuring up the precious truths of God's Word, and through prayer strengthening their faith. When they were brought into trial, the Holy Spirit would bring to their remembrance the very truths that would be needed. . . .

A daily, earnest striving to know God, and Jesus Christ whom He has sent, would bring power and efficiency to the soul. The knowledge obtained by diligent searching of the Scriptures, would be flashed into the memory at the right time. But if any had neglected to acquaint themselves with the words of Christ, if they had never tested the power of His grace in trial, they could not expect that the Holy Spirit would bring His words to their remembrance.[28]

Christ has made every provision for us to be strong. He has given us His Holy Spirit, whose office is to bring to our remembrance all the promises that Christ has made, that we may have peace and a sweet sense of forgiveness. If we will but keep our eyes fixed on the Saviour and trust in His power, we shall be filled with a sense of security; for the righteousness of Christ will become our righteousness.[29]

TO TRANSFORM MY CHARACTER

But we all, with open face beholding as in a glass the glory of the Lord, are changed into the some image from glory to glory, even as by the Spirit of the Lord.

It is by the Spirit that the heart is made pure. Through the Spirit the believer becomes a partaker of the divine nature. Christ has given His Spirit as a divine power to overcome all hereditary and cultivated tendencies to evil and to impress His own character on His church. . . .

When the Spirit of God takes possession of the heart, it transforms the life. Sinful thoughts are put away, evil deeds are renounced; love, humility, and peace take the place of anger, envy, and strife. Joy takes the place of sadness, and the countenance reflects the joy of heaven. No one sees the hand that lifts the burden or beholds the light descend from the courts above. The blessing comes when by faith the soul surrenders itself to God. Then that power which no human eye can see, creates a new being in the image of God.

The Holy Spirit is the breath of spiritual life in the soul. The impartation of the Spirit is the impartation of the life of Christ. It imbues the receiver with the attributes of Christ. . . .

The religion that comes from God is the only religion that will lead to God. In order to serve Him aright, we must be born of the divine Spirit. This will purify the heart and renew the mind, giving us a new capacity for knowing and loving God. It will give us a willing obedience to all His requirements. This is true worship. It is the fruit of the working of the Holy Spirit. By the Spirit every sincere prayer is indited, and such prayer is acceptable to God. Wherever a soul reaches out after God, there the Spirit's working is manifest, and God will reveal Himself to that soul. For such worshipers He is seeking. He waits to receive them and to make them His sons and daughters.[30]

TO ENDOW ME WITH POWER FROM ABOVE

But ye shall receive power, after that the Holy Ghost is come upon you: and ye shall be witnesses unto me both in Jerusalem, in all Judaea, and in Samaria, and unto the uttermost part of the earth.

The Holy Spirit was to descend on those who love Christ. By this they would be qualified, in and through the glorification of their Head, to receive every endowment necessary for the fulfilling of their mission. The Life-giver held in His hand not only the keys of death but a whole heaven of rich blessings. All power in heaven and earth was given to Him, and having taken His place in the heavenly courts, He could dispense these blessings to all who receive Him. The church was baptized with the Spirit's power. The disciples were fitted to go forth and proclaim Christ, first in Jerusalem, where the shameful work of dishonoring the rightful King had been done, and then to the uttermost parts of the earth. The evidence of the enthronement of Christ in His mediatorial kingdom was given.[31]

God desires that the receivers of His grace shall be witnesses to its power. Those whose course has been most offensive to Him He freely accepts; when they repent, He imparts to them His divine Spirit, places them in the highest positions of trust, and sends them forth into the camp of the disloyal to proclaim His boundless mercy.[32]

Provision is made by God Himself for every soul that turns to the Lord, to receive His immediate cooperation. The Holy Spirit becomes His efficiency.[33]

It is the Spirit's power that we need. This can do more for us in one minute than we can ever accomplish by talking.[34]

Only to those who wait humbly upon God, who watch for His guidance and grace, is the Spirit given. The power of God awaits their demand and reception. This promised blessing, claimed by faith, brings all other blessings in its train.[35]

TO RAISE A STANDARD AGAINST THE ENEMY

When the enemy shall come in like a flood, the Spirit of the Lord shall lift up a standard against him.

Jesus gives the Holy Spirit in large measure for great emergencies, to help our infirmities, to give us strong consolation.[36]

Those who are continually learning in the school of Christ will be able to pursue the even tenor of their way, and Satan's efforts to throw them off their balance will be signally defeated. Temptation is not sin. Jesus was holy and pure, yet He was tempted in all points as we are, but with a strength and power that man will never be called upon to endure. In His successful resistance He has left us a bright example, that we should follow His steps. If we are self-confident or self-righteous we shall be left to fall under the power of temptation; but if we look to Jesus and trust in Him we call to our aid a power that has conquered the foe on the field of battle, and with every temptation He will make a way of escape. When Satan comes in like a flood, we must meet his temptations with the sword of the Spirit, and Jesus will be our helper and will lift up for us a standard against him.[37]

The Holy Spirit was promised to be with those who were wrestling for victory, in demonstration of all mightiness, endowing the human agent with supernatural powers and instructing the ignorant in the mysteries of the kingdom of God. That the Holy Spirit is to be the grand helper is a wonderful promise. . . . The imparted Holy Spirit enabled His disciples, the apostles, to stand firmly against every species of idolatry and to exalt the Lord and Him alone.[38]

By His Spirit He is everywhere present. Through the agency of His Spirit and His angels He ministers to the children of men.[39]

TO GLORIFY CHRIST IN ME

He shall glorify me: for he shall receive of mine, and shall shew it unto you.

In these words Christ declares the crowning work of the Holy Spirit. The Spirit glorifies Christ by making Him the object of supreme regard, and the Saviour becomes the delight, the rejoicing, of the human agent in whose heart is wrought this transformation. . . .

Repentance toward God and faith in Jesus Christ are the fruits of the renewing power of the grace of the Spirit. Repentance represents the process by which the soul seeks to reflect the image of Christ to the world.[40]

Christ gives them the breath of His own Spirit, the life of His own life. The Holy Spirit puts forth its highest energies to work in heart and mind. The grace of God enlarges and multiplies their faculties, and every perfection of the divine nature comes to their assistance in the work of saving souls. Through cooperation with Christ they are complete in Him, and in their human weakness they are enabled to do the deeds of Omnipotence.[41]

It should be the work of the Christian's life to put on Christ and to bring himself to a more perfect likeness of Christ. The sons and daughters of God are to advance in their resemblance to Christ, our pattern. Daily they are to behold His glory and contemplate His incomparable excellence.[42]

O that the baptism of the Holy Spirit might come upon you, that you might be imbued with the Spirit of God! Then day by day you will become more and more conformed to the image of Christ, and in every action of your life the question would be, "Will it glorify my Master?" By patient continuance in well-doing you would seek for glory and honor, and would receive the gift of immortality.[43]

LOVE

The fruit of the Spirit is love, joy, peace, longsuffering, gentleness, goodness, faith, meekness, temperance: against such there is no law.

To all who believe, He is as the tree of life in the Paradise of God. His branches reach to this world, that the blessings which He has purchased for us may be brought within our reach. . . . He has given us a Comforter, the Holy Spirit, which will present to us the precious fruit from the tree of life. From this tree we may pluck and eat, and we may then guide others to it, that they also may eat.[44]

The man who loves God meditates on the law of God day and night. He is instant in season and out of season. He bears the fruit of a branch vitally connected with the Vine. As he has opportunity, he does good; and everywhere, at all times and in all places, he finds opportunity to work for God. He is one of the Lord's evergreen trees; and he carries fragrance with him wherever he goes. A wholesome atmosphere surrounds his soul. The beauty of his well-ordered life and godly conversation inspires faith and hope and courage in others. This is Christianity in practice. Seek to be an evergreen tree. Wear the ornament of a meek and quiet spirit, which is in the sight of God of great price. Cherish the grace of love, joy, peace, longsuffering, gentleness. This is the fruit of the Christian tree. Planted by the rivers of water, it always brings forth its fruit in due season.[45]

If we have the love of Christ in our souls, it will be a natural consequence for us to have all the other graces—joy, peace, longsuffering, gentleness, goodness, faith, meekness, temperance. . . .

When the love of Christ is enshrined in the heart. . . . His presence will be felt.[46]

JOY AND PEACE

Now the God of hope fill you with all joy and peace in believing, that ye may abound in hope, through the power of the Holy Ghost.

The Lord has determined that every soul who obeys His word shall have His joy, His peace, His continual keeping power. Such men and women are brought near Him always, not only when they kneel before Him in prayer, but when they take up the duties of life. He has prepared for them an abiding place with Himself, where the life is purified from all grossness, all unloveliness. By this unbroken communion with Him, they are made colaborers with Him in their lifework.[47]

Words cannot describe the peace and joy possessed by him who takes God at His word. Trials do not disturb him, slights do not vex him. Self is crucified. Day by day his duties may become more taxing, his temptations stronger, his trials more severe; but he does not falter; for he receives strength equal to his need.[48]

Those who are learning at the feet of Jesus will surely exemplify by their deportment and conversation the character of Christ. . . . Their experience is marked less with bustle and excitement than with a subdued and reverent joy. Their love for Christ is a quiet, peaceful, yet all-controlling power. The light and love of an indwelling Saviour are revealed in every word and every act.[49]

There have been times when the blessing of God has been bestowed in answer to prayer, so that when others have come into the room, no sooner did they step over the threshold than they exclaimed, "The Lord is here!" Not a word had been uttered, but the blessed influence of God's holy presence was sensibly felt. The joy that comes from Jesus Christ was there; and in this sense the Lord had been in the room just as verily as He walked through the streets of Jerusalem, or appeared to the disciples when they were in the upper chamber, and said, "Peace be unto you."[50]

LONG-SUFFERING

Strengthened with all might, according to his glorious power, unto all patience and longsuffering with joyfulness.

Love is the law of Christ's kingdom. The Lord calls upon every one to reach a high standard. The lives of His people are to reveal love, meekness, long-suffering. Long-suffering bears something, yea, many things, without seeking to be avenged by word or act.[51]

"Long-suffering" is patience with offence; long endurance. If you are long-suffering, you will not impart to others your supposed knowledge of your brother's mistakes and errors. You will seek to help and save him, because he has been purchased with the blood of Christ. "Tell him his fault between thee and him alone: if he shall hear thee, thou hast gained thy brother." "Brethren, if a man be overtaken in a fault, ye which are spiritual restore such a one in the spirit of meekness, considering thyself, lest thou also be tempted." To be long-suffering is not to be gloomy and sad, sour and hardhearted; it is to be exactly the opposite.[52]

Try to live peaceably with all men, and let the atmosphere surrounding your soul be sweet and fragrant. The Lord hears every unwise word that is spoken. If you will battle against selfish human nature, you will go forward steadily in the work of overcoming hereditary and cultivated tendencies to wrong. By patience, long-suffering, and forbearance you will accomplish much. Remember that you cannot be humiliated by the unwise speeches of someone else, but that when you answer unwisely, you lose a victory that you might have gained. Be very careful of your words.[53]

Forbearance and unselfishness mark the words and deeds of those who are born again to live the new life in Christ.[54]

GENTLENESS

Thou hast also given me the shield of thy salvation: and thy gentleness hath made me great.

You are to represent Christ in His meekness and gentleness and love.[55]

True gentleness is a gem of great value in the sight of God.[56]

We want a spirit of gentleness. We cannot live right in the family circle without it. In order to have the proper control of our children, we must manifest a spirit of gentleness and of meekness and of long-suffering. We do not want to have a faultfinding, fretful, scolding spirit. If we teach them to have a spirit of gentleness, we must have a spirit of gentleness ourselves; . . . if we would have them manifest a spirit of love toward us, we must manifest a gentle, loving spirit toward them. But at the same time there need be no weakness or unwise indulgence on the part of parents. The mother must have firmness and decision. She must be as firm as a rock, and not swerve from the right. Her laws and rules should be carried out at all times and under all hazards, but she can do this with all gentleness and meekness. . . . The children will grow up God-fearing men and women.[57]

No member of the family can enclose himself within himself, where other members of the family shall not feel his influence and spirit. The very expression of the countenance has an influence for good or evil. His spirit, his words, his actions, his attitude toward others, are unmistakable. . . . If he is filled with the love of Christ, he will manifest courtesy, kindness, tender regard for the feelings of others, and will communicate to his associates, by his acts of love, a tender, grateful, happy feeling. It will be made manifest that he is living for Jesus. . . . He will be able to say to the Lord, "Thy gentleness hath made me great."[58]

GOODNESS

A good man obtaineth favour of the Lord.

True goodness is accounted of Heaven as true greatness. The condition of the moral affections determines the worth of the man. A person may have property and intellect, and yet be valueless, because the glowing fire of goodness has never burned upon the altar of his heart.[59]

Goodness is the result of divine power transforming human nature. By believing in Christ, the fallen race he has redeemed may obtain that faith which works by love and purifies the soul from all defilement. Then Christlike attributes appear: for by beholding Christ men become changed into the same image from glory to glory, from character to character. Good fruit is produced. The character is fashioned after the divine similitude, and integrity, uprightness, and true benevolence are manifested toward the sinful race.[60]

The Lord has placed every human being on test and trial. He desires to prove and to try us, to see if we will be good and do good in this life, to see if he can trust us with eternal riches, and make us members of the royal family, children of the heavenly King.[61]

There is no limit to the good you may do. If you make the Word of God the rule of your life, and govern your actions by its precepts, making all your purposes and exertions in the fulfilling of your duty a blessing and not a curse to others, success will crown your efforts. You have placed yourself in connection with God; you have become a channel of light to others. You are honored by becoming colaborers with Jesus; and no higher honor can you receive than the blessed benediction from the lips of the Saviour: "Well done, good and faithful servant."[62]

FAITH

The just shall live by his faith.

On one occasion, when meditating concerning the future, he [Habakkuk] said, "I will stand upon my watch, and set me upon the tower, and will watch to see what He will say unto me." Graciously the Lord answered him: "Write the vision, and make it plain upon tables, that he may run that readeth it. . . . *The just shall live by his faith.*"

The faith that strengthened Habakkuk and all the holy and the just in those days of deep trial was the same faith that sustains God's people today. In the darkest hours, under circumstances the most forbidding, the Christian believer may keep his soul stayed upon the source of all light and power. Day by day, through faith in God, his hope and courage may be renewed. "The just shall live by his faith." In the service of God there need be no despondency, no wavering, no fear. The Lord will more than fulfill the highest expectations of those who put their trust in Him. He will give them the wisdom their varied necessities demand. . . .

We must cherish and cultivate the faith of which prophets and apostles have testified—the faith that lays hold on the promises of God and waits for deliverance in His appointed time and way. The sure word of prophecy will meet its final fulfillment in the glorious Advent of our Lord and Saviour Jesus Christ, as King of kings and Lord of lords. The time of waiting may seem long, the soul may be oppressed by discouraging circumstances, many in whom confidence has been placed may fall by the way; but with the prophet who endeavored to encourage Judah in a time of unparalleled apostasy, let us confidently declare, "The Lord is in His holy temple: let all the earth keep silence before Him." Let us ever hold in remembrance the cheering message, "The vision is yet for an appointed time . . . : though it tarry, wait for it; because it will surely come, it will not tarry. . . . The just shall live by his faith." [63]

MEEKNESS

The meek will he guide in judgment: and the meek will he teach his way.

Jesus loves the young. . . . He bids them learn of him meekness and lowliness of heart. This precious grace is rarely seen in the youth of the present day, even in those who profess to be Christians. Their own ways seem right in their eyes. In accepting the name of Christ they do not accept His character or submit to wear His yoke; therefore they know nothing of the joy and peace to be found in His service.[64]

Meekness is a precious grace, willing to suffer silently, willing to endure trials. Meekness is patient and labors to be happy under all circumstances. Meekness is always thankful and makes its own songs of happiness, making melody in the heart of God. Meekness will suffer disappointment and wrong and will not retaliate.[65]

A meek and quiet spirit will not be ever looking out for happiness for itself, but will seek for self-forgetfulness and find sweet content and true satisfaction in making others happy.[66]

It is not the seeking to climb to eminence that will make you great in God's sight, but it is the humble life of goodness, of fidelity that will make you the object of the heavenly angels' special guardianship. The Pattern Man . . . lived nearly thirty years in an obscure Galilean town, hidden away among the hills. All the angel host was at His command, yet He did not claim to be anything great or exalted. . . . He was a carpenter, working for wages, a servant to those for whom He labored, showing that heaven may be very near to us in the common walks of life, and that angels from the heavenly courts will take charge of the steps of those who come and go at God's command.[67]

꽃 꽃 꽃

The perfect fruit of faith, meekness, and love often matures best amid storm clouds and darkness.[68]

THE PROMISE OF POWER

For John truly baptized with water; but ye shall be baptized with the Holy Ghost.

It is not because of any restriction on God's part that the riches of His grace do not flow to men. His gift is godlike. He gave with a liberality that men do not appreciate because they do not love to receive. If all were willing to receive, all would be filled with the Spirit. . . . We are too easily satisfied with a ripple on the surface, when it is our privilege to expect the deep moving of the Spirit of God.[69]

With the reception of this gift, all other gifts would be ours; for we are to have this gift according to the plentitude of the riches of the grace of Christ, and He is ready to supply every soul according to the capacity to receive. Then let us not be satisfied with only a little of this blessing, only that amount which will keep us from the slumber of death, but let us diligently seek for the abundance of the grace of God.[70]

Promise after promise is given, assuring us of the fullness of power that God has, and yet we are so weak in faith that we do not grasp the power. O how much we need a living, earnest faith in the truths of God's Word! This great need of God's people is constantly before me. . . . What can we do to arouse them to see that we are living in the very evening of this earth's history? . . . We need to seek for a faith that will lay hold of the arm of Jehovah.[71]

Only to those who wait humbly upon God, who watch for His guidance and grace, is the Spirit given. The power of God awaits their demand and reception. This promised blessing, claimed by faith, brings all other blessings in its train. It is given according to the riches of the grace of Christ, and He is ready to supply every soul according to the capacity to receive.[72]

PREPARING FOR POWER

Repent ye therefore, and be converted, that your sins may be blotted out, when the times of refreshing shall come from the presence of the Lord.

Instead of being worked by the Holy Spirit, many, even among those engaged in the solemn work of God, are barring the way against its holy, life-giving influences. They freely criticize and judge their brethren, and yet they do not realize the necessity of earnestly looking into the divine mirror to see what spirit they themselves are manifesting. Their defects of character they regard as virtues, and cling to them. . . .

Let there be a work of reformation and repentance. Let all seek for the outpouring of the Holy Spirit. As with the disciples after the ascension of Christ, it may require several days of earnestly seeking God and putting away of sin.

When God's people are worked by the Holy Spirit, they will manifest a zeal that is according to knowledge. . . . They will reflect the light that God has been giving for years. The spirit of criticism will be put away. Filled with the spirit of humility, they will be of one mind, united with one another and with Christ.[73]

When a man is filled with the Spirit, the more severely he is tested and tried, the more dearly he proves that he is a representative of Christ. The peace that dwells in the soul is seen on the countenance. The words and actions express the love of the Saviour. There is no striving for the highest place. Self is renounced. The name of Jesus is written on all that is said and done.[74]

When the truth in its simplicity is lived in every place, then God will work through His angels as He worked on the day of Pentecost, and hearts will be changed so decidedly that there will be a manifestation of the influence of genuine truth, as is represented in the descent of the Holy Spirit.[75]

TARRYING FOR POWER

Tarry ye in the city of Jerusalem, until ye be endued with power from on high.

Every truly converted soul will be intensely desirous to bring others from the darkness of error into the marvelous light of the righteousness of Jesus Christ. The great outpouring of the Spirit of God, which lightens the whole earth with His glory, will not come until we have an enlightened people, that know by experience what it means to be laborers together with God. When we have entire, wholehearted consecration to the service of Christ, God will recognize the fact by an outpouring of His Spirit without measure; but this will not be while the largest portion of the church are not laborers together with God. God cannot pour out His Spirit when selfishness and self-indulgence are so manifest; when a spirit prevails that, if put into words, would express that answer of Cain—"Am I my brother's keeper?" . . .

When the hearts of the believers are warm with the love for God, they will do a continual work for Jesus. They will manifest the meekness of Christ and display a steadfast purpose that will not fail nor be discouraged. God will use humble men to do His work, for there is a large vineyard calling for laborers.[76]

The promise of the Holy Spirit is not limited to any age or to any race. Christ declared that the divine influence of His Spirit was to be with His followers unto the end. From the day of Pentecost to the present time, the Comforter has been sent to all who have yielded themselves fully to the Lord and to His service. . . . The more closely believers have walked with God, the more clearly and powerfully have they testified of their Redeemer's love and of His saving grace. The men and women who through the long centuries of persecution and trial enjoyed a large measure of the presence of the Spirit in their lives, have stood as signs and wonders in the world.[77]

RECEIVING THE POWER

And suddenly there came a sound from heaven as of a rushing mighty wind, and it filled all the house where they were sitting. . . . And they were all filled with the Holy Ghost.

The Spirit came upon the waiting, praying disciples with a fullness that reached every heart. The Infinite One revealed Himself in power to His church. It was as if for ages this influence had been held in restraint, and now Heaven rejoiced in being able to pour out upon the church the riches of the Spirit's grace.[78]

The outpouring of the Spirit in the days of the apostles was the "former rain," and glorious was the result. But the latter rain will be more abundant.[79]

To the end of time the presence of the Spirit is to abide with the true church.

But near the end of earth's harvest a special bestowal of the spiritual grace is promised, to prepare the church for the coming of the Son of men. This outpouring of the Spirit is likened to the falling of the latter rain; and it is for this added power that the Christians are to send their petitions to the Lord of the harvest "in the time of the latter rain." In response, "The Lord shall make bright clouds, and give them showers of rain." . . .

Those only who are constantly receiving fresh supplies of grace will have power proportionate to their daily need and their ability to use that power. Instead of looking forward to some future time when, through a special endowment of spiritual power, they will receive a miraculous fitting up for soul winning, they are yielding themselves daily to God, that He may make them vessels meet for His use. Daily they are improving the opportunities for service that lie within their reach. Daily they are witnessing for the Master wherever they may be, whether in some humble sphere of labor in the home or in a public field of usefulness.[80]

WITNESSING WITH POWER

With great power gave the apostles witness of the resurrection of the Lord Jesus: and great grace was upon them all.

What was the result of the outpouring of the Spirit? Thousands were converted in a day. The sword of the Spirit, newly edged with power and bathed in the lightnings of heaven, cut its way through unbelief, overcoming Satanic agencies and magnifying the Lord as possessing supreme power.

Everywhere the gospel was proclaimed. Those who proclaimed it had no grievous complaints to make. The hearts of the disciples were surcharged with a benevolence so full, so deep, so far reaching, that it impelled them to go to the ends of the earth, testifying, God forbid that we should glory, save in the cross of our Lord Jesus Christ. As they proclaimed the gospel as the power of God unto salvation, hearts yielded to the power of the Holy Spirit. New territory was daily added to the church. In every place converts confessed Christ. Those who had been the bitterest opponents of the truth became her champions. . . .

The disciples . . . were weighted with the burden for the salvation of souls. The gospel was to be carried to the uttermost parts of the earth, and they claimed the endowment of the power that Christ had promised. Then it was that the Holy Spirit was poured out, and thousands were converted in a day.

So may it be now. Instead of man's speculations, let the Word of God be preached. Let Christians put away their dissensions and give themselves to God for the saving of the lost. Let them ask in faith for the blessing, and it will come.[81]

Zeal for God moved the disciples to bear witness to the truth with mighty power. Should not this zeal fire our hearts with a determination to tell the story of redeeming love, of Christ, and Him crucified?[82]

I WANT THAT POWER

And is shall come to pass afterward, that I will pour out my spirit upon all flesh; and your sons and your daughters shall prophesy, your old men shall dream dreams, your young men shall see visions.

We are living in the last days, in a time when we may expect much from the Lord. These words should bring us to the throne of grace to claim great things of Him. Here the promise is given that on the men and women and on our sons and daughters the Holy Spirit is to come; and "whosoever shall call upon the name of the Lord shall be saved." This brings to view a wonderful work to be done, for which we need the converting power of God in our hearts every day. It is our privilege to experience this. Heaven is full of blessings, and it is our privilege to claim the rich promises of God for our individual selves. We need to seek the Lord day and night that we may know just what steps to take and just what we ought to do.

The Lord has a special work to do for us individually. As we see the wickedness of the world brought to light in the courts of justice and published in the daily papers, let us draw near to God, and by living faith lay hold of His promises, that the grace of Christ may be manifest in us. We may have an influence, a powerful influence, in the world. If the convicting power of God is in us, we shall be enabled to lead souls that are in sin to conversion.[83]

In the closing scenes of this earth's history, many . . . children and youth [who receive a true Christian education] will astonish people by their witness to the truth, which will be borne in simplicity, yet with spirit and power. They have been taught the fear of the Lord, and their hearts have been softened by a careful and prayerful study of the Bible. In the near future many children will be endued with the Spirit of God, and will do a work proclaiming the truth to the world. . . . They will do a work in the world that not all the powers of evil can counteract.[84]

THE WHOLE EARTH WILL BE LIGHTENED

And after these things I saw another angel come down from heaven, having great power; and the earth was lightened with his glory.

The end of all things is at hand. God is moving upon every mind that is open to receive the impressions of His Holy Spirit. He is sending out messengers that they may give the warning in every locality. God is testing the devotion of His churches and their willingness to render obedience to the Spirit's guidance. Knowledge is to be increased. The messengers of Heaven are to be seen running to and fro, seeking in every possible way to warn the people of the coming judgments and presenting the glad tidings of salvation through our Lord Jesus Christ. The standard of righteousness is to be exalted. The Spirit of God is moving upon men's hearts, and those who respond to its influence will become lights in the world. Everywhere they are seen going forth to communicate to others the light they have received as they did after the descent of the Holy Spirit on the day of Pentecost. And as they let their light shine, they receive more and more of the Spirit's power. The earth is lighted with the glory of God.[85]

This message will close with power and strength far exceeding the midnight cry. Servants of God, endowed with power from on high, with their faces lighted up, and shining with holy consecration, went forth to proclaim the message from heaven.[86]

Many were praising God. The sick were healed, and other miracles were wrought. A spirit of intercession was seen, even as was manifested before the great Day of Pentecost. Hundreds and thousands were seen visiting families and opening before them the Word of God. Hearts were convicted by the power of the Holy Spirit, and a spirit of genuine conversion was manifest. On every side doors were thrown open to the proclamation of the truth. The world seemed to be lightened with the heavenly influence.[87]

A CHALLENGING LIFE

| *March 1* | *Heroes for God* | *Esther 4:14* |

ESTHER

And who knoweth whether thou art come to the kingdom for such a time as this?

A certain day was appointed on which the Jews were to be destroyed and their property confiscated. Little did the king realize the far-reaching results that would have accompanied the complete carrying out of this decree. Satan himself, the hidden instigator of the scheme, was trying to rid the earth of those who preserved the knowledge of the true God. . . .

But the plots of the enemy were defeated by a Power that reigns among the children of men. In the providence of God, Esther, a Jewess who feared the Most High, had been made queen of the Medo-Persian kingdom. Mordecai was a near relative of hers. In their extremity they decided to appeal to Xerxes in behalf of their people. Esther was to venture into his presence as an intercessor. "Who knoweth," said Mordecai, "whether thou art come to the kingdom for such a time as this?"

The crisis that Esther faced demanded quick, earnest action; but both she and Mordecai realized that unless God should work mightily in their behalf, their own efforts would be unavailing. So Esther took time for communion with God, the source of her strength. "Go," she directed Mordecai, "gather together all the Jews that are present in Shushan, and fast ye for me, and neither eat nor drink three days, night or day: I also and my maidens will fast likewise; and so will I go in unto the king, which is not according to the law: and if I perish, I perish."[1]

To every household and every school, to every parent, teacher, and child upon whom has shone the light of the gospel, comes at this crisis the question put to Esther the queen at that momentous crisis in Israel's history, "Who knoweth whether *thou* art come to the kingdom for such a time as this?"[2]

64

PAUL

At my first answer no man stood with me, but all men forsook me.
. . . Notwithstanding the Lord stood with me, and strengthened me;
that by me the preaching might be fully known, and that all the
Gentiles might hear.

Paul before Nero—how striking the contrast! . . . In power and
greatness Nero stood unrivaled. . . . Without money, without friends,
without counsel, Paul had been brought forth from a dungeon to be
tried for his life. . . .

The countenance of the monarch bearing the shameful record of
the passions that raged within; the countenance of the prisoner
telling the story of a heart at peace with God and man. The results
of opposite systems of education stood that day contrasted—a life of
unbounded self-indulgence and a life of entire self-sacrifice. Here
were the representatives of two theories of life—all-absorbing selfishness, which counts nothing too valuable to be sacrificed for momentary gratification, and self-denying endurance, ready to give up
life itself, if need be, for the good of others. . . .

The people and the judges . . . had been present at many trials,
and had looked upon many a criminal; but never had they seen a
man wear a look of such holy calmness. . . . His words struck a
chord that vibrated in the hearts even of the most hardened. Truth,
clear and convincing, overthrew error. Light shone into the minds of
many who afterward gladly followed its rays. . . . He pointed his
hearers to the sacrifice made for the fallen race. . . .

Thus pleads the advocate of truth; faithful among the faithless,
loyal among the disloyal, he stands as God's representative, and his
voice is as a voice from heaven. There is no fear, no sadness, no discouragement, in word or look. . . . His words are as a shout of victory above the roar of battle.[3]

Let this hero of faith speak for himself. He says, "I take pleasure
in infirmities, in reproaches, in necessities, in persecution, in dis-
tresses for Christ's sake."[4]

JOSEPH

And Pharaoh said unto his servants, Can we find such a one as this is, a man in whom the Spirit of God is? And Pharaoh said unto Joseph, Forasmuch as God hath shewed thee all this, there is none so discreet and wise as thou art: thou shalt be over my house, and according unto thy word shall all my people be ruled: only in the throne will I be greater than thou.

From the dungeon Joseph was exalted to be ruler over all the land of Egypt. It was a position of high honor, yet it was beset with difficulty and peril. One cannot stand upon a lofty height without danger. As the tempest leaves unharmed the lowly flower of the valley, while it uproots the stately tree upon the mountaintop, so those who have maintained their integrity in humble life may be dragged down to the pit by the temptations that assail worldly success and honor. But Joseph's character bore the test alike of adversity and prosperity. The same fidelity to God was manifested when he stood in the palace of the Pharaohs as when in a prisoner's cell. He was still a stranger in a heathen land, separated from his kindred, the worshipers of God; but he fully believed that the divine hand had directed his steps, and in constant reliance upon God he faithfully discharged the duties of his position. Through Joseph the attention of the king and great men of Egypt was directed to the true God; and . . . they learned to respect the principles revealed in the life and character of the worshiper of Jehovah.

How was Joseph enabled to make such a record of firmness of character, uprightness, and wisdom?—In his early years he had consulted duty rather than inclination; and the integrity, the simple trust, the noble nature, of the youth, bore fruit in the deeds of the man. . . . Faithful attention to duty in every station, from the lowliest to the most exalted, had been training every power for its highest service. He who lives in accordance with the Creator's will is securing to himself the truest and noblest development of character.[5]

STEPHEN, THE FIRST MARTYR

And they stoned Stephen, calling upon God, and saying, Lord Jesus, receive my spirit. And he kneeled down, and cried with a loud voice, Lord, lay not this sin to their charge. And when he had said this, he fell asleep.

Stephen, a man loved by God, and one who was laboring to win souls to Christ, lost his life because he bore a triumphant testimony of the crucified and risen Saviour. . . . The hatred which the enemies of truth had shown for the Son of God, they revealed in their hatred for His followers. They could not bear to hear of the One whom they had crucified, and that Stephen should bear so bold a testimony filled them with rage. . . .

In the light which they saw in the face of Stephen, the men in authority had evidence from God. But they despised the evidence. O that they would heed! O that they would repent! But they would not.[6]

When Stephen was called upon to suffer for Christ's sake, he did not waver. He read his fate in the cruel faces of his persecutors, and he did not hesitate to give to them the last message which he was to bear to men. He looked up and said, "I see the heavens opened, and the Son of man standing on the right hand of God." All heaven was interested in this case. Jesus, rising from the throne of His Father, was leaning over, looking upon the face of His servant, and imparting to his countenance the beams of His own glory, and men were astonished as they saw Stephen's face lighted up as if it had been the face of an angel. The glory of God shone upon him, and while he was beholding the face of his Lord, the enemies of Christ stoned him to death. Would we not think that a hard death to die? But the fear of death was gone, and his last breath was spent in petitioning the Lord to forgive his persecutors.

Jesus has made it as easy as He possibly can for His children, and He wants us to follow in His footsteps; for if we do, we shall be partakers of Christ and His glory.[7]

THREE HEBREW WORTHIES

If it be so, our God whom we serve is able to deliver us from the burning fiery furnace, and he will deliver us out of thine hand, O king. But if not, be it known unto thee, O king, that we will not serve thy gods, nor worship the golden image which thou hast set up.

A severe test came to . . . these youth when Nebuchadnezzar issued a proclamation, calling upon all the officers of the kingdom to assemble at the dedication of the great image, and at the sound of the musical instruments, to bow down and worship it. Should any fail of doing this, they were immediately to be cast into the midst of a burning fiery furnace. The worship of this image had been brought about by the wise men of Babylon in order to make the Hebrew youth join in their idolatrous worship. They were beautiful singers, and the Chaldeans wanted them to forget their God and accept the worship of the Babylonian idols.

The appointed day came, and at the sound of the music, the vast company that had assembled at the king's command "fell down and worshiped the golden image." But these faithful young men would not bow down. . . .

Then the king commanded the furnace to be heated seven times hotter than it was wont to be heated; and when this was done, the three Hebrews were cast in. So furious were the flames that the men who cast the Hebrews in were burned to death.

Suddenly the countenance of the king paled with terror. . . . His voice trembling with excitement, the monarch exclaimed, "Lo, I see four men loose, walking in the midst of the fire, and they have no hurt; and the form of the fourth is like the Son of God."[8]

From age to age the heroes of faith have been marked by their fidelity to God, and they have been brought conspicuously before the world that their light might shine to those in darkness. Daniel and his three companions are illustrious examples of Christian heroism. . . . From their experience in the court of Babylon we may learn what God will do for those who serve Him with full purpose of heart.[9]

YOUTH TODAY

Watch ye, stand fast in the faith, quit you like men, be strong.

Christ told His disciples that in the world they should have tribulation. They would be brought before kings and rulers for His sake; all manner of evil would be spoken against them falsely, and those who destroyed their lives would think they did God service. And all, in every age, who have lived godly lives have suffered persecution in some form. . . . They have suffered every indignity, outrage, and cruelty which Satan could move upon minds to invent.

The world is as much opposed to genuine religion today as it ever has been. . . .

The spirit of persecution will . . . be aroused against the faithful ones, who make no concessions to the world, and will not be swayed by its opinions, its favor, or its opposition. A religion that bears a living testimony in favor of holiness and that rebukes pride, selfishness, avarice, and fashionable sins will be hated by the world and by superficial Christians. Marvel not, then, my youthful Christian friends, if the world hates you; for it hated your Master before you. When you suffer reproach and persecution, you are in excellent company; for Jesus endured it all, and much more. If you are faithful sentinels for God, these things are a compliment to you. It is the heroic souls, who will be true if they stand alone, who will win the imperishable crown. . . .

The way to eternal life is straight and narrow, and you will have to press through many difficulties; but by persevering effort you may win eternal life—the future, immortal inheritance. And the rest, the peace, the glory at the end of the journey, will a thousand times repay every exertion and sacrifice that you can make.[10]

MODERN HEROES

He that is slow to anger is better than the mighty; and he that ruleth his spirit than he that taketh a city.

He has conquered self—the strongest foe man has to meet. The highest evidence of nobility in a Christian is self-control. He who can stand unmoved amid a storm of abuse is one of God's heroes. . . .

He who has learned to rule his spirit will rise above the slights, the rebuffs, the annoyances to which we are daily exposed, and these will cease to cast a gloom over his spirit.

It is God's purpose that the kingly power of sanctified reason, controlled by divine grace, shall bear sway in the lives of human beings. He who rules his spirit is in possession of this power.[11]

The man or woman who preserves the balance of the mind when tempted to indulge passion, stands higher in the sight of God and heavenly angels than the most renowned general that ever led an army to battle and to victory.[12]

What young men and women need is Christian heroism. God's Word declares that he that ruleth his spirit is better than he that taketh a city. To rule the spirit means to keep self under discipline. . . . They need to seek earnestly to bring into their lives the perfection that is seen in the life of the Saviour, so that when Christ shall come, they will be prepared to enter in through the gates into the city of God. God's abounding love and presence in the heart will give the power of self-control and will mold and fashion the mind and character. The grace of Christ in the life will direct the aims and purposes and capabilities into channels that will give moral and spiritual power—power which the youth will not have to leave in this world, but which they can carry with them into the future life and retain through the eternal ages.[13]

LOVE NOT THE WORLD

Love not the world, neither the things that are in the world. If any man love the world, the love of the Father is not in him. For all that is in the world, the lust of the flesh, and the lust of the eyes, and the pride of life, is not of the Father, but is of the world.

The youth living in this age will have a stern battle to fight if they make right principles their rule of action. It is the highest effort of a large class in society to do as others do, to shape their course according to the world's standard. Like the empty bubble or the worthless weed, they drift with the current. They have no individuality, no moral independence. The approval of the world is of more value to them than the approval of God or the esteem of those whom He esteems. Their only motive or rule of action is policy. As they do not value truth or act from principle, no dependence can be placed upon them. They are the sport of Satan's temptations. They have no true respect for themselves and no real happiness in life. This class are to be pitied for their weakness and folly, and their example should be shunned by all who desire to be truly worthy of respect. But instead of this, their society is too often courted, and they seem to exert a fascinating power, well-nigh impossible to break. . . .

In forming your opinions and choosing your associates let reason and the fear of God be your guide. Be firm in your purpose here, regardless of the opinions which others may entertain concerning you. When God's requirements lead you to an opposite course from that which your associates are pursuing, go resolutely forward, whether you follow many or few. Whatever God's Word condemns, that reject even though the whole world adopt and advocate it. . . .

Those who are drifting with the tide, who love pleasure and self-indulgence, and choose the easier way, regardless of principle so long as their desires are gratified—these will never stand with the overcomers around the great white throne.[14]

PURITY IN THIS CORRUPT AGE

Who shall ascend into the hill of the Lord? or who shall stand in his holy place? He that hath clean hands, and a pure heart; who hath not lifted up his soul unto vanity, nor sworn deceitfully.

The safeguards of our purity must be watchfulness and prayer.[15]

We are living in an atmosphere of satanic witchery. The enemy will weave a spell of licentiousness around every soul that is not barricaded by the grace of Christ. Temptations will come; but if we watch against the enemy, and maintain the balance of self-control and purity, the seducing spirits will have no influence over us. Those who do nothing to encourage temptation will have strength to withstand it when it comes.[16]

If they [the youth] do not willfully rush into danger, and needlessly place themselves in the way of temptation, if they shun evil influences and vicious society, and then are unavoidably compelled to be in dangerous company, they will have strength of character to stand for the right and to preserve principle, and come forth in the strength of God with their morals untainted. If youth who have been properly educated make God their trust, their moral powers will stand the most powerful test.[17]

God's elect must stand untainted amid the corruptions teeming around them in these last days. . . . The Spirit of God should have perfect control, influencing every action.[18]

Those who enter upon active life with firm principles will be prepared to stand unsullied amid the moral pollutions of this corrupt age.[19]

"Who, O Lord, shall stand when thou appearest?" Only those who have clean hands and a pure heart shall abide in the day of His coming. . . . As you hope to be finally exalted to join the society of sinless angels and to live in an atmosphere where there is not the least taint of sin, seek purity; for nothing else will abide the searching test of the day of God and be received into a pure and holy heaven.[20]

CHOOSE THE WAY OF TRUTH

I have chosen the way of truth: thy judgments have I laid before me. I have stuck unto thy testimonies: O Lord, put me not to shame.

There are two great principles, one of loyalty, the other of disloyalty. We all need greater Christian courage, that we may uplift the standard on which is inscribed the commandments of God and the faith of Jesus. . . . The line of demarcation between the obedient and the disobedient must be plain and distinct. We must have a firm determination to do the Lord's will at all times and in all places. . . .

Christian strength is obtained by serving the Lord faithfully. Young men and young women should realize that to be one with Christ is the highest honor to which they can attain. By the strictest fidelity they should strive for moral independence, and this independence they should maintain against every influence that may try to turn them from righteous principles. Stronger minds may, yes, they will, make assertions that have no foundation in truth. Let the heavenly eyesalve be applied to the eyes of your understanding, that you may distinguish between truth and error. Search the Word; and when you find a "Thus saith the Lord," take your stand. . . .

In *Pilgrim's Progress* there is a character called Pliable. Youth, shun this character. Those represented by it are very accommodating, but they are as a reed shaken by the wind. They possess no will power. Every youth needs to cultivate decision. A divided state of the will is a snare, and will be the ruin of many youth. Be firm, else you will be left with your house, or character, built upon a sandy foundation.[21]

The Lord's philosophy is the rule of the Christian's life. The entire being should be imbued with the life-giving principles of heaven. The busy nothings which consume the time of so many shrink into their proper position before a healthy, sanctifying Bible piety.[22]

CHRIST'S ADHERENCE TO PRINCIPLE

In the volume of the book it is written of me, I delight to do thy will, O my God: yea, thy law is within my heart.

The life of Christ was distinguished from the generality of children. His strength of moral character and His firmness ever led Him to be true to His sense of duty and to adhere to the principles of right, from which no motive, however powerful, could move Him. Money or pleasure, applause or censure, could not purchase or flatter Him to consent to a wrong action. He was strong to resist temptation, wise to discover evil, and firm to abide faithful to His convictions.

The wicked and unprincipled would flatter and portray the pleasures of sinful indulgences, but His strength of principle was strong to resist the suggestions of Satan. His penetration had been cultivated, that He could discern the voice of the tempter. He would not swerve from duty to obtain the favor of any. He would not sell His principles for human praise or to avoid reproach and the envy and hatred of those who were enemies of righteousness and true goodness.[23]

He took pleasure in discharging His obligations to His parents and to society, without yielding His principles or being contaminated with the impure influence surrounding Him at Nazareth.[24]

Never did Christ deviate from loyalty to the principles of God's law. Never did He do anything contrary to the will of His Father.[25] Jesus does not, after giving us general directions, leave us to guess the way amid bypaths and dangerous passes. He leads us in a straight path, and while we follow Him our footsteps will not slide.[26]

Each soul must live in hourly communion with Christ; for he says, "Without me ye can do nothing." His principles are to be our principles; for these principles are the everlasting truth, proclaimed in righteousness, goodness, mercy, and love.[27]

His principles are the only steadfast things our world knows.[28]

DANIEL LIVED BY PRINCIPLE

Then the presidents and princes sought to find occasion against Daniel concerning the kingdom; but they could find none occasion nor fault; forasmuch as he was faithful, neither was there any error or fault found in him.

Daniel was subjected to the severest temptations that can assail the youth today, yet he was true to the religious instruction received in early life. He was surrounded with influences calculated to subvert those who would vacillate between principle and inclination, yet the Word of God presents him as a faultless character. Daniel dared not trust to his own moral power. Prayer was to him a necessity. He made God his strength, and the fear of God was continually before him in all the transactions of his life. . . . He sought to live in peace with all, while he was unbending as the lofty cedar wherever principle was involved. In everything that did not come in collision with his allegiance to God, he was respectful and obedient to those who had authority over him. . . .

In the experience of Daniel and his companions we have an instance of the triumph of principle over temptation to indulge the appetite. It shows us that through religious principle young men may triumph over the lusts of the flesh, and remain true to God's requirements. . . . What if Daniel and his companions had made a compromise with those heathen officers, and had yielded to the pressure of the occasion, by eating and drinking as was customary with the Babylonians? That single instance of departure from principle would have weakened their sense of right and their abhorrence of wrong. Indulgence of appetite would have involved the sacrifice of physical vigor, clearness of intellect, and spiritual power. One wrong step would probably have led to others, until, their connection with Heaven being severed, they would have been swept away by temptation.[29]

75

JOSEPH, A MAN OF PRINCIPLE

How can I do this great wickedness, and sin against God?

Joseph's gentleness and fidelity won the heart of the chief captain, who came to regard him as a son rather than a slave. . . . But Joseph's faith and integrity were to be tested by fiery trials. His master's wife endeavored to entice the young man to transgress the law of God. Heretofore he had remained untainted by the corruption teeming in that heathen land; but this temptation, so sudden, so strong, so seductive—how should it be met? Joseph knew well what would be the consequence of resistance. On the one hand were concealment, favor, and rewards; on the other, disgrace, imprisonment, perhaps death. His whole future life depended upon the decision of the moment. Would principle triumph? Would Joseph still be true to God? With inexpressible anxiety, the angels looked upon the scene.

Joseph's answer reveals the power of religious principle. He would not betray the confidence of his master on earth, and, whatever the consequences, he would be true to his Master in heaven. . . .

Joseph suffered for his integrity; for his tempter revenged herself by accusing him of a foul crime, and causing him to be thrust into prison. Had Potiphar believed his wife's charge against Joseph, the young Hebrew would have lost his life; but the modesty and uprightness that had uniformly characterized his conduct were proof of his innocence; and yet, to save the reputation of his master's house, he was abandoned to disgrace and bondage. . . .

But Joseph's real character shines out, even in the darkness of the dungeon. He held fast his faith and patience; his years of faithful service had been most cruelly repaid, yet this did not render him morose or distrustful. He had the peace that comes from conscious innocence, and he trusted his case with God.[30]

PRINCIPLE NOT TO BE SACRIFICED FOR PEACE

Peace I leave with you, my peace I give unto you: not as the world giveth, give I unto you. Let not your heart be troubled, neither let it be afraid.

There always have been and always will be two classes on the earth to the end of time—the believers in Jesus, and those who reject Him. Sinners, however wicked, abominable, and corrupt, by faith in Him will be purified, made clean, through the doing of His word. . . . Those who reject Christ and refuse to believe the truth will be filled with bitterness against those who accept Jesus as a personal Saviour. But those who receive Christ are melted and subdued by the manifestation of His love and His humiliation, suffering, and death in their behalf. . . .

The peace that Christ gave to His disciples, and for which we pray, is the peace that is born of truth, a peace that is not to be quenched because of division. Without may be wars and fightings, jealousies, envies, hatred, strife; but the peace of Christ is not that which the world giveth or taketh away. It could endure amid the hunting of spies and the fiercest opposition of His enemies. . . . Christ did not for an instant seek to purchase peace by a betrayal of sacred trusts. Peace could not be made by a compromise of principles. . . . It is a grave mistake on the part of those who are children of God to seek to bridge the gulf that separates the children of light from the children of darkness by yielding principle, by compromising the truth. It would be surrendering the peace of Christ in order to make peace or fraternize with the world. The sacrifice is too costly to be made by the children of God to make peace with the world by giving up the principles of truth. . . . Then let the followers of Christ settle it in their minds that they will never compromise truth, never yield one iota of principle for the favor of the world. Let them hold to the peace of Christ.[31]

77

I KEEP MY BODY IN SUBJECTION

But I keep under my body, and bring it into subjection: lest that by any means, when I have preached to others, I myself should be a castaway.

The body is the only medium through which the mind and the soul are developed for the upbuilding of character. Hence it is that the adversary of souls directs his temptations to the enfeebling and degrading of the physical powers. His success here means the surrender to evil of the whole being. The tendencies of our physical nature, unless under the dominion of a higher power, will surely work ruin and death.

The body is to be brought into subjection. The higher powers of the being are to rule. The passions are to be controlled by the will, which is itself to be under the control of God. . . .

The requirements of God must be brought home to the conscience. Men and women must be awakened to the duty of self-mastery, the need of purity, freedom from every depraving appetite and defiling habit. They need to be impressed with the fact that all their powers of mind and body are the gift of God, and are to be preserved in the best possible condition for His service. . . .

Human barriers against natural and cultivated tendencies are but as the sandbank against the torrent. Not until the life of Christ becomes a vitalizing power in our lives can we resist the temptations that assail us from within and from without. . . . By becoming one with Christ, man is free. Subjection to the will of Christ means restoration to perfect manhood.

Obedience to God is liberty from the thraldom of sin, deliverance from human passion and impulse. Man may stand conqueror of himself, conqueror of his own inclinations, conqueror of principalities and powers, and of "the rulers of the darkness of this world," and of "spiritual wickedness in high places." [32]

I LIVE BY GOD'S RULES

Make me to go in the path of thy commandments, for therein do I delight. Incline my heart unto thy testimonies, and not to covetousness.

Youth is the time to lay up knowledge in those lines that can be put into daily practice throughout the life. Youth is the time to establish good habits, to correct wrong ones, to gain and hold the power of self-control, to accustom oneself to ordering all the acts of life with reference to the will of God and the welfare of one's fellow creatures. Youth is the sowing time that determines the harvest of this life and the life beyond the grave. The habits formed in childhood and youth, the tastes acquired, the self-control gained, are almost certain to determine the future of the man or woman.[33]

One selfish thought indulged, one duty neglected, prepares the way for another. What we venture to do once, we are more apt to do again. Habits of sobriety, of self-control, of economy, of close application, of sound, sensible conversation, of patience and true courtesy, are not gained without diligent, close watching over self. It is much easier to become demoralized and depraved than to conquer defects, keeping self in control and cherishing true virtues. Persevering efforts will be required if the Christian graces are ever perfected in our lives.[34]

Let the habit of self-control be early established. Let the youth be impressed with the thought that they are to be masters, and not slaves. Of the kingdom within them God has made them rulers, and they are to exercise their Heaven-appointed kingship. When such instruction is faithfully given, the results will extend far beyond the youth themselves. Influences will reach out that will save thousands of men and women who are on the very brink of ruin.[35]

I WILL LOVE AS CHRIST LOVED

By this shall all men know that ye are my disciples, if ye have love one to another.

If we would be true lights in the world, we must manifest the loving, compassionate spirit of Christ. To love as Christ loved means that we must practice self-control. It means that we must show unselfishness at all times and in all places. It means that we must scatter round us kind words and pleasant looks. These cost the giver nothing, but they leave behind a precious fragrance. Their influence for good cannot be estimated. Not only to the receiver, but to the giver, they are a blessing; for they react upon him. Genuine love is a precious attribute of heavenly origin, which increases in fragrance in proportion as it is dispensed to others. . . .

God desires His children to remember that in order to glorify Him, they must bestow their affection on those who need it most. None with whom we come in contact are to be neglected. No selfishness in look, word, or deed is to be manifested to our fellow beings, whatever their position, whether they be high or low, rich or poor. The love that gives kind words to only a few, while others are treated with coldness and indifference, is not love, but selfishness. It will not in any way work for the good of souls or the glory of God. We are not to confine our love to one or two objects.

Those who gather the sunshine of Christ's righteousness, and refuse to let it shine into the lives of others, will soon lose the sweet, bright rays of heavenly grace, selfishly reserved to be lavished upon a few. . . . Self should not be allowed to gather to itself a select few, giving nothing to those who need help the most. Our love is not to be sealed up for special ones. Break the bottle, and the fragrance will fill the house.[36]

I WILL SET A WATCH OVER MY LIPS

Set a watch, O Lord, before my mouth; keep the door of my lips.

In the use of language there is perhaps no error that old and young are more ready to pass over lightly in themselves than hasty, impatient speech. They think it is a sufficient excuse to plead, "I was off my guard, and did not really mean what I said." But God's Word does not treat it lightly. . . .

The largest share of life's annoyances, its heartaches, its irritations, is due to uncontrolled temper. In one moment, by hasty, passionate, careless words, may be wrought evil that a whole lifetime's repentance cannot undo. Oh, the hearts that are broken, the friends estranged, the lives wrecked, by the harsh, hasty words of those who might have brought help and healing! . . . In his own strength man cannot rule his spirit. But through Christ he may gain self-control.[37]

Uniform firmness and unimpassioned control are necessary to the discipline of every family. Say what you mean calmly, move with consideration, and carry out what you say without deviation. . . . Never let a frown gather upon your brow or a harsh word escape your lips. God writes all these words in His book of records.[38]

Overwork sometimes causes a loss of self-control. But the Lord never compels hurried, complicated movements. Many gather to themselves burdens that the merciful heavenly Father did not place on them. Duties He never designed them to perform chase one another wildly. God desires us to realize that we do not glorify His name when we take so many burdens that we are overtasked and, becoming heart weary and brain weary, chafe and fret and scold. We are to bear only the responsibilities that the Lord gives us, trusting in Him, and thus keeping our hearts pure and sweet and sympathetic.[39]

I WILL USE SELF-CONTROL IN EATING

Blessed art thou, O land, when . . . thy princes eat in due season, for strength, and not for drunkenness!

The observance of temperance and regularity in all things has a wonderful power. It will do more than circumstances or natural endowments in promoting that sweetness and serenity of disposition which count so much in smoothing life's pathway. At the same time the power of self-control thus acquired will be found one of the most valuable equipments for grappling successfully with the stern duties and realities that await every human being.[40]

We urge that the principles of temperance be carried into all the details of home life; . . . that self-denial and self-control should be taught to the children, and enforced upon them, so far as consistent, from babyhood.[41]

Children should be taught that they must not have their own way, but that the will of their parents must guide them. One of the most important lessons in this connection is the control of appetite. They should learn to eat at regular periods and to allow nothing to pass their lips between these stated meals. . . .

Children reared in this way are much more easily controlled than those who are indulged in eating everything their appetite craves, and at all times. They are usually cheerful, contented, and healthy. Even the most stubborn, passionate, and wayward have become submissive, patient, and possessed of self-control by persistently following up this order of diet, united with a firm but kind management in regard to other matters.[42]

Let every youth in our land, with the possibilities before him of a destiny higher than that of crowned kings, ponder the lesson conveyed in the words of the wise man, "Blessed art thou, O land, when . . . thy princes eat in due season, for strength, and not for drunkenness!"[43]

I WILL BE MASTER OF MY MIND

Gird up the loins of your mind, be sober, and hope to the end for the grace that is to be brought unto you at the revelation of Jesus Christ.

We have each of us an individual work to do, to gird up the loins of our minds, to be sober, to watch unto prayer. The mind must be firmly controlled to dwell upon subjects that will strengthen the moral powers. . . . The thoughts must be pure, the meditations of the heart must be clean, if the words of the mouth are to be words acceptable to Heaven and helpful to your associates.[44]

The mind should be guarded carefully. Nothing should be allowed to enter that will harm or destroy its healthy vigor. But to prevent this, it should be preoccupied with good seed, which, springing to life, will bring forth fruit-bearing branches. . . . A field left uncultivated speedily produces a rank growth of thistles and tangled vines, which exhaust the soil and are worthless to the owner. The ground is full of seeds blown and carried by the wind from every quarter; and if it is left uncultivated, they spring up to life spontaneously, choking every precious fruit-bearing plant that is struggling for existence. If the field were tilled and sown to grain, these valueless weeds would be extinguished, and could not flourish.[45]

The youth who finds joy and happiness in reading the Word of God and in the hour of prayer is constantly refreshed by drafts from the Fountain of life. He will attain a height of moral excellence and a breadth of thought of which others cannot conceive. Communion with God encourages good thoughts, noble aspirations, clear perceptions of truth, and lofty purposes of action. Those who thus connect their souls with God are acknowledged by Him as His sons and daughters. They are constantly reaching higher and still higher, obtaining clear views of God and of eternity, until the Lord makes them channels of light and wisdom to the world.[46]

I WILL BE A CHRISTIAN AT HOME

[Love] doth not behave itself unseemly, seeketh not her own, is not easily provoked, thinketh no evil.

Much may be gained by self discipline in the home. . . . Let each make life as pleasant as possible for the other. Cultivate respect in the speech. Preserve unity and love. Satan will have no power over those who fully control themselves in the home.[47]

We must have the Spirit of God, or we can never have harmony in the home. . . . We cannot cherish home affection with too much care; for the home, if the Spirit of the Lord dwells there, is a type of heaven. . . . Everything that would tend to mar the peace and unity of the family circle must be repressed. Kindness and love, the spirit of tenderness and forbearance, will be cherished. If one errs, the other will exercise Christlike forbearance.[48]

He who manifests the spirit of tenderness, forbearance, and love will find that the same spirit will be reflected upon him. . . . If Christ indeed is formed within, the hope of glory, there will be union and love in the home. Christ abiding in the heart of the wife will be at agreement with Christ abiding in the heart of the husband. They will be striving together for the mansions Christ has gone to prepare for those who love Him. . . . Tender affection should ever be cherished between husband and wife, parents and children, brothers and sisters. . . . It is the duty of everyone in the family to be pleasant, to speak kindly.[49]

A house with love in it, where love is expressed in words and looks and deeds, is a place where angels love to manifest their presence and hallow the scene by rays of light from glory. . . . Love should be seen in the looks and manners and heard in the tones of the voice.[50]

જ જ જ

Self-control on the part of all the members of the family will make home almost a paradise.[51]

I WILL KEEP THE DOOR OF MY HEART

Keep thy heart with all diligence; for out of it are the issues of life.

"Keep thy heart with all diligence," is the counsel of the wise man; "for out of it are the issues of life." As a man "thinketh in his heart, so is he." The heart must be renewed by divine grace, or it will be in vain to seek for purity of life. He who attempts to build up a noble, virtuous character independent of the grace of Christ is building his house upon the shifting sand. In the fierce storms of temptation it will surely be overthrown. David's prayer should be the petition of every soul: "Create in me a clean heart, O God; and renew a right spirit within me." And having become partakers of the heavenly gift, we are to go on unto perfection, being "kept by the power of God, through faith."

Yet we have a work to do to resist temptation. Those who would not fall a prey to Satan's devices must guard well the avenues of the soul; they must avoid reading, seeing, or hearing that which will suggest impure thoughts. The mind should not be left to wander at random upon every subject that the adversary of souls may suggest. . . . This will require earnest prayer and unceasing watchfulness. We must be aided by the abiding influence of the Holy Spirit, which will attract the mind upward and habituate it to dwell on pure and holy things. And we must give diligent study to the Word of God. "Wherewithal shall a young man cleanse his way? By taking heed thereto according to Thy word." "Thy word," says the psalmist, "have I hid in mine heart, that I might not sin against Thee."[52]

You will have to become a faithful sentinel over your eyes, ears, and all your senses, if you would control your mind and prevent vain and corrupt thoughts from staining your soul. The power of grace alone can accomplish this most desirable work.[53]

I WILL SET NO WICKED THING BEFORE MINE EYES

"I will set no wicked thing before mine eyes: I hate the work of them that turn aside; it shall not cleave to me.

All should guard the senses, lest Satan gain victory over them; for these are the avenues to the soul.[54]

Avoid reading and seeing things which will suggest impure thoughts. Cultivate the moral and intellectual powers.[55]

Among the most dangerous resorts of pleasure is the theater. Instead of being a school of morality and virtue, as is so often claimed, it is the very hotbed of immorality. Vicious habits and sinful propensities are strengthened and confirmed by these entertainments. Low songs, lewd gestures, expressions, and attitudes deprave the imagination and debase the morals. Every youth who habitually attends such exhibitions will be corrupted in principle. There is no influence in our land more powerful to poison the imagination, to destroy religious impressions, and to blunt the relish for the tranquil pleasures and sober realities of life than theatrical amusements.

The love for these scenes increases with every indulgence, as the desire for intoxicating drink strengthens with its use. The only safe course is to shun the theater, the circus, and every other questionable place of amusement.

There are modes of recreation which are highly beneficial to both mind and body. An enlightened, discriminating mind will find abundant means for entertainment and diversion, from sources not only innocent, but instructive. . . . The great God whose glory shines from the heavens, and whose divine hand upholds millions of worlds, is our Father. We have only to love Him, trust in Him, as little children in faith and confidence, and He will accept us as His sons and daughters, and we shall be heirs to all the inexpressible glory of the eternal world.[56]

I WILL SEEK THE GOOD, THAT I MAY LIVE

Seek good, and not evil, that ye may live: and so the Lord, the God of hosts, shall be with you.

Satan is using every means to make crime and debasing vice popular. We cannot walk the streets of our cities without encountering flaring notices of crime presented in some novel or to be acted at some theater. The mind is educated to familiarity with sin. The course pursued by the base and vile is kept before the people in the periodicals of the day, and everything that can excite passion is brought before them in exciting stories. They hear and read so much of debasing crime that the once tender conscience, which would have recoiled with horror from such scenes, becomes hardened, and they dwell upon these things with greedy interest.

Many of the amusements popular in the world today, even with those who claim to be Christians, tend to the same end as did those of the heathen. There are indeed few among them that Satan does not turn to account in destroying souls. Through the drama he has worked for ages to excite passion and glorify vice. The opera, with its fascinating display and bewildering music, the masquerade, the dance, the card table, Satan employs to break down the barriers of principle and open the door to sensual indulgence. In every gathering for pleasure where pride is fostered or appetite indulged, where one is led to forget God and lose sight of eternal interests, there Satan is binding his chains about the soul.[57]

Our only safety is to be shielded by the grace of God every moment, and not put out our own spiritual eyesight so that we will call evil, good, and good, evil. Without hesitation or argument, we must close and guard the avenues of the soul against evil.[58]

I WILL TUNE MY EAR TO HEAVEN

And thine ears shall hear a word behind thee, saying, This is the way, walk ye in it, when ye shall turn to the right hand, and when ye shall turn to the left.

Many narratives of the Inspired Word are given to teach us that the human family is the object of the special care of God and heavenly beings. Man is not left to become the sport of Satan's temptations. All heaven is actively engaged in the work of communicating light to the inhabitants of the world, that they may not be left in the darkness of midnight without spiritual guidance. An Eye that never slumbers or sleeps is guarding the camp of Israel. Ten thousand times ten thousand and thousands of thousands of angels are ministering to the needs of the children of men. Voices inspired by God are crying, This is the way, walk ye in it.[59]

We can avoid seeing many of the evils that are multiplying so fast in these last days. We can avoid hearing about much of the wickedness and crime that exist.[60]

To the active minds of children and youth, the scenes pictured in imaginary revelations of the future are realities. As revolutions are predicted, and all manner of proceedings described that break down the barriers of law and self-restraint, many catch the spirit of these representations. They are led to the commission of crimes even worse, if possible, than these sensational writers depict. Through such influences as these society is becoming demoralized. The seeds of lawlessness are sown broadcast. None need marvel that a harvest of crime is the result.[61]

Say firmly: ". . . I will close my eyes to frivolous and sinful things. My ears are the Lord's and I will not listen to the subtle reasoning of the enemy. My voice shall not in any way be subject to a will that is not under the influence of the Spirit of God. My body is the temple of the Holy Spirit, and every power of my being shall be consecrated to worthy pursuits."[62]

I WILL LOVE GOOD BOOKS

Till I come, give attendance to reading, to exhortation, to doctrine.

God has given to His people the choicest reading matter. Let the Word of God find a place in every room in the house. Keep the Bible, the bread of life, in plain sight. Let the money spent for magazines be spent instead for publications containing present truth, and let them be given a prominent place in the home. With all safety these may be placed before the children and youth. Novels should not find a place in the homes of those who believe in Christ. Do not keep before the youth that which is represented as wood, hay, and stubble, for it will poison the appetite for that which is represented as gold, silver, and precious stones. The inclination for light, trashy reading is to be strictly denied.

Keep choice, elevating literature ever before the members of the family. Read our books and papers. Study them. Become familiar with the truths they contain. As you do this, you will feel the influence of the Holy Spirit. Every moment of life is precious, and should be spent in preparing for the future immortal life. Let the mind be stored with the elevating, ennobling themes of the Word of God, that you may be ready to speak a word in season to those who come within the sphere of your influence. The reading of our publications will not make us mental dyspeptics. None of us will receive the bread of life to our injury, but as these books are read, the mind will be furnished with that which will establish the heart in the truth.[63]

We must prepare ourselves for most solemn duties. A world is to be saved. . . . In view of the great work to be done, how can anyone afford to waste precious time and God-given means in doing those things that are not for his best good or for the glory of God?[64]

I WILL KEEP A SONG IN MY HEART

Be filled with the Spirit; speaking to yourself in psalms and hymns and spiritual songs, singing and making melody in your heart to the Lord.

God is glorified by songs of praise from a pure heart filled with love and devotion to Him. . . . The gratitude which they [Christians] feel and the peace of God ruling within cause them to make melody in their hearts unto the Lord and by words to make mention of the debt of love and thankfulness due the dear Saviour, who so loved them as to die that they might have life.[65]

The history of the songs of the Bible is full of suggestion as to the uses and benefits of music and song. Music is often perverted to serve purposes of evil, and thus becomes one of the most alluring agencies of temptation. But, rightly employed, it is a precious gift of God, designed to uplift the thoughts to high and noble themes, to inspire and elevate the soul.

As the children of Israel, journeying through the wilderness, cheered their way by the music of sacred song, so God bids His children today gladden their pilgrim life. There are few means more effective for fixing His words in the memory than repeating them in song. And such song has wonderful power. It has power to subdue rude and uncultivated natures; power to quicken thought and to awaken sympathy, to promote harmony of action, and to banish the gloom and foreboding that destroy courage and weaken effort.

It is one of the most effective means of impressing the heart with spiritual truth. How often to the soul hard pressed and ready to despair, memory recalls some word of God's—the long-forgotten burden of a childhood song—and temptations lose their power, life takes on new meaning and new purpose, and courage and gladness are imparted to other souls![66]

I WILL SING UNTO THE LORD

Whoso offereth praise glorifieth me: and to him that ordereth his conversation aright will I shew the salvation of God.

Come to Jesus just as you are, sinful, weak, and needy, and He will give you the water of life. You want a faith that reaches through the hellish shadow that Satan casts athwart your pathway. He is busily inventing amusements and fashions which will so take up men's minds that they shall not be able to spare any time for meditation. Teach your children to glorify God, not to please themselves. They are His children—His by creation and by redemption. Teach them to shun the amusements and follies of this degenerate age. Keep their minds clean and pure in the sight of God. . . . Praise God. Let your conversation, your music, your songs all praise Him who has done so much for us. Praise God here, and then you will be fitted to join the heavenly choir when you enter the city of God. Then you can cast your glittering crowns at the feet of Jesus, take your golden harps, and fill all heaven with melody. We shall praise Him with an immortal tongue.[67]

As our Redeemer leads us to the threshold of the Infinite, flushed with the glory of God, we may catch the themes of praise and thanksgiving from the heavenly choir round about the throne; and as the echo of the angels' song is awakened in our earthly homes, hearts will be drawn closer to the heavenly singers. Heaven's communion begins on earth. We learn here the keynote of its praise.[68]

Praise the Lord; talk of His goodness; tell of His power. Sweeten the atmosphere that surrounds your soul. . . . Praise, with heart and soul and voice, Him who is the health of your countenance, your Saviour, and your God.[69]

GOD PERMITS TRIAL AND AFFLICTION TO PURIFY ME

But who may abide the day of his coming? and who shall stand when he appeareth? for he is like a refiner's fire, and like fullers' soap: and he shall sit as a refiner and purifier of silver: and he shall purify the sons of Levi, and purge them as gold and silver, that they may offer unto the Lord an offering in righteousness.

A refining, purifying process is going on among the people of God, and the Lord of hosts has set His hand to this work. This process is most trying to the soul, but it is necessary in order that defilement may be removed. Trials are essential in order that we may be brought close to our heavenly Father, in submission to His will, that we may offer unto the Lord an offering in righteousness. . . . The Lord brings His children over the same ground again and again, increasing the pressure until perfect humility fills the mind, and the character is transformed; then they are victorious over self, and in harmony with Christ and the Spirit of heaven. The purification of God's people cannot be accomplished without suffering. . . . He passes us from one fire to another, testing our true worth. True grace is willing to be tried. If we are loath to be searched by the Lord, our condition is one of peril. . . .

It is in mercy that the Lord reveals to men their hidden defects. He would have them critically examine the complicated emotions and motives of their own hearts, and detect that which is wrong, and modify their dispositions and refine their manners. God would have His servants become acquainted with their own hearts. In order to bring to them a true knowledge of their condition, He permits the fire of affliction to assail them, so that they may be purified. The trials of life are God's workmen to remove the impurities, infirmities, and roughness from our characters, and fit them for the society of pure, heavenly angels in glory. . . . The fire will not consume us, but only remove the dross, and we shall come forth seven times purified, bearing the impress of the Divine.[70]

GOD HAS A PURPOSE IN EVERY AFFLICTION

Beloved, think it not strange concerning the fiery trial which is to try you, as though some strange thing happened unto you: but rejoice, inasmuch as ye are partakers of Christ's sufferings; that, when his glory shall be revealed, ye may be glad also with exceeding joy.

One evening a gentleman who was much depressed because of deep affliction was walking in a garden, where he observed a pomegranate tree nearly cut through the stem. Greatly wondering, he asked the gardener why the tree was in this condition, and he received an answer that explained to his satisfaction the wounds of his own bleeding heart. "Sir," said the gardener, "this tree used to shoot out so strong that it bore nothing but leaves. I was obliged to cut it in this manner; and when it was almost cut through, it began to bear fruit."

Our sorrows do not spring out of the ground. In every affliction God has a purpose to work out for our good. Every blow that destroys an idol, every providence that weakens our hold upon earth and fastens our affections more firmly upon God, is a blessing. The pruning may be painful for a time, but afterward it "yieldeth the peaceable fruit of righteousness." We should receive with gratitude whatever will quicken the conscience, elevate the thoughts, and ennoble the life. The fruitless branches are cut off and cast into the fire. Let us be thankful that through painful pruning we may retain a connection with the living Vine; for if we suffer with Christ, we shall also reign with Him. The very trial that taxes our faith the most severely and makes it seem as though God had forsaken us is to lead us more closely to Him, that we may lay all our burdens at the feet of Christ and experience the peace which He will give us in exchange. . . . God loves and cares for the feeblest of His creatures, and we cannot dishonor Him more than by doubting His love to us. O let us cultivate that living faith that will trust Him in the hour of darkness and trial![71]

GOD GIVES POWER TO BEAR EVERY TRIAL

There hath no temptation taken you but such as is common to man: but God is faithful, who will not suffer you to be tempted above that ye are able; but will with the temptation also make a way to escape, that ye may be able to bear it.

Christ will never abandon the soul for whom He has died. The soul may leave Him, and be overwhelmed with temptation; but Christ can never turn from one for whom He has paid the ransom of His own life. Could our spiritual vision be quickened, we should see souls bowed under oppression and burdened with grief, pressed as a cart beneath sheaves, and ready to die in discouragement. We should see angels flying swiftly to aid these tempted ones, who are standing as on the brink of a precipice. The angels from heaven force back the hosts of evil that encompass these souls, and guide them to plant their feet on the sure foundation. The battles waging between the two armies are as real as those fought by the armies of this world, and on the issue of the spiritual conflict eternal destinies depend.

To us, as to Peter, the word is spoken, "Satan hath desired to have you, that he may sift you as wheat; but I have prayed for thee, that thy faith fail not." Thank God, we are not left alone.[72]

We are coming to the crisis. Let us stand the test manfully, grasping the hand of Infinite Power. God will work for us. We have only to live one day at a time, and if we get acquainted with God, He will give us strength for what is coming tomorrow, grace sufficient for each day, and every day will find its own victories, just as it finds its trials. We shall have the power of the Highest with us, for we shall be clad with the armor of Christ's righteousness. We have the same God that has worked for His people in ages past. Jesus stands by our side, and shall we falter?—No, as the trials come, the power of God will come with them. God will help us to stand in faith on His Word, and when we are united, He will work with special power in our behalf.[73]

A PROGRESSIVE LIFE

April 1   *Christian Growth*   *2 Peter 1:5-8*

THE LADDER OF CHRISTIAN PROGRESS

Giving all diligence, add to your faith virtue; and to virtue knowledge; and to knowledge temperance; and to temperance patience; and to patience godliness; and to godliness brotherly kindness; and to brotherly kindness charity. For if these things be in you, and abound, they make you that ye shall neither be barren nor unfruitful in the knowledge of our Lord Jesus Christ.

These words are full of instruction, and strike the keynote of victory. The apostle presents before the believers the ladder of Christian progress, every step of which represents advancement in the knowledge of God, and in the climbing of which there is to be no standstill. Faith, virtue, knowledge, temperance, patience, godliness, brotherly kindness, and charity are the rounds of the ladder. We are saved by climbing round after round, mounting step after step, to the height of Christ's ideal for us. Thus He is made unto us wisdom, and righteousness and sanctification, and redemption.[1]

All these successive steps are not to be kept before the mind's eye, and counted as you start; but fixing the eye upon Jesus, with an eye single to the glory of God, you will make advancement. . . .

By taking one step after another, the highest ascent may be climbed, and the summit of the mount may be reached at last. Do not become overwhelmed with the great amount of work you must do in your lifetime, for you are not required to do it all at once. Let every power of your being go to each day's work, improve each precious opportunity, appreciate the helps that God gives you, and make advancement up the ladder of progress step by step. Remember that you are to live but one day at a time, that God has given you one day, and heavenly records will show how you have valued its privileges and opportunities. May you so improve every day given you of God that at last you may hear the Master say, "Well done, thou good and faithful servant."[2]

ADD TO YOUR FAITH VIRTUE: AND TO VIRTUE KNOWLEDGE

His divine power hath given unto us all things that pertain unto life and godliness, through the knowledge of him that hath called us to glory and virtue.

After receiving the faith of the gospel, our first work is to seek to add virtuous and pure principles, and thus cleanse the mind and heart for the reception of true knowledge.[3]

The apostle has presented before us the importance of making continual advancement in the Christian life. There is no excuse for our lack of spiritual understanding. . . .

Faith is the first round in the ladder of advancement. Without faith it is impossible to please God. But many stop on this round and never ascend higher. They seem to think that when they have professed Christ, when their names are on the church record, their work is completed. Faith is essential; but the Inspired Word says, "Add to your faith, virtue." Those who are seeking for eternal life and a home in the kingdom of God must lay for their character building the foundation of virtue. Jesus must be the chief cornerstone. The things that defile the soul must be banished from the mind and life. When temptations are presented, they must be resisted in the strength of Christ. The virtue of the spotless lamb of God must be woven into the character till the soul can stand in its integrity. . . . Joseph is an example of how the youth may stand unspotted, amid the evil of the world, and add to their faith, virtue. . . .

Every moment of our lives is intensely real, and charged with solemn responsibilities. Ignorance will be no excuse for lack of spiritual understanding and attainment; for we are exhorted to add to virtue, knowledge. . . . The uncultured fishermen became men of refinement and ability; and the lessons that they were privileged to learn are written for our admonition and instruction. We are invited to become learners in the school of Christ. We need to acquire all the knowledge possible.

ADD TO TEMPERANCE PATIENCE

Let patience have her perfect work, that ye may be perfect and entire, wanting nothing.

"And to knowledge, temperance." This is the third step in the path toward perfection of character. On every side there is indulgence and dissipation, and the result is degeneration and corruption. The inhabitants of our earth are depreciating in mental, moral, and physical power, because of the intemperate habits of society. Appetite, passion, and love of display are carrying the multitudes into the greatest excesses and extravagance. . . . The people of God must take an opposite course from the world. They must take up the warfare against these sinful practices, deny appetite, and keep the lower nature in subjection. . . . It is for us to "search the Scriptures," and bring our habits into harmony with the instruction of the Bible. . . .

"And to temperance, patience." The need of becoming temperate is made manifest as we try to take this step. It is next to an impossibility for an intemperate person to be patient.[5]

Some of us have a nervous temperament, and are naturally as quick as a flash to think and to act; but let no one think that he cannot learn to become patient. Patience is a plant that will make rapid growth if carefully cultivated. By becoming thoroughly acquainted with ourselves, and then combining with the grace of God a firm determination on our part, we may be conquerors, and become perfect in all things, wanting in nothing.[6]

Patience pours the balm of peace and love into the experiences of the home life. . . . Patience will seek for unity in the church, in the family, and in the community. This grace must be woven into our lives.[7]

ADD TO GODLINESS BROTHERLY KINDNESS AND CHARITY

But thou, O man of God, . . . follow after righteousness, godliness, faith, love, patience, meekness.

We must have a close and intimate connection with heaven, if we bear the grace of godliness. Jesus must be a guest in our homes, a member of our households, if we reflect His image and show that we are sons and daughters of the Most High. Religion is a beautiful thing in the home. If the Lord abides with us, we shall feel that we are members of Christ's family in heaven. We shall realize that angels are watching us, and our manners will be gentle and forbearing. We shall be fitting up for an entrance into the courts of heaven by cultivating courtesy and godliness. . . .

Enoch walked with God. He honored God in every affair of life. In his home and in his business he inquired, "Will this be acceptable to the Lord?" And by remembering God and following His counsel, he was transformed in character, and became a godly man, whose ways pleased the Lord. We are exhorted to add to godliness, brotherly kindness. O how much we need to take this step, to add this quality to our characters! . . . We should have that love for others that Christ has had for us. A man is estimated at his true value by the Lord of heaven. If he is unkind in his earthly home, he is unfit for the heavenly home. If he will have his own way, no matter whom it grieves, he would not be content in heaven, unless he could rule there. The love of Christ must control our hearts. . . . Seek God with a broken and contrite spirit, and you will be melted with compassion toward your brethren. You will be prepared to add to brotherly kindness, charity, or love. . . .

It will bring heaven nearer to us. We may have the sweet peace and consolation of God in doing this work. These steps will take us into the atmosphere of heaven.[8]

THE GRACE OF GOD IS FOR ME

By the grace of God I am what I am: and his grace which was bestowed upon me was not in vain; but I laboured more abundantly than they all: yet not I, but the grace of God which was with me.

There are those who attempt to ascend the ladder of Christian progress; but as they advance, they begin to put their trust in the power of man, and soon lose sight of Jesus, the author and finisher of their faith. The result is failure—the loss of all that has been gained. Sad indeed is the condition of those who, becoming weary of the way, allow the enemy of souls to rob them of the Christian graces.[9]

The love of God in the soul will have a direct influence upon the life and will call the intellect and the affections into active, healthful exercise. The child of God will not rest satisfied until he is clothed with the righteousness of Christ and sustained by His life-giving power. When he sees a weakness in his character, it is not enough to confess it again and again; he must go to work with determination and energy to overcome his defects by building up opposite traits of character. He will not shun this work because it is difficult. Untiring energy is required of the Christian; but he is not obliged to work in his own strength; divine power awaits his demand. Everyone who is sincerely striving for the victory over self will appropriate the promise, "My grace is sufficient for thee."

Through personal effort joined with the prayer of faith the soul is trained. Day by day the character grows into the likeness of Christ. . . . It may cost a severe conflict to overcome habits which have been long indulged, but we may triumph through the grace of Christ. . . .

If we are true to the promptings of the Spirit of God, we shall go on from grace to grace and from glory to glory until we shall receive the finishing touch of immortality.[10]

THE EXCEEDING RICHES OF HIS GRACE

But God, who is rich in mercy, for his great love wherewith he loved us, even when we were dead in sins, hath quickened us together with Christ, . . . and hath raised us up together, and made us sit together in heavenly places in Christ Jesus: that in the ages to come he might shew the exceeding riches of his grace in his kindness toward us through Christ Jesus.

We would never have learned the meaning of this word "grace" had we not fallen. God loves the sinless angels who do His service and are obedient to all His commands, but He does not give them grace. These heavenly beings know naught of grace; they have never needed it, for they have never sinned. Grace is an attribute of God shown to undeserving human beings. We did not seek after it, but it was sent in search of us. God rejoices to bestow this grace on everyone who hungers for it, not because we are worthy, but because we are so utterly unworthy. Our need is the qualification which gives us the assurance that we will receive this gift.

But God does not use this grace to make His law of none effect or to take the place of His law. "The Lord is well pleased for His righteousness' sake; He will magnify the law, and make it honorable." His law is truth. . . .

God's grace and the law of His kingdom are in perfect harmony; they walk hand in hand. His grace makes it possible for us to draw nigh to Him by faith. By receiving it, and letting it work in our lives, we testify to the validity of the law; we exalt the law and make it honorable by carrying out its living principles. . . .

How may we witness for God? . . . By rendering pure, wholehearted obedience to God's law. If we will let Him, He will manifest Himself in us, and we shall be witnesses, before the universe of heaven and before an apostate world who are making void the law of God, to the power of redemption.[11]

There is but one power that can bring us into conformity to the likeness of Christ, that can make us steadfast and keep us constant. It is the grace of God that comes to us through obedience to the law of God.[12]

I MUST GROW IN GRACE

Grow in grace, and in the knowledge of our Lord and Saviour Jesus Christ.

God requires that every human agent shall improve all the means of grace Heaven has provided, and become more and more efficient in the work of God. Every provision has been made that the piety, purity, and love of the Christian shall ever increase, that his talents may double and his ability increase in the service of his divine Master. But though this provision has been made, many who profess to believe in Jesus do not make it manifest by growth that testifies to the sanctifying power of the truth upon life and character. When we first receive Jesus into our hearts, we are as babes in religion; but we are not to remain babes in experience. We are to grow in grace and in the knowledge of our Lord and Saviour Jesus Christ; we are to attain to the full measure of the stature of men and women in Him. We are to make advances, to gain new and rich experiences through faith, growing in trust and confidence and love, knowing God and Jesus Christ whom He hath sent.[13]

The work of transformation from unholiness to holiness is a continuous one. Day by day God labors for man's sanctification, and man is to cooperate with Him, putting forth persevering efforts in the cultivation of right habits. He is to add grace to grace; and as he thus works on the plan of addition, God works for him on the plan of multiplication. Our Saviour is always ready to hear and answer the prayer of the contrite heart, and grace and peace are multiplied to His faithful ones. Gladly He grants them the blessings they need in their struggle against the evils that beset them. . . . Glorious is the hope before the believer as he advances by faith toward the heights of Christian perfection![14]

GROWTH IN GRACE BEGINS AT HOME

The Lord will give grace and glory: no good thing will he withhold from them that walk uprightly.

There are many who do not grow in grace because they fail of cultivating home religion.[15]

The members of the family are to show that they are in constant possession of a power received from Christ. They are to improve in every habit and practice, thus showing that they keep constantly before them what it means to be a Christian.[16]

Those who are Christians in the home will be Christians in the church and in the world.[17]

Grace can thrive only in the heart that is being constantly prepared for the precious seeds of truth. The thorns of sin will grow in any soil; they need no cultivation; but grace must be carefully cultivated. The briers and thorns are always ready to spring up, and the work of purification must advance continually.[18]

That which will make the character lovely in the home is that which will make it lovely in the heavenly mansions.[19] If you are . . . to be the light of the world, that light is to shine in your home. Here you are to exemplify the Christian graces, to be lovable, patient, kind, yet firm. . . . You need to seek constantly the highest culture of mind and soul. . . . As a humble child of God, learn in the school of Christ; seek constantly to improve your powers, that you may do the most perfect, thorough work at home, by both precept and example. . . . Let the light of heavenly grace irradiate your character, that there may be sunlight in the home.[20]

The measure of your Christianity is gauged by the character of your home life. The grace of Christ enables its possessors to make the home a happy place, full of peace and rest.[21]

HOW TO GROW IN GRACE

God is able to make all grace abound toward you; that ye, always having all sufficiency in all things, may abound to every good work: (As it is written, He hath dispersed abroad; he hath given to the poor: his righteousness remaineth for ever.)

Many are longing to grow in grace; they pray over the matter, and are surprised that their prayers are not answered. The Master has given them a work to do whereby they shall grow. Of what value is it to pray when there is need of work? The question is, Are they seeking to save souls for whom Christ died? Spiritual growth depends upon giving to others the light that God has given to you. You are to put forth your best thoughts in active labor to do good, and only good, in your family, in your church, and in your neighborhood.

In place of growing anxious with the thought that you are not growing in grace, just do every duty that presents itself, carry the burden of souls on your heart, and by every conceivable means seek to save the lost. Be kind, be courteous, be pitiful; speak in humility of the blessed hope; talk of the love of Jesus; tell of His goodness, His mercy, and His righteousness; and cease to worry as to whether or not you are growing. Plants do not grow through any conscious effort. . . . The plant is not in continual worriment about its growth; it just grows under the supervision of God.[22]

The only way to grow in grace is to be interestedly doing the very work Christ has enjoined upon us to do—interestedly engaged to the very extent of our ability to be helping and blessing those who need the help we can give them. . . . Christians who are constantly growing in earnestness, in zeal, in fervor, in love—such Christians never backslide. . . . Their wisdom is increasing, [and] their ability [in] how to work. They seem to comprehend the largest plans. They are ready to engage in the most stirring enterprises, and they have no room for slothfulness; they cannot find a place for stagnation.[23]

❧ ❧ ❧

The treasures of grace are absolutely unlimited.[24]

103

THE PATH OF THE CHRISTIAN LEADS TO HEAVEN

The path of the just is as the shining light, that shineth more and more unto the perfect day.

The youth may receive grace from Christ daily, and find their light growing brighter and brighter as they follow in the path of holiness. . . .

Growth in grace will not lead you to be proud, self-confident, and boastful, but will make you more conscious of your own nothingness, of your entire dependence upon the Lord. He who is growing in grace will be ever reaching heavenward, obtaining clear views of the fullness of the provisions of the gospel.

The youth may be free in Christ; they may be the children of light, and not of darkness. God calls upon every young man and young woman to renounce every evil habit, to be diligent in business, fervent in spirit, serving the Lord. Jesus will help you, so that you need not remain in indolence, making no effort to correct your wrongs or improve your conduct. The sincerity of your prayers will be proved by the vigor of the effort you make to obey all of God's commandments. You may move intelligently, and at every step renounce evil habits and associations, believing that the Lord will renovate your heart by the power of His Spirit. . . .

Do not excuse your defects of character, but in the grace of Christ overcome them. Wrestle with the evil passions which the Word of God condemns; for in yielding to them, you abase yourself. Repent of sin while Mercy's sweet voice invites you; for it is the first step in the noblest work you can do. Strive for the mastery with all the powers God hath given you.[25]

The path of the just is a progressive one, from strength to strength, from grace to grace, and from glory to glory. The divine illumination will increase more and more, corresponding with our onward movements, qualifying us to meet the responsibilities and emergencies before us.[26]

O GOD! HELP ME TO HIGHER LEVELS

Hear my cry, O God; attend unto my prayer. From the end of the earth will I cry unto thee, when my heart is overwhelmed: lead me to the rock that is higher than I. For thou hast been a shelter for me, and a strong tower from the enemy.

Have you ever watched a hawk in pursuit of a timid dove? Instinct has taught the dove that in order for the hawk to seize his prey, he must gain a loftier flight than his victim. So she rises higher and still higher into the blue dome of heaven, ever pursued by the hawk, which is seeking to obtain the advantage. But in vain. The dove is safe as long as she allows nothing to stop her in her flight, or draw her earthward; but let her once falter, and take a lower flight, and her watchful enemy will swoop down upon his victim. Again and again have we watched this scene with almost breathless interest, all our sympathies with the little dove. How sad we should have felt to see it fall a victim to the cruel hawk!

We have before us a warfare—a lifelong conflict with Satan and his seductive temptations. The enemy will use every argument, every deception, to entangle the soul; and in order to win the crown of life, we must put forth earnest, persevering effort. We must not lay off the armor or leave the battlefield until we have gained the victory, and can triumph in our Redeemer.

As long as we continue to keep our eyes fixed upon the Author and Finisher of our faith we shall be safe. But our affections must be placed upon things above, not on things on the earth. By faith we must rise higher and still higher in the attainments of the graces of Christ. By daily contemplating His matchless charms, we must grow more and more into His glorious image. While we thus live in communion with Heaven, Satan will lay his nets for us in vain.[27]

THE BEGINNING OF WISDOM

The fear of the Lord is the beginning of wisdom: and the knowledge of the holy is understanding.

Christ was the greatest teacher the world ever saw. He brought to man knowledge direct from heaven. The lessons which He has given us are what we need for both the present and the future state. He sets before us the true aims of life and how we may secure them.

In the school of Christ students are never graduated. Among the pupils are both old and young. Those who give heed to the instructions of the divine Teacher constantly advance in wisdom, refinement, and nobility of soul, and thus they are prepared to enter that higher school where advancement will continue throughout eternity.

Infinite Wisdom sets before us the great lessons of life—lessons of duty and happiness. These are often hard to learn, but without them we can make no real progress. They may cost us effort and tears, and even agony, but we must not falter or grow weary. We shall at last hear the Master's call, "Child, come up higher." . . .

Every faculty, every attribute, with which the Creator has endowed the children of men is to be employed for His glory; and in this employment is found its purest, holiest, happiest exercise. While religious principle is held paramount, every advance step taken in the acquirement of knowledge or in the culture of the intellect is a step toward the assimilation of the human with the Divine, the finite with the Infinite.[28]

If the youth will but learn of the heavenly Teacher, . . . they will know for themselves that the fear of the Lord is indeed the beginning of wisdom. Having thus laid a sure foundation, they . . . turn every privilege and opportunity to the very best account, and may rise to any height in intellectual attainments.[29]

WISDOM GIVETH LIFE

The excellency of knowledge is, that wisdom giveth life to them that have it.

Pointing out the way of salvation, the Bible is our guide to a higher, better life.[30]

In turning from God's Word to feed on the writings of uninspired men, the mind becomes dwarfed and cheapened. It is not brought in contact with deep, broad principles of eternal truth. . . .

The work of every teacher, every parent, should be to fasten the minds of the children and youth upon the grand truths of the Word of inspiration. This is the education essential for this life and for the life to come. And let it not be thought that this will prevent the study of the sciences or cause a lower standard in education. The knowledge of God is as high as heaven and as broad as the universe. There is nothing so ennobling and invigorating as the study of the great themes which concern our eternal life. Let the youth seek to grasp these God-given truths, and their minds will expand and grow strong in the effort. It will bring every student who is a doer of the Word into a broader field of thought and secure for him a wealth of knowledge that is imperishable.[31]

In God's Word only we find an authentic account of creation. . . . In this Word only can we find a history of our race unsullied by human prejudice or human pride. . . Here we may hold communion with patriarchs and prophets and listen to the voice of the Eternal as He speaks with men. Here we behold the Majesty of Heaven, as He humbled Himself to become our substitute and surety, to cope single-handed with the powers of darkness and to gain the victory in our behalf. A reverent contemplation of such themes as these cannot fail to soften, purify, and ennoble the heart and at the same time to inspire the mind with new strength and vigor.[32]

HOW TO GAIN KNOWLEDGE

If thou criest after knowledge, and liftest up thy voice for understanding; if thou seekest her as silver, and searchest for her as for hid treasures; then shalt thou understand the fear of the Lord, and find the knowledge of God.

Let none think that there is no more knowledge for them to gain. The depth of human intellect may be measured; the works of human authors may be mastered; but the highest, deepest, broadest flight of the imagination cannot find out God. There is infinity beyond all that we can comprehend. We have seen only the glimmering of divine glory and of the infinitude of knowledge and wisdom; we have, as it were, been working on the surface of the mine, when rich, golden ore is beneath the surface, to reward the one who will dig for it. The shaft must be sunk deeper and yet deeper in the mine, and the result will be glorious treasure. Through a correct faith divine knowledge will become human knowledge.

No one can search the Scriptures in the Spirit of Christ without being rewarded. When a man is willing to be instructed as a little child, when he submits wholly to Christ, he will find the truth in His Word. If men would be obedient, they would understand the plan of God's government. The heavenly world would open its treasures of grace and glory for exploration. Human beings would be altogether different from what they are now; for by exploring the mines of truth, men would be ennobled. The mystery of redemption, the incarnation of Christ, His atoning sacrifice, would not be, as they are now, vague in our minds. They would be, not only better understood, but altogether more highly appreciated. . . .

The experimental knowledge of God and of Christ transforms man into the image of God. It gives man the mastery of himself, bringing every impulse and passion . . . under the control of the higher powers of the mind. It makes its possessor a son of God and an heir of heaven. It brings him into communion with the mind of the Infinite and opens to him the rich treasures of the universe.[33]

KEEP SOUND WISDOM AND DISCRETION

My son, . . . keep sound wisdom and discretion: so shall they be life unto thy soul, and grace to thy neck. Then shalt thou walk in thy way safely, and thy foot shall not stumble.

As little children we are to sit at the feet of Christ, learning of Him how to work successfully. We are to ask God for sound judgment and for light to impart to others. There is need of knowledge that is the fruit of experience. We should not allow a day to pass without gaining an increase of knowledge in temporal and spiritual things. We are to plant no stakes that we are not willing to take up and plant further on, nearer the heights we hope to ascend. The highest education is to be found in training the mind to advance day by day. The close of each day should find us a day's march nearer the overcomer's reward. Day by day our understanding is to ripen. Day by day we are to work out conclusions that will bring a rich reward in this life and in the life to come. Looking daily to Jesus, instead of to what we ourselves have done, we shall make decided advancement in temporal as well as spiritual knowledge.

The end of all things is at hand. What we have done must not be allowed to place the period to our work. The Captain of our salvation says, "Advance. The night cometh, in which no man can work." Constantly we are to increase in usefulness. Our lives are always to be under the power of Christ. Our lamps are to be kept burning brightly. . . .

In all ages God has given human beings divine revelations, that thus He may fulfill His purpose of unfolding gradually to the mind the doctrines of grace. His manner of imparting the truth is illustrated by the words, "His going forth is prepared as the morning." He who places himself where God can enlighten him, advances, as it were, from the partial obscurity of dawn to the full radiance of noonday.[34]

WISDOM FOR MY WORK

I have filled him with the spirit of God, in wisdom, and in understanding, and in knowledge, and in all manner of workmanship.

You need not go to the end of the earth for wisdom, for God is near. . . . He longs to have you reach after Him by faith. He longs to have you expect great things from Him. He longs to give you understanding in temporal as well as in spiritual matters. He can sharpen the intellect. He can give tact and skill. Put your talents into the work, ask God for wisdom, and it will be given you.[35]

To every one who constantly yields his will to the will of the Infinite, to be led and taught of God, there is promised an ever-increasing development of spiritual things. God fixes no limit to the advancement of those who are "filled with the knowledge of His will and in all wisdom and spiritual understanding."[36]

Those who make God their efficiency realize their own weakness, and the Lord supplies them with His wisdom. As day by day they depend upon God, carrying out His will with humility and wholeheartedness and strictest integrity, they increase in knowledge and ability. By willing obedience they show reverence and honor to God, and are honored by Him.[37]

The case of Daniel reveals to us the fact that the Lord is always ready to hear the prayers of the contrite soul, and when we seek the Lord with all our hearts, He will answer our petitions. Here is revealed where Daniel obtained his skill and understanding; and if we will only ask of God wisdom, we may be blessed with increased ability and with power from heaven.[38]

WISDOM SHOWN BY MY CONVERSATION

Who is a wise man and endued with knowledge among you? let him shew out of a good conversation his works with meekness of wisdom.

How many sins this consistent conduct would prevent! How many souls it would turn from crooked paths into paths of righteousness. By a well-ordered life and godly conversation God's people are to demonstrate the power of the great truths which He has given them. . . .

A contrast is drawn between those who think themselves to be wise and those whom God has gifted with wisdom because they will not use their powers to hurt or destroy. A man may speak fair words, but unless his life reveals good works, his wisdom is human. Genuine wisdom is full of gentleness, mercy, and love. The worldly policy which men call wisdom is by God called foolishness. Many in the church have become spiritual bankrupts because they have been satisfied with this wisdom. They have lost the opportunity to obtain knowledge and to use knowledge aright, because they have not realized that the efficiency of Christ is essential to make a successful merchant for God, one who can trade wisely on his entrusted goods. They have failed to supply themselves with heavenly merchandise, and the value of their stock in trade has continually decreased.

It is not enough to have knowledge. We must have the ability to use knowledge aright. God calls upon us to show a good conversation, free from all roughness and vanity. Speak no words of vanity, no words of harsh command; for they will gender strife. Speak instead words that will give light, knowledge, information, words that will restore and build up. A man shows that he has true wisdom by using the talent of speech to produce music in the souls of those who are trying to do their appointed work and who are in need of encouragement.[39]

&a; &a; &a;

When the heart is pure, rich treasures of wisdom will flow forth.[40]

NATURE, THE KEY TO UNLOCK TREASURE HOUSE OF GOD'S WORD

Consider the wondrous works of God . . . the wondrous works of him which is perfect in knowledge.

The whole natural world is designed to be an interpreter of the things of God. To Adam and Eve in their Eden home nature was full of the knowledge of God, teeming with divine instruction. To their attentive ears it was vocal with the voice of wisdom. Wisdom spoke to the eye, and was received into the heart; for they communed with God in His created works. . . . In the natural world God has placed in the hands of the children of men the key to unlock the treasure house of His Word. The unseen is illustrated by the seen; divine wisdom, eternal truth, infinite grace, are understood by the things that God has made.[41]

As the dwellers of Eden learned from nature's pages, as Moses discerned God's handwriting on the Arabian plains and mountains, and the Child Jesus on the hillsides of Nazareth, so the children of today may learn of Him. . . . On everything upon the earth, from the loftiest tree of the forest to the lichen that clings to the rock, from the boundless ocean to the tiniest shell on the shore, they may behold the image and superscription of God.[42]

Here are mysteries that the mind will become strong in searching out. . . . All may find themes for study in . . . the spires of grass covering the earth with their green velvet carpet, the plants and flowers, . . . the lofty mountains, the granite rocks, . . . the precious gems of light studding the heavens to make the night beautiful, the exhaustless riches of the sunlight, the solemn glories of the moon, the winter's cold, the summer's heat, the changing, recurring seasons, in perfect order and harmony, controlled by infinite power; here are subjects which call for deep thought, for the stretch of the imagination.[43]

HE MULTIPLIES MY TALENTS

Well done, thou good and faithful servant: thou hast been faithful over a few things, I will make thee ruler over many things: enter thou into the joy of thy lord.

God has given us talents to use for Him. To one He gives five talents, to another two, and to another one. Let not him who has but one talent think to hide it from God. The Lord knows where it is hidden. He knows that it is doing nothing for Him. When the Lord comes, He will ask His servants, What have you done with the talents I entrusted to you? And as he who received five and he who received two tell Him that by trading they have doubled their talents, He will say to them, "Well done, good and faithful servant. Thou hast been faithful over a few things, I will make thee ruler over many things. . . . Enter thou into the joy of thy Lord." Thus He will say also to him who has improved the one talent lent him. . . .

To him who has but one talent I would say, Do you know that one talent, rightly used and improved, will bring to the Lord one hundred talents? How? you ask. Use your gift in the conversion of one man of intellect, who sees what God is to him, and what he should be to God. Let him place himself on the side of the Lord, and as he imparts the light to others, he will be the means of bringing many souls to the Saviour. Through the right use of one talent one hundred souls may receive the truth. It is not to those who have the greatest number of talents to whom the "Well done" is spoken, but to those who in sincerity and faithfulness have used their gifts for the Master. . . .

There is a great work to be done in our world, and we are accountable for every ray of light that shines upon our pathway. Impart that light, and you will receive more light to impart. Great blessing will come to those who use their talents aright.[44]

THE TALENT OF SPEECH

Let your speech be alway with grace, seasoned with salt, that ye may know how ye ought to answer every man.

The voice is an entrusted talent, and it should be used to help and encourage and strengthen our fellowmen. If parents will love God and keep the way of the Lord to do justice and judgment, their language . . . will be of a sound, pure, edifying character. Whether they are at home or abroad, their words will be well chosen.[45]

The very best school for voice culture is in the home life. Study in every way, not to annoy, but to cultivate a soft voice, distinct and plain. . . . Mothers should themselves act like Christ, speaking tender, loving words in the home.[46]

The right culture and use of the power of speech has to do with every line of Christian work; it enters into the home life and into all our intercourse with one another. We should accustom ourselves to speak in pleasant tones, to use pure and correct language, and words that are kind and courteous. Sweet, kind words are as dew and gentle showers to the soul. The Scripture says of Christ that grace was poured into His lips, that He might "know how to speak a word in season to him that is weary." And the Lord bids us, "Let your speech be alway with grace," "that it may minister grace unto the hearers.". . . If we follow Christ's example in doing good, hearts will open to us as they did to Him.

Not abruptly, but with tact born of divine love, we can tell them of Him who is the "Chiefest among ten thousand," and the One "altogether lovely." This is the very highest work in which we can employ the talent of speech.[47]

Righteous words and deeds have a more powerful influence for good than all the sermons that can be preached.[48]

114

THE TALENT OF TIME

See then that ye walk circumspectly, not as fools, but as wise, redeeming the time, because the days are evil.

God bestows talents upon men, not that these talents may lie unused or be employed in self-gratification, but that they may be used to bless others. God grants men the gift of time for the purpose of promoting His glory. When this time is used in selfish pleasure, the hours thus spent are lost for all eternity.[49]

Our time belongs to God. Every moment is His, and we are under the most solemn obligation to improve it to His glory. Of no talent He has given will He require a more strict account than of our time.

The value of time is beyond computation. Christ regarded every moment as precious, and it is thus that we should regard it. Life is too short to be trifled away. We have but a few days of probation in which to prepare for eternity. . . .

The human family have scarcely begun to live when they begin to die, and the world's incessant labor ends in nothingness unless a true knowledge in regard to eternal life is gained. The man who appreciates time as his working day will fit himself for a mansion and for a life that is immortal. It is well that he was born. . . .

Life is too solemn to be absorbed in temporal and earthly matters, in a treadmill of care and anxiety for the things that are but an atom in comparison with the things of eternal interest. Yet God has called us to serve Him in the temporal affairs of life. Diligence in this work is as much a part of true religion as is devotion. The Bible gives no endorsement to idleness. It is the greatest curse that afflicts our world. Every man and woman who is truly converted will be a diligent worker.[50]

≈ ≈ ≈

The moments are freighted with eternal consequences.[51]

THE TALENT OF MONEY

He which soweth sparingly shall reap also sparingly; and he which soweth bountifully shall reap also bountifully. Every man according as he purposeth in his heart, so let him give; not grudgingly, or of necessity: for God loveth a cheerful giver.

In the parable of the talents we have two classes brought to view. One class is represented by the diligent servant, and the other by the wicked and slothful servant. They had both been entrusted with their Lord's money. One went to work with earnestness, seeking opportunities to use his entrusted gift in such a way that others would be blessed and benefited. He does not live simply to please himself, to gratify selfish desires, to delight in pleasure parties and in places of amusement, seeking for gratification of his fleshly lusts, as though this were the object of life; but he thinks soberly, and remembers that his religious life is short.[52]

It is God who gives men power to get wealth, and He has bestowed this ability, not as a means of gratifying self, but as a means of returning to God His own. With this object it is not a sin to acquire means. Money is to be earned by labor. Every youth should be trained to habits of industry. The Bible condemns no man for being rich if he has acquired his riches honestly. . . . Wealth will prove a blessing if we regard it as the Lord's, to be received with thankfulness and with thankfulness returned to the Giver.[53]

Money has great value, because it can do great good. In the hands of God's children it is food for the hungry, drink for the thirsty, and clothing for the naked. It is a defense for the oppressed and a means of help to the sick. But money is of no more value than sand, only as it is put to use in providing for the necessities of life, in blessing others, and advancing the cause of Christ.[54]

STRENGTH IS A TALENT

A wise man is strong; yea, a man of knowledge increaseth strength.

We are to love God, not only with all the heart, mind, and soul, but with all the strength. This covers the full, intelligent use of the physical powers. . . .

It was Christ who planned . . . every specification in regard to the building of Solomon's temple. The One who in His earthly life worked as a carpenter in the village of Nazareth was the heavenly architect who marked out the plan for the sacred building where His name was to be honored. . . .

All right inventions and improvements have their source in Him who is wonderful in counsel and excellent in working. The skillful touch of the physician's hand, his power over nerve and muscle, his knowledge of the delicate organism of the body, is the wisdom of divine power, to be used in behalf of the suffering. The skill with which the carpenter uses the hammer, the strength with which the blacksmith makes the anvil ring, comes from God. He has entrusted men with talents, and He expects them to look to Him for counsel. . . .

Bible religion is to be interwoven with all we do or say. . . . They are to be united in all human pursuits, in mechanical and agricultural labors, in mercantile and scientific enterprises. . . . It is just as essential to do the will of God when erecting a building as when taking part in a religious service. . . .

Of Daniel we learn that in all his business transactions, when subjected to the closest scrutiny, not one fault or error could be found. He was a sample of what every businessman may be. His history shows what may be accomplished by one who consecrates the strength of brain and bone and muscle, of heart and life, to the service of God.[55]

GOD GIVES ME POWER TO DO GOOD

He that doeth good is of God.

There are many ways in which the youth can be putting to usury the talents entrusted to them of God, to build up the work and cause of God, not to please themselves but to glorify God. The Majesty of heaven, the King of glory, made the infinite sacrifice in coming to our world in order that He might elevate and ennoble humanity. . . . We read, "He went about doing good." . . .

He has a vineyard in which everyone can perform good work. Suffering humanity needs help everywhere. The students may win their way to hearts by speaking words in season, by doing favors for those who need even physical labor. This will not degrade any of you, but it will bring a consciousness of the approval of God. It will be putting the talents entrusted to you for wise improvement to the exchangers. It will increase them by trading upon them. . . .

It is our duty ever to seek to do good in the use of the muscles and brain God has given to youth, that they may be useful to others, making their labors lighter, soothing the sorrowing, lifting up the discouraged, speaking words of comfort to the hopeless, turning the minds of the students from fun and frolic which often carries them beyond the dignity of manhood and womanhood to shame and disgrace. The Lord would have the mind elevated, seeking higher, nobler channels of usefulness.[56]

The true man is one who is willing to sacrifice his own interest for the good of others, and who exercises himself in binding up the brokenhearted.[57]

All power to do good is God-given. . . . To God belongs all the glory for the wise and good deeds of human agents.[58]

AFFECTIONS AND IMPULSES ARE PRECIOUS TALENTS

Be kindly affectioned one to another with brotherly love; in honour preferring one another.

Kindly affections, generous impulses, and a quick apprehension of spiritual things are precious talents and lay their possessor under a weighty responsibility. All are to be used in God's service. But here many err. Satisfied with the possession of these qualities, they fail to bring them into active service for others. . . . Those who possess large affections are under obligation to God to bestow them, not merely on their friends, but on all who need their help. Social advantages are talents, and are to be used for the benefit of all within reach of our influence. . . .

Talents used are talents multiplied. Success is not the result of chance or of destiny; it is the outworking of God's own providence, the reward of faith and discretion, of virtue and persevering effort. The Lord desires us to use every gift we have; and if we do this, we shall have greater gifts to use. He does not supernaturally endow us with the qualifications we lack; but while we use that which we have, He will work with us to increase and strengthen every faculty. By every wholehearted, earnest sacrifice for the Master's service, our powers will increase. . . . As we cherish and obey the promptings of the Spirit, our hearts are enlarged to receive more and more of His power and to do more and better work. Dormant energies are aroused and palsied faculties receive new life. . . .

As we seek to win others to Christ, bearing the burdens of souls in our prayers, our own hearts will throb with the quickening influence of God's grace; our own affections will glow with more divine fervor; our whole Christian life will be more of a reality, more earnest, more prayerful.[59]

BE STRONG AND COURAGEOUS

Be thou strong and very courageous, that thou mayest observe to do according to all the law, which Moses my servant commanded thee: turn not from it to the right hand or to the left, that thou mayest prosper whithersoever thou goest.

In the history of Joseph, Daniel, and his fellows we see how the golden chain of truth may bind the youth to the throne of God. They could not be tempted to turn aside from their course of integrity. They valued the favor of God far above the favor and praise of princes, and God loved them, and spread His shield over them. Because of their faithful integrity, because of their determination to honor God above every human power, the Lord signally honored them before men. They were honored by the Lord God of hosts, whose power is over all the works of His hand in heaven above and the earth beneath. These youth were not ashamed to display their true colors. Even in the court of the king, in their words, their habits, their practices, they confessed their faith in the Lord God of heaven. They refused to bow to any earthly mandate that detracted from the honor of God. They had strength from heaven to confess their allegiance to God. . . .

Never be ashamed of your colors; put them up, unfurl them to the gaze of men and angels. . . . The world has a right to know just what may be expected from every intelligent human being. He who is a living embodiment of firm, decided, righteous principles will be a living power upon his associates; and he will influence others by his Christianity. Many do not discern and appreciate how great is the influence of each one for good or evil. . . .

Your happiness for this life and for the future, immortal life lies with yourself. . . . How important it is that everyone shall consider where he is leading souls. We are in view of the eternal world, and how diligently we should count the cost of our influence.[60]

BE AN EXAMPLE TO FELLOW BELIEVERS

Be thou an example of the believers, in word, in conversation, in charity, in spirit, in faith, in purity.

By the atmosphere surrounding us, every person with whom we come in contact is consciously or unconsciously affected. . . . Our words, our acts, our dress, our deportment, even the expression of the countenance, has an influence. . . . Every impulse thus imparted is seed sown which will produce its harvest. It is a link in the long chain of human events, extending we know not whither. If by our example we aid others in the development of good principles, we give them power to do good. In their turn they exert the same influence upon others, and they upon still others. Thus by our unconscious influence thousands may be blessed.

Throw a pebble into the lake, and a wave is formed; and another and another; and as they increase, the circle widens, until it reaches the very shore. So with our influence. Beyond our knowledge or control it tells upon others in blessing or cursing. . . .

And the wider the sphere of our influence the more good we may do. When those who profess to serve God follow Christ's example, practicing the principles of the law in their daily life; when every act bears witness that they love God supremely and their neighbor as themselves, then will the church have power to move the world.[61]

If young men make their model an exalted one, having pure morals and firm principles, and if blended with this are affability and true Christian courtesy, there is a refined perfection to the character which will win its way anywhere, and a powerful influence will be wielded in favor of virtue, temperance, and righteousness. Such characters will be of the highest value to society, more precious than gold. Their influence is for time and for eternity.[62]

A SAVING INFLUENCE OVER ASSOCIATES AND UNBELIEVERS

*Ye were ensamples to all that believe in Macedonia and Achaia.
For from you sounded out the word of the Lord not only in
Macedonia and Achaia, but also in every place your faith to God-
ward is spread abroad; so that we need not to speak any thing.*

If you can exert a saving influence over one soul, remember
there is joy in heaven over the one that repented. . . . You may, by
judicious effort, be the means of bringing back the lost sheep to
Jesus' fold. Although you may be young, you must work with Christ;
with His spirit in your heart you can do much more than it now
seems possible for you to do.[63]

If your example is Christlike, that alone, if you do not say a
word, will be a help to many. Patient continuance in well-doing will
help others to place their feet in the path of truth and righteousness.
. . . Be careful to start right, and then keep quietly on.[64]

The firm purposes you may possess in carrying out good principles will have an influence to balance souls in the right direction.
There is no limit to the good you may do. If you make the Word of
God the rule of your life, and govern your actions by its precepts,
making all your purposes and exertions in the fulfilling of your duty
a blessing . . . , success will crown your efforts.[65]

The youth who are consecrated to God sway a mighty influence
for good. Preachers or laymen advanced in years cannot have one
half the influence for good upon the young that the youth, if devoted to God, can have upon their associates.[66]

The silent witness of a true, unselfish, godly life carries an almost
irresistible influence.[67]

The unstudied, unconscious influence of a holy life is the most
convincing sermon that can be given in favor of Christianity.[68]

THE INFLUENCE OF A MEEK AND QUIET SPIRIT

Whose adorning let it not be that outward adorning of plaiting the hair, and of wearing of gold, or of putting on of apparel; but let it be the hidden man of the heart, in that which is not corruptible, even the ornament of a meek and quiet spirit, which is in the sight of God of great price.

The apostle presents the inward adorning, in contrast with the outward, and tells us what the great God values. The outward is corruptible. But the meek and quiet spirit, the development of a beautifully symmetrical character, will never decay. It is an adornment which is not perishable. In the sight of the Creator of everything that is valuable, lovely, and beautiful it is declared to be of great price.[69]

Shall we not seek earnestly to gain that which God estimates as more valuable than costly dress, or pearls, or gold? The inward adorning, the grace of meekness, a spirit in harmony with the heavenly angels, will not lessen true dignity of character or make us less lovely here in this world. The Redeemer has warned us against the pride of life, but not against its grace and natural beauty.[70]

Self-denial in dress is a part of our Christian duty. To dress plainly and abstain from display of jewelry and ornaments of every kind is in keeping with our faith.[71]

It is of the greatest importance that we . . . show by precept and example that we are cultivating that which the Monarch of the universe estimates of great value. In doing this what an influence for good can we have.[72]

Children and youth who devote time and means to make themselves objects of attraction by outward display and affected manners are not working in the right direction. They need to cultivate true, Christian politeness and nobility of soul. . . . The beauty of mind, the purity of the soul, revealed in the countenance, will have more power to attract and exert an influence upon hearts than any outward adorning.[73]

THE INFLUENCE OF A CHRISTIAN FAMILY

For I know him, that he will command his children, and his household after him, and they shall keep the way of the Lord, to do justice and judgment.

Every Christian family should illustrate to the world the power and excellence of Christian influences.[74]

The home in which the members are kindly, courteous Christians exerts a far-reaching influence for good. Other families mark the results attained by such a home and follow the example set, in their turn guarding their homes against evil influences. Angels of heaven often visit the home in which the will of God bears sway. Under the power of divine grace such a home becomes a place of refreshing to worn, weary pilgrims. Self is kept from asserting itself. Right habits are formed. There is a careful recognition of the rights of others. The faith that works by love and purifies the soul stands at the helm, presiding over the entire household.[75]

One well-ordered, well-disciplined family tells more in behalf of Christianity than all the sermons that can be preached.[76]

A lamp, however small, if kept steadily burning, may be the means of lighting many other lamps. Our sphere of influence may seem narrow, our ability small, our opportunities few, our acquirements limited; yet wonderful possibilities are ours through a faithful use of the opportunities of our own homes. If we will open our hearts and home to the divine principles of life, we shall become channels for currents of life-giving power. From our homes will flow streams of healing, bringing life, and beauty, and fruitfulness.[77]

❧ ❧ ❧

The influence of a carefully guarded Christian home in the years of childhood and youth is the surest safeguard against the corruptions of the world.[78]

M A Y

A HEALTHFUL LIFE

MY BODY BELONGS TO GOD

What? know ye not that your body is the temple of the Holy Ghost which is in you, which ye have of God, and ye are not your own? for ye are bought with a price: therefore glorify God in your body, and in your spirit, which are God's.

Life is a gift of God. Our bodies have been given us to use in God's service, and He desires that we shall care for and appreciate them. Our bodies must be kept in the best possible condition physically, and under the most spiritual influences. . . .

A pure, healthy life is most favorable for the perfection of Christian character and for the development of the powers of mind and body.

The law of temperance must control the life of every Christian. God is to be in all our thoughts; His glory is ever to be kept in view. We must break away from every influence that would captivate our thoughts and lead us from God. We are under sacred obligations to God so to govern our bodies and rule our appetites and passions that they will not lead us away from purity and holiness, or take our minds from the work God requires us to do.[1]

Those who serve God in sincerity and truth will be a peculiar people, unlike the world, separate from the world. Their food will be prepared, not to encourage gluttony or gratify a perverted taste, but to secure to themselves the greatest physical strength, and consequently the best mental conditions. . . .

Our heavenly Father has bestowed upon us the great blessing of health reform, that we may glorify Him by obeying the claims He has upon us. . . . The harmonious, healthy action of all the powers of body and mind results in happiness; the more elevated and refined the powers, the more pure and unalloyed the happiness.[2]

MAN CREATED IN GOD'S IMAGE

And God said, Let us make man in our image, after our likeness.

Man was the crowning act of the creation of God, made in the image of God, and designed to be a counterpart of God. . . . Man is very dear to God, because he was formed in His own image.[3]

As Adam came forth from the hand of his Creator he was of noble height and of beautiful symmetry. He was more than twice as tall as men now living upon the earth, and was well proportioned. His features were perfect and beautiful. His complexion was neither white nor sallow, but ruddy, glowing with the rich tint of health. Eve was not quite as tall as Adam. Her head reached a little above his shoulders. She too was noble, perfect in symmetry, and very beautiful.[4]

Man came from the hand of God perfect in every faculty of mind and body; in perfect soundness, therefore in perfect health.[5]

God endowed man with so great vital force that he has withstood the accumulation of disease brought upon the race in consequence of perverted habits, and has continued for six thousand years. . . .

If Adam, at his creation, had not been endowed with twenty times as much vital force as men now have, the race, with their present habits of living in violation of natural law, would have become extinct.[6]

Created to be "the image and glory of God," Adam and Eve had received endowments not unworthy of their high destiny. Graceful and symmetrical in form, regular and beautiful in feature, their countenances glowing with the tint of health and the light of joy and hope, they bore in outward resemblance the likeness of their Maker.[7]

MY WONDERFUL BODY

I will praise thee; for I am fearfully and wonderfully made: marvellous are thy works; and that my soul knoweth right well.

The mechanism of the human body cannot be fully understood; it presents mysteries that baffle the most intelligent. It is not as the result of a mechanism, which, once set in motion, continues its work, that the pulse beats, and breath follows breath. . . . The beating heart, the throbbing pulse, every nerve and muscle in the living organism, is kept in order and activity by the power of an ever-present God.[8]

The Creator of man has arranged the living machinery of our bodies. Every function is wonderfully and wisely made. And God has pledged Himself to keep this human machinery in healthful action if the human agent will obey His laws and cooperate with God. Every law governing the human machinery is to be considered just as truly divine in origin, in character, and in importance as the Word of God. Every careless, inattentive action, any abuse put upon the Lord's wonderful mechanism, by disregarding His specified laws in the human habitation, is a violation of God's law. We may behold and admire the work of God in the natural world, but the human habitation is the most wonderful.[9]

This living machinery is to be understood. Every part of its wonderful mechanism is to be carefully studied.[10]

As in the study of physiology they see that they are indeed "fearfully and wonderfully made," they will be inspired with reverence. Instead of marring God's handiwork, they will have an ambition to make all that is possible of themselves, in order to fulfill the Creator's glorious plan. Thus they will come to regard obedience to the laws of health, not as a matter of sacrifice or self-denial, but as it really is an inestimable privilege and blessing.[11]

GOD MADE MAN UPRIGHT

God hath made man upright; but they have sought out many inventions.

The health reform is an important part of the third angel's message; and as a people professing this reform, we should not retrograde, but make continual advancement. It is a great thing to ensure health by placing ourselves in right relations to the laws of life.[12]

Among the first things to be aimed at should be a correct position, both in sitting and in standing. God made man upright, and He desires him to possess not only the physical but the mental and moral benefit, the grace and dignity and self-possession, the courage and self-reliance, which an erect bearing so greatly tends to promote.[13]

The lungs should be allowed the greatest freedom possible. Their capacity is developed by free action; it diminishes if they are cramped and compressed. Hence the ill effects of the practice so common, especially in sedentary pursuits of stooping at one's work. In this position it is impossible to breathe deeply. Superficial breathing soon becomes a habit, and the lungs lose their power to expand. . . . Thus an insufficient supply of oxygen is received. The blood moves sluggishly.[14]

Next in importance to right position are respiration and vocal culture. The one who sits and stands erect is more likely than others to breathe properly. . . . To ensure correct delivery in reading and speaking, see that the abdominal muscles have full play in breathing, and that the respiratory organs are unrestricted. Let the strain come on the muscles of the abdomen rather than on those of the throat. Great weariness and serious disease of the throat and lungs may thus be prevented.[15]

In order to enjoy good health, we must ask the Lord to bless us, and then do what we can to place ourselves under conditions the most favorable to health.[16]

CLEANLINESS

Let us draw near with a true heart in full assurance of faith, having our hearts sprinkled from an evil conscience, and out bodies washed with pure water.

Scrupulous cleanliness is essential to both physical and mental health. Impurities are constantly thrown off from the body through the skin. Its millions of pores are quickly clogged unless kept clean by frequent bathing, and the impurities which should pass off through the skin become an additional burden to the other eliminating organs. . . . A bath, properly taken, fortifies against cold, because it improves the circulation; the blood is brought to the surface, and a more easy and regular flow is obtained. The mind and the body are alike invigorated. The muscles become more flexible, the intellect is made brighter. The bath is a soother of the nerves.[17]

Teach the little ones that God is not pleased to see them with unclean bodies and untidy, torn garments. . . . Having the clothing neat and clean will be one means of keeping the thoughts pure and sweet. . . . Especially should every article which comes in contact with the skin be kept clean.[18]

Truth never places her delicate feet in a path of uncleanness or impurity. . . . He who was so particular that the children of Israel should cherish habits of cleanliness will not sanction any impurity in the homes of His people today. God looks with disfavor on uncleanness of any kind.[19]

Unclean, neglected corners in the house will tend to make impure, neglected corners in the soul.[20]

Perfect cleanliness, plenty of sunlight, careful attention to sanitation in every detail of the home life, are essential to freedom from disease and to the cheerfulness and vigor of the inmates of the home.[21]

Heaven is pure and holy, and those who pass through the gates of the city of God must here be clothed with inward and outward purity.[22]

EXERCISE

The glory of young men is their strength.

Another precious blessing is proper exercise.[23] Each organ and muscle has its work to do in the living organism. Every wheel in the machinery must be a living, active, working wheel. Nature's fine and wonderful works need to be kept in active motion in order to accomplish the object for which they were designed.[24]

Bind up an arm, even for a few weeks, then free it from its bands, and you will see that it is weaker than the one you have been using moderately during the same time. Inactivity produces the same effect upon the whole muscular system.

Inactivity is a fruitful cause of disease. Exercise quickens and equalizes the circulation of the blood.[25]

For a healthy young man, stern, severe exercise is strengthening to the whole system. . . . Without such exercise the mind cannot be kept in working order. It becomes inactive, unable to put forth the sharp, quick action that will give scope to its powers. . . .

All the heavenly beings are in constant activity, and the Lord Jesus, in His lifework, has given an example for every one. He went about "doing good." God has established the law of obedient action. Silent but ceaseless, the objects of His creation do their appointed work. The ocean is in constant motion. The springing grass, which today is, and tomorrow is cast into the oven, does its errand, clothing the fields with beauty. The leaves are stirred to motion, and yet no hand is seen to touch them. The sun, moon, and stars are useful and glorious in fulfilling their mission. . . . And man, his mind and body created in God's own similitude, must be active in order to fill his appointed place.[26]

Action gives power.[27]

INDUSTRY

Whatsoever thy hand findeth to do, do it with thy might.

The life of Jesus was filled with industry, and He took exercise in performing varied tasks in harmony with His developing physical strength. In doing the work that was marked out for Him, He had no time for indulgence in exciting, useless amusements. He . . . was trained in useful labor, and even for the endurance of hardship. . . .

Christ presents before us a pattern for youth and children. His early life was lived under conditions favorable to the obtaining of physical development and to the acquisition of moral power to resist temptation, so that He might remain untainted amid the corruption of wicked Nazareth. . . .

The education of Christ, during the time He was subject to His parents, was of the most valuable kind. . . . The physical and mental exercise that was necessary to the performance of His tasks developed both physical and mental strength. His life of industry and retirement closed the avenues through which Satan could enter to tempt Him to the love of vanity and display. He waxed strong in body and spirit, thus gaining a preparation for the duties of manhood and for the performance of the important duties that afterward devolved upon Him.[28]

Jesus was an earnest, constant worker. Never lived there among men another so weighted with responsibilities. Never another carried so heavy a burden of the world's sorrow and sin. Never another toiled with such self-consuming zeal for the good of men. Yet His life was a life of health. Physically as well as spiritually He was represented by the sacrificial lamb, "without blemish and without spot." In body as in soul He was an example of what God designed all humanity to be through obedience to His laws.[29]

A NUTRITIOUS DIET

Wherefore do ye spend money for that which is not bread? and your labour for that which satisfieth not? hearken diligently unto me, and eat ye that which is good, and let your soul delight itself in fatness.

Health reform is an intelligent selection of the most healthful article of food prepared in the most healthful, simplest form.[30]

Our bodies are built up from the food we eat. There is a constant breaking down of the tissues of the body; every movement of every organ involves waste, and this waste is repaired from our food. Each organ of the body requires its share of nutrition. The brain must be supplied with its portion; the bones, muscles, and nerves demand theirs. It is a wonderful process that transforms the food into blood and uses this blood to build up the varied parts of the body; but this process is going on continually, supplying with life and strength each nerve, muscle, and tissue.[31]

God has furnished man with abundant means for the gratification of an unperverted appetite. He has spread before him the products of the earth—a bountiful variety of food that is palatable to the taste and nutritious to the system. Of these our benevolent heavenly Father says we may freely eat. Fruits, grains, and vegetables, prepared in a simple way, free from spice and grease of all kinds, make, with milk or cream, the most healthful diet. They impart nourishment to the body and give a power of endurance and a vigor of intellect that are not produced by a stimulating diet.[32]

Let the table be made inviting and attractive, as it is supplied with the good things which God has so bountifully bestowed. Let mealtime be a cheerful, happy time. As we enjoy the gifts of God, let us respond by grateful praise to the Giver.[33]

God has given us the fruits and grains of the earth for food, that we might have unfevered blood, calm nerves, and clear minds.[34]

REST

And he said unto them, Come ye yourselves apart into a desert place, and rest a while: for there were many coming and going, and they had no leisure so much as to eat.

Though time is short, and there is a great work to be done, the Lord is not pleased to have us so prolong our seasons of activity that there will not be time for periods of rest, for the study of the Bible, and for communion with God. All this is essential to fortify the soul, to place us in a position where we shall receive wisdom from God to employ our talents in the Master's service to the highest account.[35]

When Jesus said the harvest was great and the laborers were few, He did not urge upon His disciples the necessity of ceaseless toil. . . . He tells His disciples that their strength has been severely tried, that they will be unfitted for future labor unless they rest awhile. . . . In the name of Jesus, economize your powers, that after being refreshed with rest, you may do more and better work.[36]

When the disciples related all their experience to Jesus, He understood their need. Their labor had greatly elated and encouraged them, but it had also worn upon them. . . . A desert place did not mean a waste and solitary wilderness, but a place of retirement and quiet, pleasant to the eyes and invigorating to the body. They sought such a place near a favorite resort on the sea of Galilee. . . . The Christian life is not made up of unceasing activity or of continual meditation. . . . He knew that a season of rest and recreation, apart from the multitude and the scene of their labors, would invigorate them, and He sought to withdraw them from the busy cities to a quiet resort where they might have a season of precious fellowship with Him and with each other. . . . The disciples of Jesus needed to be educated as to how they should labor and how they should rest. Today there is need that God's chosen workmen should listen to the command of Christ to go apart and rest awhile.[37]

PRESERVE THE BODY TEMPLE

Know ye not that ye are the temple of God, and that the Spirit of God dwelleth in you?

God has given you a habitation to care for and preserve in the best condition for His service and glory. Your bodies are not your own. . . . "Know ye not that ye are the temple of God, and that the Spirit of God dwelleth in you?"[38]

Health is a blessing of which few appreciate the value. . . . Life is a holy trust, which God alone can enable us to keep, and to use to His glory. But He who formed the wonderful structure of the body will take special care to keep it in order if men do not work at cross-purposes with Him. Every talent entrusted to us He will help us to improve and use in accordance to the will of the Giver.[39]

Youth is the time to establish good habits, to correct wrong ones already contracted, to gain and to hold the power of self-control, and to lay the plan, and accustom one's self to the practice of ordering all the acts of life with reference to the will of God.[40]

The sacred temple of the body must be kept pure and uncontaminated, that God's Holy Spirit may dwell therein. We need to guard faithfully the Lord's property, for any abuse of our powers shortens the time that our lives could be used for the glory of God. Bear in mind that we must consecrate all—soul, body, and spirit—to God. All is His purchased possession, and must be used intelligently, to the end that we may preserve the talent of life. By properly using our powers to their fullest extent in the most useful employment, by keeping every organ in health, by so preserving every organ that mind, sinew, and muscle shall work harmoniously, we may do the most precious service for God.[41]

When we do all we can on our part to have health, then may we expect that the blessed results will follow, and we can ask God in faith to bless our efforts for the preservation of health.[42]

PROSPER AND BE IN HEALTH

Beloved, I wish above all things that thou mayest prosper and be in health, even as thy soul prospereth.

The Saviour in His miracles revealed the power that is continually at work in man's behalf to sustain and to heal him. Through the agencies of nature, God is working, day by day, hour by hour, moment by moment, to keep us alive, to build up and restore us. When any part of the body sustains injury, a healing process is at once begun; nature's agencies are set at work to restore soundness. But the power working through these agencies is the power of God. All life-giving power is from Him. When one recovers from disease, it is God who restores him. . . .

The words spoken to Israel are true today of those who recover health of body or health of soul. "I am the Lord that healeth thee."

The desire of God for every human being is expressed in the words, "Beloved, I wish above all things that thou mayest prosper and be in health, even as thy soul prospereth.[43]

Pure air, sunlight, abstemiousness, rest, exercise, proper diet, the use of water, trust in divine power—these are the true remedies.[44]

The things of nature are God's blessings, provided to give health to body, mind, and soul. They are given to the well to keep them well and to the sick to make them well. . . .

Nature is God's physician. The pure air, the glad sunshine, the beautiful flowers and trees, the orchards and vineyards, and outdoor exercise amid these surroundings are health giving—the elixir of life.

Nothing so tends to restore health and happiness as living amid attractive country surroundings.[45]

Life in the open air is good for body and mind. It is God's medicine for the restoration of health.[46]

❀ ❀ ❀

True religion and the laws of health go hand in hand.[47]

OUTDOOR ACTIVITY

The Lord God planted a garden eastward in Eden; and there he put the man whom he had formed. . . . And the Lord God took the man, and put him into the garden of Eden to dress it and to keep it.

To Adam and Eve was committed the care of the garden, "to dress it and to keep it." Though rich in all that the Owner of the universe could supply, they were not to be idle. Useful occupation was appointed them as a blessing, to strengthen the body, to expand the mind, and to develop the character.[48]

Let men and women work in field and orchard and garden. This will bring health and strength to nerve and muscle. . . . Every part of the human organism should be equally taxed. This is necessary for the harmonious development and action of every part. . . . God made nerve and muscle in order that they might be used. It is the inaction of the human machinery that brings suffering and disease.[49]

More people die for want of exercise than through overfatigue; very many more rust out than wear out. Those who accustom themselves to proper exercise in the open air will generally have a good and vigorous circulation.[50]

Morning exercise, in walking in the free, invigorating air of heaven, or cultivating flowers, small fruits, and vegetables, is necessary to a healthful circulation of the blood. It is the surest safeguard against colds, coughs, congestions of brain and lungs, inflammation of the liver, the kidneys, and the lungs, and a hundred other diseases.[51]

Go out and exercise every day, even though some things indoors have to be neglected.[52]

The more nearly we come into harmony with God's original plan, the more favorable will be our position for the recovery and preservation of health.[53]

THE AIR WE BREATHE

He giveth to all life, and breath, and all things.

Air is the free blessing of heaven, calculated to electrify the whole system.[54]

The lungs are constantly throwing off impurities, and they need to be constantly supplied with fresh air.[55]

We are more dependent upon the air we breathe than upon the food we eat. Men and women, young and old, who desire health, and who would enjoy active life, should remember that they cannot have these without a good circulation. Whatever their business and inclinations, they should make up their minds to exercise in the open air as much as they can. They should feel it a religious duty to overcome the conditions of health which have kept them confined indoors, deprived of exercise in the open air.[56]

Air, the precious boon of heaven, which all may have, will bless you with its invigorating influence if you will not refuse it entrance. Welcome it, cultivate a love for it, and it will prove a precious soother of the nerves. . . . The influence of pure, fresh air is to cause the blood to circulate healthfully through the system. It refreshes the body and tends to render it strong and healthy, while at the same time its influence is decidedly felt upon the mind, imparting a degree of composure and serenity. It excites the appetite and renders the digestion of food more perfect, and induces sound, sweet sleep.[57]

The pure, invigorating air of heaven is God's free gift to men and women, and it is impossible for them to be cheerful, healthful, and happy unless they appreciate these rich bounties and allow them to answer the purpose for which they were designed.[58]

ea ea ea

The free, pure air of heaven is one of the richest blessings we can enjoy.[59]

SUNLIGHT

Truly the light is sweet, and a pleasant thing it is for the eyes to behold the sun.

There are but few who realize that, in order to enjoy health and cheerfulness, they must have an abundance of sunlight, pure air, and physical exercise. We pity little children who are kept confined indoors when the sun is shining gloriously without.[60]

Clothe your boys and girls comfortably and properly. . . . Then let them go out and exercise in the open air, and live to enjoy health and happiness.[61]

The pale and sickly grain-blade that has struggled up out of the cold of early spring puts out the natural and healthy deep green after enjoying for a few days the health-and-life-giving rays of the sun. Go out into the light and warmth of the glorious sun, . . . and share with vegetation its life-giving, healing power.[62]

No room in the house should be considered furnished and adorned without the cheering, enlivening light and sunshine, which are Heaven's own free gift to man. . . .

When God had made our world, and darkness was upon the face of the deep, he said, Let there be light, and there was light. And God saw the light that it was good. Shall we close our houses, and exclude from them the light which God has pronounced good?[63]

If you would have your homes sweet and inviting, make them bright with air and sunshine. . . . The precious sunlight may fade your carpets, but it will give a healthful color to the cheeks of your children. If you have God's presence, and possess earnest, loving hearts, a humble home, made bright with air and sunlight . . . will be to your family . . . a heaven below.[64]

Exercise and a free abundant use of the air and sunlight—blessings which Heaven has freely bestowed upon all—would give life and strength.[65]

138

WATER

Jesus answered and said unto her, Whosoever drinketh of this water shall thirst again: but whosoever drinketh of the water that I shall give him shall never thirst; but the water that I shall give him shall be in him a well of water springing up into everlasting life.

In health and in sickness pure water is one of Heaven's choicest blessings. Its proper use promotes health. It is the beverage which God provided to quench the thirst of animals and man. Drunk freely, it helps to supply the necessities of the system and assists nature to resist disease. The external application of water is one of the easiest and most satisfactory ways of regulating the circulation of the blood.[66]

Pure water to drink and fresh air to breathe invigorate the vital organs, purify the blood, and help nature in her task of overcoming the bad conditions of the system.[67]

Water is the best liquid possible to cleanse the tissues.[68]

If those who are afflicted would assist nature in her efforts by the use of pure, soft water, much suffering would be prevented.[69]

Water treatments, wisely and skillfully given, may be the means of saving many lives. Let diligent study be united with careful treatments. Let prayers of faith be offered by the bedside of the sick. Let the sick be encouraged to claim the promises of God for themselves.[70]

The refreshing water, welling up in a parched and barren land, causing the desert place to blossom and flowing out to give life to the perishing, is an emblem of the divine grace which Christ alone can bestow, and which is as the living water, purifying, refreshing, and invigorating the soul.[71]

❧ ❧ ❧

In the East water was called the "gift of God."[72]

139

ENJOY GOD'S CREATED WORKS

On the seventh day God ended his work which he had made; and he rested on the seventh day from all his work which he had made.

God reserved the seventh day as a period of rest for man, for the good of man as well as for His own glory. He saw that the wants of man required a day of rest from toil and care, that his health and life would be endangered without a period of relaxation from the labor and anxiety of the six days.[73]

The Sabbath of the Lord is to be made a blessing to us and to our children. . . . They can be pointed to the blooming flowers and the opening buds, the lofty trees and beautiful spires of grass, and taught that God made all these in six days, and rested on the seventh day, and hallowed it. Thus the parents may bind up their lessons of instruction to their children, so that when these children look upon the things of nature, they will call to mind the great Creator of them all. Their thoughts will be carried up to nature's God—back to the creation of our world, when the foundation of the Sabbath was laid, and all the sons of God shouted for joy.[74]

Happy is the family who can go to the place of worship on the Sabbath as Jesus and His disciples went to the synagogue—across the fields, along the shores of the lake, or through the groves.[75]

The Sabbath bids us behold in His created works the glory of the Creator. And it is because He desired us to do this that Jesus bound up His precious lessons with the beauty of natural things. On the holy rest day, above all other days, we should study the messages that God has written for us in nature. We should study the Saviour's parables where He spoke them, in the fields and groves, under the open sky, among the grass and flowers. As we come close to the heart of nature, Christ makes His presence real to us and speaks to our hearts of His peace and love.[76]

DO ALL TO THE GLORY OF GOD

Whether therefore ye eat. or drink, or whatsoever ye do, do all to the glory of God.

In order to preserve health, temperance in all things is necessary—temperance in labor, temperance in eating and drinking. Our heavenly Father sent the light of health reform . . . that those who love purity and holiness may know how to use with discretion the good things He has provided for them, and that by exercising temperance in daily life they may be sanctified through the truth.[77]

Great care should be taken to form right habits of eating and drinking. The food eaten should be that which will make the best blood. The delicate organs of digestion should be respected. God requires us, by being temperate in all things, to act our part toward keeping ourselves in health. . . . The spiritual experience is greatly affected by the way in which the stomach is treated. Eating and drinking in accordance with the laws of health promote virtuous actions.[78]

Principle should rule instead of appetite or fancy. . . . It means much to be true to God. He has claims upon all who are engaged in His service. He desires that mind and body be preserved in the best condition of health, every power and endowment under the divine control, and as vigorous as careful, strictly temperate habits can make them. . . . Temperance in eating, drinking, sleeping, and dressing is one of the grand principles of the religious life, Truth brought into the sanctuary of the soul will guide in the treatment of the body.[79]

The better you observe the laws of health, the more clearly can you discern temptations, and resist them, and the more clearly you discern the value of eternal things. May the Lord help you to make the most of your present opportunities and privileges, that you may daily gain new victories, and finally enter the city of God, as those who have overcome by the blood of the Lamb and the word of their testimony.[80]

TEMPERATE IN LABOR

Behold that which I have seen: it is good and comely for one to eat and to drink, and to enjoy the good of all his labour that he taketh under the sun all the days of his life, which God giveth him: for it is his portion.

That time is spent to the very best account which is directed to the establishment and preservation of sound physical and mental health. . . . It is an easy matter to lose the health, but it is difficult to regain it . . . We cannot afford to dwarf or cripple a single function of the mind or body by overwork or abuse of any part of the living machinery.[81]

Those who make great exertions to accomplish just so much work in a given time, and continue to labor when their judgment tells them they should rest, are never gainers. They are living on borrowed capital. They are expending the vital force which they will need at a future time. And when the energy they have so recklessly used is demanded, they fail for want of it. . . . Their time of need has come, but their physical resources are exhausted. Everyone who violates the laws of health must sometime be a sufferer to a greater or less degree.[82]

Much of the fatigue and labor under which they are wearing and growing old are not burdens that God has bound upon them, but which they have brought upon themselves by doing the very things the Word of God has told them not to do.[83]

It is not our duty to place ourselves where we shall be overworked. Some may at times be placed where this is necessary, but it should be the exception, not the rule. . . . If we honor the Lord by acting our part, He will on His part preserve our health. . . . By practicing temperance in eating, in drinking, in dressing, in labor, and in all things, we can do for ourselves what no physician can for us.[84]

                        ❧ ❧ ❧

Do not try to crowd into one day the work of two.[85]

DO NOT TURN DAY INTO NIGHT

How long will thou sleep, O sluggard? when wilt thou arise out of thy sleep?

Health is a great treasure. It is the richest possession mortals can have. Wealth, honor, or learning is dearly purchased if it be at the loss of the vigor of health. None of these attainments can secure happiness if health is wanting. It is a terrible sin to abuse the health that God has given us; for every abuse of health enfeebles us for life, and makes us losers.[86]

How prevalent is the habit of turning day into night and night into day. Many youth sleep soundly in the morning, when they should be up with the early singing birds, and be stirring when all nature is awake. Let youth practice regularity in the hours for going to bed and for rising. . . . Let them purpose in their hearts that they will bring themselves under discipline, and practice orderly rules. God is a God of order, and it is the duty of the youth to observe strict rules, for such practices will work for their advantage.[87]

Since the work of building up the body takes place during the hours of rest, it is essential, especially in youth, that sleep should be regular and abundant.[88]

The majority of pleasure lovers attend the fashionable night gatherings, and spend in exciting amusements the hours God has given them for quiet rest and sleep in order to invigorate the body. . . . They are robbing the cheeks of the glow of health, and then to supply the deficiency use cosmetics.[89]

Would it not be better, therefore, to break up this habit of turning night into day, and the fresh hours of morning into night? If the youth would form habits of regularity and order, they would improve in health, in spirits, in memory, and in disposition.[90]

143

TEMPERATE IN STUDY

*And further, by these, my son, be admonished: of making many
books there is no end; and much study is a weariness of the flesh.*

Mental effort without corresponding physical exercise calls an
undue proportion of blood to the brain, and thus the circulation is un-
balanced. The brain has too much blood, while the extremities have
too little. The hours of study and recreation should be carefully regu-
lated, and a portion of the time should be spent in physical labor. . . .

The health cannot be preserved unless some portion of each day
is given to muscular exertion in the open air. Stated hours should be
devoted to manual labor of some kind, anything which will call into
action all parts of the body. Equalize the taxation of the mental and
the physical power, and the mind . . . will be refreshed.[91]

The minds of thinking men labor too hard. They frequently use
their mental powers prodigally, while there is another class whose
highest aim in life is physical labor. The latter class do not exercise
the mind. Their muscles are exercised, but their brains are robbed
of intellectual strength; just as the minds of thinking men are
worked, but their bodies are robbed of strength and vigor by their
neglect to exercise the muscles. . . . Health should be a sufficient in-
ducement to lead them to unite physical with mental labor.

Moral, intellectual, and physical culture should be combined in
order to have well-developed, well-balanced men and women.
Some are qualified to exercise great intellectual strength, while others are inclined to love and enjoy physical labor. Both of these
classes should seek to improve where they are deficient, that they
may present to God their entire being, a living sacrifice, holy and
acceptable to Him, which is their reasonable service.[92]

The health should be as carefully guarded as the character.[93]

APPROPRIATE ATTIRE

She is not afraid of the snow for her household: for all her household are clothed with scarlet (double garments, margin).

Our clothing, while modest and simple, should be of good quality, of becoming colors, and suited for service. It should be chosen for durability rather than display. It should provide warmth and proper protection. The wise woman described in the Proverbs "is not afraid of the snow for her household: for all her household are clothed with double garments."

Our dress should be cleanly. Uncleanliness in dress is unhealthful, and thus defiling to the body and to the soul. . . .

In all respects the dress should be healthful. "Above all things" God desires us to be "in health"—health of body and of soul. And we are to be workers together with Him for the health of both soul and body. Both are promoted by healthful dress.

It should have the grace, the beauty, the appropriateness of natural simplicity. Christ has warned us against the pride of life, but not against its grace and natural beauty. He pointed to the flowers of the field, to the lily unfolding in its purity, and said, "Even Solomon in all his glory was not arrayed like one of these." Thus by the things of nature Christ illustrates the beauty that Heaven values, the modest grace, the simplicity, the purity, the appropriateness, that would make our attire pleasing to Him.[94]

Perfect health depends upon perfect circulation. Special attention should be given to the extremities, that they may be as thoroughly clothed as the chest and region over the heart.[95]

ða ða ða

Let our sisters dress plainly, as many do, having the dress of good material, durable, modest, appropriate for this age, and let not the dress question fill the mind.[96]

REGULARITY IN EATING

Let your moderation be known unto all men. The Lord is at hand.

Regularity in eating is very important for health of body and serenity of mind.[97]

Children are generally untaught in regard to the importance of when, how, and what they should eat. They are permitted to indulge their tastes freely, to eat at all hours, to help themselves to fruit when it tempts their eyes, and this, with the pie, cake, bread and butter, and sweetmeats eaten almost constantly, makes them gormands and dyspeptics. The digestive organs, like a mill which is continually kept running, become enfeebled, vital force is called from the brain to aid the stomach in its overwork, and thus the mental powers are weakened. The unnatural stimulation and wear of the vital forces make them nervous, impatient of restraint, self-willed, and irritable. . . . It is difficult to arouse them to a sense of the shame and grievous nature of sin.[98]

Nothing should be eaten between meals, no confectionery, nuts, fruits, or food of any kind. Irregularities in eating destroy the healthful tone of the digestive organs, to the detriment of health and cheerfulness.[99]

Another pernicious habit is that of eating just before bedtime. . . . The sleep is often disturbed with unpleasant dreams, and in the morning the persons awake unrefreshed and with little relish for breakfast. When we lie down to rest, the stomach should have its work all done, that it, as well as the other organs of the body, may enjoy rest.[100]

Every prohibition of God is for the health and eternal well-being of man.[101]

When they [God's people] break away from all health-destroying indulgences, they will have a clearer perception of what constitutes true godliness. A wonderful change will be seen in the religious experience.[102]

DANIEL AN EXAMPLE IN TEMPERANCE

And the king communed with them; and among them all was found none like Daniel, Hananiah, Mishael, and Azariah. . . . And in all matters of wisdom and understanding, that the king enquired of them, he found them ten times better than all the magicians and astrologers that were in all his realm.

During their three years of training, Daniel and his associates maintained their abstemious habits, their allegiance to God, and their constant dependence upon His power. When the time came for their abilities and acquirements to be tested by the king, they were examined with other candidates for the service of the kingdom. . . . Their keen apprehension, their choice and exact language, their extensive knowledge, testified to the unimpaired strength and vigor of their mental power. . . .

God always honors the right. The most promising youths from all the lands subdued by the great conqueror had been gathered at Babylon, yet amid them all the Hebrew captives were without a rival. The erect form, the firm, elastic step, the fair countenance, the undimmed senses, the untainted breath—all these were insignia of the nobility with which nature honors those who are obedient to her laws. . . .

Amid the seductive influences of the luxurious courts of Babylon they stood firm. The youth of today are surrounded with allurements to self-indulgence. Especially in our large cities, every form of sensual gratification is made easy and inviting. Those who, like Daniel, refuse to defile themselves will reap the reward of temperate habits. . . .

Daniel's clearness of mind and firmness of purpose, his power in acquiring knowledge and in resisting temptation, were due in a great degree to the plainness of his diet, in connection with his life of prayer. . . .

Stand forth in your God-given manhood and womanhood. . . . God will reward you with calm nerves, a clear brain, an unimpaired judgment, keen perceptions. The youth of today whose principles are firm and unwavering will be blessed with health of body, mind, and soul.[103]

THE BODY IS TO BE SERVANT OF THE MIND

For God hath not given us the spirit of fear; but of power, and of love, and of a sound mind.

Every organ of the body was made to be servant of the mind.[104] The brain is the capital of the body, the seat of all the nervous forces and of mental action. The nerves proceeding from the brain control the body. By the brain nerves, mental impressions are conveyed to all the nerves of the body as by telegraph wires; and they control the vital action of every part of the system. All the organs of motion are governed by the communications they receive from the brain.[105]

The brain nerves which communicate with the entire system are the only medium through which Heaven can communicate with man and affect his inmost life. Whatever disturbs the circulation of the electric currents in the nervous system lessens the strength of the vital powers, and the result is a deadening of the sensibilities of the mind.[106]

Any part of the body that is not treated with consideration will telegraph its injury to the brain.[107]

It is not only the privilege, but the sacred duty, of all to understand the laws God has established in their beings. . . . And as they more fully understand the human body, . . . they will seek to bring their bodies into subjection to the noble powers of the mind. The body will be regarded by them as a wonderful structure, formed by the Infinite Designer, and given in their charge to keep this harp of a thousand strings in harmonious action.[108]

To make a success of Christian life, the development of sound minds in sound bodies is of the greatest importance.[109]

The harmonious, healthy action of all the powers of body and mind results in happiness; the more elevated and refined the powers, the more pure and unalloyed the happiness.[110]

SECURITY IN CHRIST IMPROVES HEALTH

The fear of the Lord prolongeth days.

All who are under the training of God need the quiet hour for communion with their own hearts, with nature, and with God. . . . We must individually hear Him speaking to the heart. When every other voice is hushed, and in quietness we wait before Him, the silence of the soul makes more distinct the voice of God. He bids us, "Be still, and know that I am God." . . . Amidst the hurrying throngs and the strain of life's intense activities, he who is thus refreshed will be surrounded with an atmosphere of light and peace. He will receive a new endowment of both physical and mental strength.[111]

Let the mind become intelligent and the will be placed on the Lord's side, and there will be a wonderful improvement in the physical health.[112]

Sickness of the mind prevails everywhere. Nine tenths of the diseases from which men suffer have their foundation here. . . . The religion of Christ . . . is one of its most effectual remedies, for it is a potent soother of the nerves.[113]

Heaven is all health; and the more deeply heavenly influences are realized, the more sure will be the recovery. . . .

Godliness does not conflict with the laws of health, but is in harmony with them. The fear of the Lord is the foundation of all real prosperity.[114]

We should cooperate with God in the care of our bodies. Love for God is essential for life and health. Faith in God is essential for health. In order to have perfect health, our hearts must be filled with love and hope and joy in the Lord.[115]

PEACE THROUGH A CONSCIOUSNESS OF RIGHTDOING

Great peace have they which love thy law: and nothing shall offend them.

If the mind is free and happy, from a consciousness of rightdoing and a sense of satisfaction in causing happiness to others, it creates a cheerfulness that will react upon the whole system, causing a freer circulation of the blood and a toning up of the entire body. The blessing of God is a healing power, and those who are abundant in benefiting others will realize that wondrous blessing in both heart and life.[116]

Those who follow the path of wisdom and holiness will not be troubled with vain regrets over misspent hours, neither will they be troubled with gloom or horror of mind, as some are, unless engaged in vain, trifling amusements. . . .

Amusements excite the mind, but depression is sure to follow. Useful labor and physical exercise will have a more healthful influence upon the mind and will strengthen the muscles, improve the circulation, and will prove a powerful agent in the recovery of health. . . .

The consciousness of rightdoing is the best medicine for diseased bodies and minds. The special blessing of God resting upon the receiver is health and strength.[117]

Doing good is a work that benefits both giver and receiver. If you forget self in your interest for others, you gain a victory over your infirmities. The satisfaction you will realize in doing good will greatly aid you in the recovery of the healthy tone of the imagination. The pleasure of doing good animates the mind and vibrates through the whole body.[118]

        ❧ ❧ ❧

A person whose mind is quiet and satisfied in God is in the pathway to health.[119]

A MERRY HEART IS GOOD MEDICINE

A merry (rejoicing) heart doeth good like a medicine.

The relation that exists between the mind and the body is very intimate. When one is affected the other sympathizes. The condition of the mind affects the health to a far greater degree than many realize. Many of the diseases from which men suffer are the result of mental depression. Grief, anxiety, discontent, remorse, guilt, distrust, all tend to break down the life forces and to invite decay and death.

Disease is sometimes produced, and is often greatly aggravated, by the imagination. Many are lifelong invalids who might be well if they only thought so. . . .

Courage, hope, faith, sympathy, love, promote health and prolong life. A contented mind, a cheerful spirit, is health to the body and strength to the soul.[120]

Gratitude, rejoicing, benevolence, trust in God's love and care—these are health's greatest safeguard.[121]

The power of the will and the importance of self-control, both in the preservation and in the recovery of health, the depressing and even ruinous effect of anger, discontent, selfishness, or impurity, and, on the other hand, the marvelous life-giving power to be found in cheerfulness, unselfishness, gratitude, should also be shown.

There is a physiological truth—truth that we need to consider—in the scripture, "A merry [rejoicing] heart doeth good like a medicine."[122]

The true principles of Christianity open before all a source of inestimable happiness.[123]

We should encourage a cheerful, hopeful, peaceful frame of mind; for our health depends upon our so doing.[124]

KIND ACTS AND PLEASANT WORDS PROMOTE HEALTH

Pleasant words are as an honeycomb, sweet to the soul, and health to the bones.

Kind, cheerful, encouraging words will prove more effective than the most healing medicines. These will bring courage to the heart of the desponding and discouraged, and the happiness and sunshine brought into the family by kind acts and encouraging words will repay the effort tenfold. The husband should remember that much of the burden of training his children rests upon the mother, that she has much to do with molding their minds. This should call into exercise his tenderest feelings, and with care should he lighten her burdens. He should encourage her to lean upon his large affections and direct her mind to heaven, where there is strength and peace and a final rest for the weary.[125]

His kindness and loving courtesy will be to her a precious encouragement, and the happiness he imparts will bring joy and peace to his own heart.[126]

The sweetest type of heaven is a home where the Spirit of the Lord presides. . . . Anything that would mar the peace and unity of the family should be firmly repressed, and kindness and love should be cherished.[127]

Home should be a place where cheerfulness, courtesy, and love abide; and where these graces dwell, there will abide happiness and peace.[128]

Those who are fighting the battle of life at great odds may be refreshed and strengthened and encouraged by little attentions which cost nothing. Kindly words simply spoken, little attentions simply bestowed, will sweep away the clouds of temptation which gather over the horizon of the soul.[129]

Under the influence of meekness, kindness, and gentleness, an atmosphere is created that will heal and not destroy.[130]

HEALTH AND HAPPINESS

I have set the Lord always before me: because he is at my right hand, I shall not be moved. Therefore my heart is glad, and my glory rejoiceth: my flesh also shall rest in hope.

The Christian should live so near to God that he may approve things that are excellent, "being filled with the fruits of righteousness, which are by Jesus Christ, unto the glory and praise of God." His heart should be attuned to gratitude and praise. He should be ever ready to acknowledge the blessings he is receiving, remembering who it is that has said, "Whoso offereth praise glorifieth me.". . .

It is the duty of every one to cultivate cheerfulness instead of brooding over sorrow and troubles. Many not only make themselves wretched in this way, but they sacrifice health and happiness to a morbid imagination. There are things in their surroundings that are not agreeable, and their countenances wear a continual frown that, more plainly than words, expresses discontent. These depressing emotions are a great injury to them healthwise, for by hindering the process of digestion they interfere with nutrition. While grief and anxiety cannot remedy a single evil, they can do great harm; but cheerfulness and hope, while they brighten the pathway of others, "are life unto those that find them, and health to all their flesh."

Christ came to restore to its original loveliness a world ruined by sin. . . . In the new earth there will be no sin nor disease. . . . And the body will be restored to its original perfection. We shall wear the spotless image of our Lord. . . .

The development of Christian character, tending toward this state of perfection, is a growth toward beauty. . . . As the heart becomes transformed by the renewing of the mind, the graces of the Spirit leave their impress on the face, and it expresses the refinement, delicacy, peace, benevolence, and pure and tender love that reign in the heart. . . .

ə♣ ə♣ ə♣

Give "thanks always for all things unto God." [131]

FORGIVENESS OF SIN BRINGS HEALING

Bless the Lord, O my soul, and forget not all his benefits: who forgiveth all thine iniquities; who healeth all thy diseases.

The Saviour ministered to both the soul and the body. The gospel which He taught was a message of spiritual life and of physical restoration. Deliverance from sin and healing of disease were linked together. The same ministry is committed to the Christian physician. He is to unite with Christ in relieving both the physical and spiritual needs of his fellow men. He is to be to the sick a messenger of mercy, bringing to them a remedy for the diseased body and for the sin-sick soul.[132]

When the poor paralytic was brought to the house where Jesus was teaching, a dense crowd surrounded the door, barring every way of access to the Saviour. But faith and hope had been kindled in the heart of the poor sufferer, and he proposed that his friends take him to the rear of the house, break up the roof, and let him down into the presence of Christ. The suggestion was acted upon; as the afflicted one lay at the feet of the mighty Healer, all that man could do for his restoration had been done. Jesus knew that the sufferer had been tortured with a sense of his sins, and that he must first find relief from this burden. With a look of tenderest compassion, the Saviour addressed him, not as a stranger, or even a friend, but as one who had even then been received into the family of God: "Son, be of good cheer; thy sins be forgiven thee."[133]

Many are suffering from maladies of the soul far more than from diseases of the body, and they will find no relief until they shall come to Christ, the wellspring of life. Complaints of weariness, loneliness, and dissatisfaction will then cease. Satisfying joys will give vigor to the mind and health and vital energy to the body.[134]

Today Christ is feeling the woes of every sufferer. . . . He knows how to speak the word, "Be whole," and bid the sufferer, "Go, and sin no more."[135]

A PRESCRIPTION FOR HEALING OF ALL ILLS

Come unto me, all ye that labour and are heavy laden, and I will give you rest.

God's healing power runs all through nature. If a tree is cut, if a human being is wounded or breaks a bone, nature begins at once to repair the injury. Even before the need exists, the healing agencies are in readiness; and as soon as a part is wounded, every energy is bent to the work of restoration. So it is in the spiritual realm. Before sin created the need, God had provided the remedy. Every soul that yields to temptation is wounded, bruised, by the adversary; but wherever there is sin, there is the Saviour.[136]

When the gospel is received in its purity and power, it is a cure for the maladies that originated in sin. The Sun of Righteousness arises, "with healing in His wings.". . .

The love which Christ diffuses through the whole being is vitalizing power. Every vital part—the brain, the heart, the nerves—it touches with healing. By it the highest energies of the being are roused to activity. It frees the soul from the guilt and sorrow, the anxiety and care, that crush the life forces. With it come serenity and composure. It implants in the soul joy that nothing earthly can destroy—joy in the Holy Spirit—health-giving, life-giving joy.

Our Saviour's words, "Come unto Me, . . . and I will give you rest," are a prescription for the healing of physical, mental, and spiritual ills. Though men have brought suffering upon themselves by their own wrongdoing He regards them with pity. In Him they may find help. He will do great things for those who trust in Him. . . .

If human beings would open the windows of the soul heavenward, in appreciation of the divine gifts, a flood of healing virtue would flow in.[137]

A HAPPY LIFE

REMEMBER YOUR CREATOR IN YOUR YOUTH

Remember now thy Creator in the days of thy youth, while the evil days come not, nor the years draw nigh, when thou shalt say, I have no pleasure in them.

I wish I could portray the beauty of the Christian life. Beginning in the morning of life, controlled by the laws of nature and of God, the Christian moves steadily onward and upward, daily drawing nearer his heavenly home, where await for him a crown of life, and a new name, "which no man knoweth saving him that receiveth it." Constantly he grows in happiness, in holiness, in usefulness. The progress of each year exceeds that of the past year.

God has given the youth a ladder to climb, a ladder that reaches from earth to heaven. Above this ladder is God, and on every round fall the bright beams of his glory. He is watching those who are climbing, ready, when the grasp relaxes and the steps falter, to send help. Yes, tell it in words full of cheer, that no one who perseveringly climbs the ladder will fail of gaining an entrance into the heavenly city.[1]

Angels of God, that ascend and descend the ladder that Jacob saw in vision, will help every soul who will to climb even to the highest heaven. They are guarding the people of God and watching how every step is taken. Those who climb the shining way will be rewarded; they will enter into the joy of their Lord.[2]

Early piety ensures to its possessor the full enjoyment of all that makes life happy. . . . Those who wait until the span of life is almost ended before they seek God, lose a life of pure, elevated happiness—happiness that never comes in pursuit of the pleasures that this life affords. Those who have been long acquainted with God, who from their youth have drawn their happiness from the pure fountain of heaven, are prepared to enter the family of God.[3]

CHRIST WITHIN THE SOURCE OF HAPPINESS

Glory ye in his holy name: let the heart of them rejoice that seek the Lord.

Multitudes . . . crave something which they do not have. They are spending their money for that which is not bread and their labor for that which satisfieth not. The hungering, thirsting soul will continue to hunger and thirst as long as it partakes of these unsatisfying pleasures. O that every such one would listen to the voice of Jesus, "If any man thirst, let him come unto Me, and drink." Those who drink of the living water will thirst no more. . . . Christ, the wellspring of life, is the fountain of peace and happiness. . . .

Let the youth magnify the name of the Lord for His great goodness, His loving mercy, His tender compassion. They can magnify His name by revealing His grace through a well-ordered life and a godly conversation. And as they do this the disposition is sweetened; irritability passes away.[4]

That heart is the happiest that has Christ as an abiding guest. That home is the most blessed where godliness is a controlling principle. . . . In the workshop where the peace and heavenly presence of Christ dwells, the workers will be the most trustworthy, the most faithful, and the most efficient. The fear and love of God are seen.[5]

In this world there is neither comfort nor happiness without Jesus. Let us acknowledge Him as our Friend and Saviour. . . . In Him are matchless charms. O may we all so live during this brief period of probationary time that we shall reign with Him throughout the ceaseless ages of eternity![6]

❧ ❧ ❧

If Christ abides in the heart by faith, . . . you will be happy, full of praise and joy.[7]

NO REAL JOY APART FROM CHRIST

Enter thou into the joy of thy lord.

The reason why some are restless is that they do not go to the only true source of happiness. They are ever trying to find *out* of Christ that enjoyment which is found alone *in* Him. In Him are no disappointed hopes. Oh, how is the precious privilege of prayer neglected! . . . Prayer is the strength of the Christian. When alone, he is not alone; he feels the presence of the One who said, "Lo, I am with you alway."

The young want just what they have not, namely, *religion.* Nothing can take the place of it.[8]

The Christian's hope is just what is needed. Religion will prove to the believer a comforter, a sure guide to the Fountain of true happiness.[9]

There is no true joy except Christ's joy. All the supposed happiness a man fancies he can gain without Christ will prove to be as ashes, a disappointment. Do not suppose for a moment that an irreligious man can be a happy man.[10]

No man can really enjoy life without religion. Love to God purifies and ennobles every taste and every desire, intensifies every affection, and brightens every worthy pleasure. It enables men to appreciate and enjoy all that is true, and good, and beautiful.[11]

You will ever find with the true Christian a marked cheerfulness, a holy, happy confidence in God, a submission to His providences, that is refreshing to the soul.[12]

Faith in God's love and overruling providence lightens the burdens of anxiety and care. It fills the heart with joy and contentment in the highest or the lowliest lot. Religion tends directly to promote health, to lengthen life, and to heighten our enjoyment of all its blessings. It opens to the soul a never-failing fountain of happiness.[13]

WISDOM AND UNDERSTANDING BRING HAPPINESS

Happy is the man that findeth wisdom, and the man that getteth understanding.

The ceremony of anointing David . . . was an intimation to the youth of the high destiny awaiting him. . . .

Notwithstanding the high position which he was to occupy, he quietly continued his employment, content to await the development of the Lord's plans in His own time and way. As humble and modest as before his anointing, the shepherd boy returned to the hills, and watched and guarded his flocks as tenderly as ever. But with new inspiration he composed his melodies and played upon his harp. Before him spread a landscape of rich and varied beauty. . . .

David, in the beauty and vigor of his young manhood, was preparing to take a high position with the noblest of the earth. His talents, as precious gifts from God, were employed to extol the glory of the divine Giver. His opportunities of contemplation and meditation served to enrich him with that wisdom and piety that made him beloved of God and angels. As he contemplated the perfections of his Creator, clearer conceptions of God opened before his soul. Obscure themes were illuminated, difficulties were made plain, perplexities were harmonized, and each ray of new light called forth fresh bursts of rapture and sweeter anthems of devotion, to the glory of God and the Redeemer. The love that moved him, the sorrows that beset him, the triumphs that attended him, were all themes for his active thought; and as he beheld the love of God in all the providences of his life, his heart throbbed with more fervent adoration and gratitude, his voice rang out in a richer melody, his harp was swept with more exultant joy; and the shepherd boy proceeded from strength to strength, from knowledge to knowledge; for the Spirit of the Lord was upon him.[14]

THE BIBLE SHOWS THE WAY TO TRUE HAPPINESS

I have rejoiced in the way of thy testimonies, as much as in all riches. . . . I will delight myself in thy statutes: I will not forget thy word.

The Bible presents to our view the unsearchable riches and immortal treasures of heaven. Man's strongest impulse urges him to seek his own happiness, and the Bible recognizes this desire and shows us that all heaven will unite with man in his efforts to gain true happiness. It reveals the condition upon which the peace of Christ is given to men. It describes a home of everlasting happiness and sunshine, where no tears nor want shall ever be known.[15]

That blessed book will teach you to be honest, temperate in all things, frugal, industrious, truthful, and upright. Its counsels heeded will make you a faithful companion of youth, giving you an influence that will ever lead upward, to purity of character; an influence that will lead away from sin, into paths of righteousness.

Will such a life be without enjoyment? Ah, no! It will be full of comfort, full of satisfaction, because you are bringing heaven into your life, peace into your soul, and leaving a testimony that "the law of the Lord is perfect, converting the soul.". . .

I would that all the young could understand how precious is the offering of a youthful heart to God. How lovingly the angels guard the steps of God-fearing, God-loving youth. Jesus knows them by name, and their example is helping other youth to do right. The youth who has hidden within the heart and mind a store of God's words of caution and encouragement, of His precious pearls of promise, from which he can draw at any time, will be a living channel of light. He has connection with the Source of all light. The Sun of Righteousness sends its light and healing beams into his soul, irradiating rays of light to all around him.[16]

THE HAPPIEST PEOPLE IN THE WORLD

Happy is that people, whose God is the Lord.

If you would find happiness and peace in all you do, you must do everything in reference to the glory of God. If you would have peace in your hearts, you must seek earnestly to imitate the life of Christ. Then there will be no need of affecting cheerfulness or of your seeking for pleasure in the indulgence of pride and the frivolities of the world. You will have a serenity and happiness in rightdoing that you can never realize in a course of wrong. Jesus took human nature, passing through infancy, childhood, and youth, that He might know how to sympathize with all and leave an example for all children and youth. He is acquainted with the temptations and weaknesses of children. He has, in His love, opened a fountain of pleasure and joy for the soul that trusts in Him. By seeking to honor Christ and to follow His example, children and youth can be truly happy. They may feel their accountability to labor with Jesus Christ in the great plan of saving souls. If youth will feel their responsibility before God, they will be elevated above everything that is mean, selfish, and impure. Life to such will be full of importance. They will realize that they have something great and glorious to live for. This will have an influence upon youth to make them earnest, cheerful, and strong under all the burdens, discouragements, and difficulties of life, as was their divine Pattern. . . . I entreat of you to ever cultivate thoughtful responsibility to God. The consciousness that you are doing those things which God can approve, will make you strong in His strength; and by copying the Pattern, you may, like Him, increase in wisdom and in favor with God and man.[17]

Those who in everything make God first and last and best are the happiest people in the world.[18]

161

OBEDIENCE

The Lord commanded us to do all these statutes, to fear the Lord our God, for our good always, that he might preserve us alive, as it is at this day. And it shall be our righteousness, if we observe to do all these commandments.

Happiness must be sought in the right way and from the right source. Some think they may surely find happiness in a course of indulgence in sinful pleasures or in deceptive worldly attractions. And some sacrifice physical and moral obligations, thinking to find happiness, and they lose both soul and body. Others will seek their happiness in the indulgence of an unnatural appetite, and consider the indulgence of taste more desirable than health and life. Many suffer themselves to be enchained by sensual passions, and will sacrifice physical strength, intellect, and moral powers to the gratification of lust. They will bring themselves to untimely graves, and in the judgment will be charged with self-murder.

Is this the happiness desirable which is to be found in the path of disobedience and transgression of physical and moral law? Christ's life points out the true source of happiness and how it is to be attained. . . . If they would be happy indeed, they should cheerfully seek to be found at the post of duty, doing the work which devolves upon them with fidelity, conforming their hearts and lives to the perfect pattern.[19]

Upon obedience depends life and happiness, health and joy, of men, women, and children. Obedience is for their well-being in this life and in the life to come.[20]

Where can we find a surer guide than the only true God? . . . Where is a safer path than that in which the Eternal leads the way? When we follow Him we are in no cheap, tangled bush path.[21]

The path of obedience to God is the path of virtue, of health, and happiness.[22]

DELIGHT TO DO GOD'S WILL

Where there is no vision the people perish: but he that keepeth the law, happy is he.

To those who love God it will be the highest delight to keep His commandments and to do those things that are pleasing in His sight. . . .

Says the psalmist, "The law of the Lord is perfect." How wonderful in its simplicity, its comprehensiveness and perfection, is the law of Jehovah! It is so brief that we can easily commit every precept to memory, and yet so far-reaching as to express the whole will of God and to take cognizance, not only of the outward actions, but of the thoughts and intents, the desires and emotions, of the heart. Human laws cannot do this. They can deal with the outward actions only. . . . The law of God takes note of the jealousy, envy, hatred, malignity, revenge, lust, and ambition that surge through the soul, but have not found expression in the outward action; . . . and these sinful emotions will be brought into account in the day when "God shall bring every work into judgment, with every secret thing, whether it be good, or whether it be evil.". . .

There is no mystery in the law of God. All can comprehend the great truths which it embodies. The feeblest intellect can grasp these rules. . . .

Obedience to the law is essential, not only to our salvation, but to our own happiness and the happiness of all with whom we are connected.[23]

Man's happiness must always be guarded by the law of God. . . . The law is the hedge which God has placed about His vineyard. By it those who obey are protected from evil.[24]

We owe to Him all that makes life desirable, and He asks of us the affections of the heart and the obedience of the life. His precepts, if obeyed, will bring happiness into the home life, happiness to every individual.[25]

૪ ૪ ૪

Rightdoing will bring peace and holy joy.[26]

WILLING AND OBEDIENT

If ye be willing and obedient, ye shall eat the good of the land.

In requiring obedience to the laws of His kingdom, God gives His people health and happiness, peace and joy.[27]

To the great principle of love and loyalty to God, the Father of all, the principle of filial love and obedience is closely related. Contempt for parental authority will soon lead to contempt for the authority of God.[28]

At a very early age children can comprehend what is plainly and simply told them, and by kind and judicious management can be taught to obey. . . . The mother should not allow her child to gain an advantage over her in a single instance. And in order to maintain this authority it is not necessary to resort to harsh measures; a firm, steady hand and a kindness which convinces the child of your love will accomplish the purpose.[29]

When children love and repose confidence in their mother, and have become obedient to her, they have been taught the first lessons in becoming Christians. They must be obedient to and love and trust Jesus as they are obedient to and love and trust their parents.[30]

Prompt and continual obedience to wise parental rule will promote the happiness of the children themselves as well as the honor of God and the good of society. Children should learn that in submission to the laws of the household is their perfect liberty. Christians will learn the same lesson—that in their obedience to God's law is their perfect freedom.[31]

❧ ❧ ❧

Children will be happier, far happier, under proper discipline than if left to do as their untrained impulses shall suggest.[32]

THE GOLDEN RULE

All things whatsoever ye would that men should do to you, do ye even so to them: for this is the law and the prophets.

The Saviour taught this principle [the golden rule] to make mankind happy, not unhappy; for in no other way can happiness come. God desires men and women to live the higher life. He gives them the boon of life, not to enable them merely to gain wealth, but to improve their higher powers by doing the work He has entrusted to mankind—the work of searching out and relieving the necessities of their fellow men. Man should not work for his own selfish interest, but for the interest of every one about him, blessing others by his influence and kindly deeds. This purpose of God is exemplified in Christ's life.[33]

Seize every opportunity to contribute to the happiness of those around you, sharing with them your affection. Words of kindness, looks of sympathy, expression of appreciation, would to many a struggling, lonely one be as a cup of cold water to a thirsty soul. A word of cheer, an act of kindness, would go far to lighten the burdens that are resting heavily upon weary shoulders. It is in unselfish ministry that true happiness is found. And every word and deed of such service is recorded in the books of heaven as done to Christ. . . . Live in the sunshine of Christ's love. Then your influence will bless the world.[34]

The spirit of unselfish labor for others gives depth, stability, and Christlike loveliness to the character and brings peace and happiness to its possessor.[35]

Every duty performed, every sacrifice made in the name of Jesus, brings an exceeding great reward. In the very act of duty, God speaks and gives His blessing.[36]

REJOICE AND DO GOOD

I know that there is no good . . . but for a man to rejoice, and to do good in his life.

The youth may think to find happiness by seeking their own pleasure, but true happiness will never be theirs while they pursue this course. The Saviour lived not to please Himself. We read of Him that He went about "doing good." He spent His life in loving service, comforting the sorrowing, ministering to the needy, lifting up the bowed down, He had no home in this world, only as the kindness of His friends provided one for Him as a wayfarer. Yet it was heaven to be in His presence. Day by day He met trials and temptations, yet He did not fail or become discouraged. . . . He was always patient and cheerful, and the afflicted hailed Him as a messenger of life and peace and health. . . .

What a wonderful example Christ has left for us in His lifework. Who of His children are living, as He did, for the glory of God? He is the Light of the world, and the one who works successfully for the Master must kindle his taper from that divine life.

To His disciples Christ said, "Ye are the salt of the earth: but if the salt have lost his savor, wherewith shall it be salted? it is thenceforth good for nothing, but to be cast out, and to be trodden under foot of men." How careful, then, we should be to follow the example of Christ. Unless we do this we are worthless—salt which has lost its savor.

Only by following Christ's example can we find true happiness. When He is accepted the heart is subdued and its purposes are changed.[37]

His service will place upon you no restriction that will not increase your happiness. In complying with His requirements, you will find a peace, contentment, and enjoyment that you can never have in the path of . . . sin.[38]

PATIENT CONTINUANCE IN WELL-DOING

Let us hear the conclusion of the whole matter: Fear God, and keep his commandments: for this is the whole duty of man.

He [Solomon] gives us the history of his search for happiness. He engaged in intellectual pursuits; he gratified his love for pleasure; he carried out his schemes of commercial enterprise. He was surrounded by the fascinating splendor of court life. . . .

Solomon sat upon a throne of ivory, the steps of which were of solid gold, flanked by six golden lions. His eyes rested upon highly cultivated and beautiful gardens just before him. These grounds were visions of loveliness, arranged to resemble, as far as possible, the Garden of Eden. Choice trees and shrubs and flowers of every variety had been brought from foreign lands to beautify them. Birds of every variety of brilliant plumage flitted from tree to tree, making the air vocal with sweet songs. Youthful attendants, gorgeously dressed and decorated, waited to obey his lightest wish. Scenes of revelry, music, sports, and games were arranged for his diversion at an extravagant expenditure of money.

But all this did not bring happiness to the king. . . . Dissipation had left its impress upon his once fair and intellectual face. He was sadly changed from the youthful Solomon. His brow was furrowed with care and unhappiness. . . . His lips were prepared to break forth into reproaches at the slightest deviation from his wishes.

His shattered nerves and wasted frame showed the result of violating Nature's laws. He confessed to a wasted life, an unsuccessful chase after happiness.[39]

The way to true happiness remains the same in all ages. Patient continuance in well-doing will lead to honor, happiness, and eternal life.[40]

BEING GOOD AND DOING GOOD

Trust in the Lord, and do good; so shalt thou dwell in the land, and verily thou shalt be fed.

Real happiness is found only in being good and doing good. The purest, highest enjoyment comes to those who faithfully fulfill their appointed duties. . . .

To all Christ has given the work of ministry. He is the King of glory, yet He declared, "The Son of man came not to be ministered unto, but to minister." He is the Majesty of heaven, yet He willingly consented to come to this earth to do the work laid upon Him by His Father. He has ennobled labor. That He might set us an example of industry, He worked with His hands at the carpenter's trade. From a very early age He acted His part in sustaining the family. He realized that He was a part of the family firm, and willingly bore His share of the burdens.

Children and youth should take pleasure in making lighter the cares of father and mother, showing an unselfish interest in the home. As they cheerfully lift the burdens that fall to their share, they are receiving a training which will fit them for positions of trust and usefulness. Each year they are to make steady advancement, gradually but surely laying aside the inexperience of boyhood and girlhood for the experience of manhood and womanhood. In the faithful performance of the simple duties of the home, boys and girls lay the foundation for mental, moral, and spiritual excellence.[41]

Riches and idleness are thought by some to be blessings indeed; but those who are always busy, and who cheerfully go about their daily tasks, are the most happy and enjoy the best health. The healthful weariness which results from well-regulated labor secures to them the benefits of refreshing sleep. The sentence that man must toil for his daily bread, and the promise of future happiness and glory, both came from the same throne, and both are blessings.[42]

CONTENTMENT

Godliness with contentment is great gain.

Too many cares and burdens are brought into our families, and too little of natural simplicity and peace and happiness is cherished. There should be less care for what the outside world will say and more thoughtful attention to the members of the family circle. There should be less display and affectation of worldly politeness, and much more tenderness and love, cheerfulness and Christian courtesy, among the members of the household. Many need to learn how to make home attractive, a place of enjoyment. Thankful hearts and kind looks are more valuable than wealth and luxury, and contentment with simple things will make home happy if love be there.

Jesus, our Redeemer, walked the earth with the dignity of a king; yet He was meek and lowly of heart. He was a light and blessing in every home because He carried cheerfulness, hope, and courage with Him. Oh, that we could be satisfied with less heart longings, less striving for things difficult to obtain wherewith to beautify our homes, while that which God values above jewels, the meek and quiet spirit, is not cherished. The grace of simplicity, meekness, and true affection would make a paradise of the humblest home. It is better to endure cheerfully every inconvenience than to part with peace and contentment.[43]

Here is the secret of content and peace and happiness. . . . The true Christian . . . seeks to live a life of usefulness and conform his habits to the example of Jesus. Such a one will find the truest happiness, the reward of well-doing. Such a one will be lifted above the slavery of an artificial life into the freedom and grace of Christlike simplicity.[44]

GRATITUDE

I will sing unto the Lord, because he hath dealt bountifully with me.

Every earthly wish may be gratified, and yet men pass on as did the ungrateful lepers who had been cleansed and healed of their obnoxious disease. These lepers had been restored to health by Christ, and the parts that had been destroyed by the disease were re-created; but only one, on finding himself made whole, returned to give God glory. . . .

The lesson which is recorded concerning the ten lepers should awaken in every heart a most earnest desire to change the existing order of ingratitude into one of praise and thanksgiving. Let the professed people of God stop murmuring and complaining. Let us remember who is the first great Giver of all our blessings. We are fed and clothed and sustained in life, and should we not educate ourselves and our children to respond with gratitude to our heavenly Father?[45]

Have we not reason to talk of God's goodness and to tell of His power? When friends are kind to us we esteem it a privilege to thank them for their kindness. How much more should we count it a joy to return thanks to the Friend who has given us every good and perfect gift. Then let us, in every church, cultivate thanksgiving to God. Let us educate our lips to praise God in the family circle. . . . Let our gifts and offerings declare our gratitude for the favors we daily receive. In everything we should show forth the joy of the Lord and make known the message of God's saving grace.[46]

The hearts of those who reveal the attributes of Christ glow with divine love. They are imbued with the spirit of gratitude. . . . Lift up Jesus. Lift Him up, the man of Calvary, with the voice of song and prayer. Seek earnestly to spread the gospel. Tell the precious story of God's love for man. In this work you will find a satisfaction that will last through the eternal ages.[47]

THANKSGIVING AND PRAISE

Enter into his gates with thanksgiving, and into his courts with praise: be thankful unto him, and bless his name.

If we will consecrate heart and mind to the service of God, doing the work He has for us to do and walking in the footsteps of Jesus, our hearts will become sacred harps, every chord of which will send forth praise and thanksgiving to the Lamb sent by God to take away the sins of the world. . . .

Christ would have our thoughts center upon Him. . . . Look away from self to Jesus Christ, the life of every blessing, every grace, the life of all that is precious and valuable to the children of God. . . .

The Lord Jesus is our strength and happiness, the great storehouse from which, on every occasion, men may draw strength. As we study Him, talk of Him, become more and more able to behold Him—as we avail ourselves of His grace and receive the blessings He proffers us, we have something with which to help others. Filled with gratitude, we communicate to others the blessings that have been freely given us. Thus receiving and imparting, we grow in grace; and a rich current of praise and gratitude constantly flows from our lips; the sweet spirit of Jesus kindles thanksgiving in our hearts, and our souls are uplifted with a sense of security. The unfailing, inexhaustible righteousness of Christ becomes our righteousness by faith.[48]

Let the fresh blessings of each new day awaken praise in our hearts for these tokens of His loving care.

When you open your eyes in the morning, thank God that He has kept you through the night. Thank Him for His peace in your heart. Morning, noon, and night let gratitude as a sweet perfume ascend to heaven. . . .

The angels of God, thousands upon thousands, . . . guard us against evil and press back the powers of darkness that are seeking our destruction. Have we not reason to be thankful every moment, thankful even when there are apparent difficulties in our pathway?[49]

171

FAITHFUL IN THE LITTLE THINGS OF LIFE

Take us the foxes, the little foxes, that spoil the vines.

In many ways life's happiness is bound up with the faithfulness of common duties.[50]

It is the neglect of the littles, the trifles, that poisons life's happiness. A faithful performance of the littles composes the sum of happiness to be realized in this life. He that is faithful in little is faithful also in much. He that is unfaithful or unjust in small matters will be in greater matters.[51]

Until you can cheerfully and happily take up these duties you are not fitted for greater and higher duties. The humble tasks before us are to be taken up by someone; and those who do them should feel that they are doing a necessary and honorable work, and that in their mission, humble though it may be, they are doing the work of God just as surely as was Gabriel when sent to the prophets.[52]

It is the little things of life that develop the spirit in men and women and determine the character. . . . In words, in tones, in gestures, in looks, you can represent the spirit of Jesus. He who neglects these little things, and yet flatters himself that he is ready to do wonderful things for the Master, will be in danger of failing altogether. Life is not made up of great sacrifices and wonderful achievements, but of little things.[53]

Examine under the microscope the smallest and commonest of wayside blossoms, and note in all its parts the exquisite beauty and completeness. So in the humblest lot true excellence may be found; the commonest tasks, wrought with loving faithfulness, are beautiful in God's sight.[54]

The little attentions, the small acts of love and self-sacrifice, that flow out from the life as quietly as the fragrance from a flower—these constitute no small share of the blessings and happiness of life.[55]

LOVING THOUGHTFULNESS IN THE HOME

If we love one another, God dwelleth in us, and his love is perfected in us.

Make your home atmosphere fragrant with tender thoughtfulness.[56]

Home is to be the center of the purest and most elevated affection. Peace, harmony, affection, and happiness should be perseveringly cherished every day, until these precious things abide in the hearts of those who compose the family.[57]

The reason there are so many hardhearted men and women in our world is that true affection has been regarded as weakness and has been discouraged and repressed. The better part of the nature of persons of this class was perverted and dwarfed in childhood, and unless rays of divine light can melt away their coldness and hardhearted selfishness, the happiness of such is buried forever. If we would have tender hearts, such as Jesus had when He was upon the earth, and sanctified sympathy, such as the angels have for sinful mortals, we must cultivate the sympathies of childhood, which are simplicity itself.[58]

Commend your children whenever you can. Make their lives as happy as possible. . . . Keep the soil of the heart mellow by the manifestation of love and affection, thus preparing it for the seed of truth. . . . The Lord gives the earth not only clouds and rain but the beautiful, smiling sunshine, causing the seed to germinate and the blossoms to appear.[59]

An approving glance, a word of encouragement or commendation, will be like sunshine in their hearts, often making the whole day happy.[60]

The happiness of husband and children should be more sacred to every wife and mother than that of all others.[61]

SING AND THE WORLD SINGS WITH YOU

He hath put a new song in my mouth, even praise unto our God: many shall see it, and fear, and shall trust in the Lord.

God wants us to be happy. He desires to put a new song on our lips, even praise to our God. He wants us to believe that He forgives our sins and takes away our unrighteousness. He wants us to make melody in our hearts to Him. . . .

Let every word we utter, every line we write, be fraught with encouragement and unwavering faith. . . . Think not that Jesus is the Saviour of your brother only. He is your personal Saviour. If you entertain this precious thought, you will . . . make melody to God in your soul. It is our privilege to triumph in God. It is our privilege to lead others to see that their only hope is in God, and to flee to Him for refuge.

Every act of consecration to God brings joy; for as we appreciate the light He has given us, more and greater light will come. We must . . . open the heart to the bright beams of the Sun of Righteousness. There is peace in perfect submission. . . .

Let the peace of God reign in your soul. Then you will have strength to bear all suffering, and you will rejoice that you have grace to endure. Praise the Lord; talk of His goodness; tell of His power. Sweeten the atmosphere that surrounds your soul. . . . Praise, with heart and soul and voice, Him who is the health of your countenance, your Saviour, and your God.[62]

Let praise and thanksgiving be expressed in song. When tempted, instead of giving utterance to our feelings, let us by faith lift up a song of thanksgiving to God. Song is a weapon that we can always use against discouragement. As we thus open the heart to the sunlight of the Saviour's presence, we shall have . . . His blessing.[63]

THE BEAUTIES OF NATURE

The works of the Lord are great, sought out of all them that have pleasure therein. . . . He hath made his wonderful works to be remembered.

God, who made the Eden home of our first parents so surpassingly lovely, has also given the noble trees, the beautiful flowers, and everything lovely in nature for our happiness.[64]

Wherever we turn are traces of primal loveliness. Wherever we may turn we hear the voice of God and behold His handiwork. . . .

Nature's ten thousand voices speak His praise. In earth, and air, and sky, with their marvelous tint and color, varying in gorgeous contrast or softly blended in harmony, we behold His glory. The everlasting hills tell us of His power. The trees wave their green banners in the sunlight, and point us upward to their Creator. The flowers that gem the earth with their beauty whisper to us of Eden and fill us with longings for its unfading loveliness. The living green that carpets the brown earth tells us of God's care for the humblest of His creatures. The caves of the sea and the depths of the earth reveal His treasures. He who placed the pearls in the ocean and the amethyst and the chrysolite among the rocks is a lover of the beautiful. The sun rising in the heavens is the representative of Him who is the light and life of all that He has made. All the brightness and beauty that adorn the earth and light up the heavens speak of God.

Shall we, in the enjoyment of the gifts, forget the Giver? Let them rather lead us to contemplate His goodness and His love. Let all that is beautiful in our earthly home remind us of the crystal river and green fields, the waving trees and the living fountains, the shining city and the white-robed singers, of our heavenly home—that world of beauty that no artist can picture and no mortal tongue describe.[65]

PEACE AND ASSURANCE

And the work of righteousness shall be peace; and the effect of righteousness quietness and assurance for ever.

The true principles of psychology are found in the Holy Scriptures. Man knows not his own value. He acts according to his unconverted temperament of character, because he does not look unto Jesus, the Author and Finisher of his faith. He who comes to Jesus, he who believes on Him and makes Him his Example, realizes the meaning of the words, "To them gave He power to become the sons of God.". . .

Those who pass through the experience of true conversion will realize, with keenness of perception, their responsibility to God to work out their own salvation with fear and trembling, their responsibility to make complete their recovery from the leprosy of sin. Such an experience will lead them humbly and trustfully to place their dependence upon God.[66]

To have a consciousness that the eyes of the Lord are upon us and His ears open to hear our prayers is a satisfaction indeed. To know that we have a never-failing Friend in whom we can confide all the secrets of the soul is a privilege which words can never express.[67]

Men and women enjoying the religion of Jesus Christ will not be uneasy, restless, discontented, changeable; the peace of Christ in the heart will give solidity to character.[68]

You must not let anything rob your soul of peace, of restfulness, of the assurance that you are accepted just now. Appropriate every promise; all are yours on condition of your complying with the Lord's prescribed terms. Entire surrender of your ways, which seem so very wise, and taking Christ's ways, is the secret of perfect rest in His love.[69]

The soul consecrated to the service of Christ has a peace that the world cannot give or take away.[70]

A MERRY HEART MAKES A CHEERFUL COUNTENANCE

A merry heart maketh a cheerful countenance: but by sorrow of the heart the spirit is broken.

If you are burdened and weary, you need not curl up like leaves upon a withered branch. Cheerfulness and a clear conscience are better than drugs, and will be an effective agent in your restoration to health. . . .

You will be benefited with the effort you make to be cheerful. . . . Get out of doors as much as possible, and be benefited with the breezes and the blessed sunshine. Let the songs of the birds and the beauties of nature awaken holy and grateful feelings in your hearts and lead you to adore your Creator who has anticipated your wants and surrounded you with unnumbered tokens of His love and constant care. . . .

Have an aim in life while you do live. Gather sunshine about you instead of clouds. Seek to be a fresh, beautiful flower in God's garden, imparting fragrance to all around you. Do this, and you will not die a whit sooner; but you will surely shorten your days by unhappy complainings. . . .

Prune off every decaying leaf and withered branch from your life and manifest only freshness and vigor.[71]

The cheerfulness of the Christian is created by the consideration of the great blessings we enjoy because we are the children of God. "Therefore, my brethren dearly beloved," he says, "and longed for, my joy and crown, so stand fast in the Lord, my dearly beloved." The cheerful enlightenment of the mind and the soul temple by the assurance that we have reconciliation with God, the hope we have of everlasting life through Christ, and the pleasure of blessing others, are joys which bring no sorrow with them.[72]

ଽ ଽ ଽ

Christians should be the most cheerful and happy people that live.[73]

177

KINDNESS THE MARK OF A CHRISTIAN

She openeth her mouth with wisdom; and in her tongue is the law of kindness.

Your influence reaches the soul; you touch not a wire but that vibrates back to God. . . . It is your duty to be Christians in the highest sense of the word—"Christlike." It is through the unseen lines that attract you to other minds with which you are brought in contact that may, if you are in constant connection with God, leave impressions that will make you a savor of life unto life. Otherwise, if you are selfish, if you are self-exalted, if you are worldly-minded, no matter what your position, no matter what your experience has been, or how much you know, if you are not having the law of kindness on your lips, sweet fragrance of love springing from your heart, you can do nothing as it ought to be done.[74]

Kindness and love and courtesy are the marks of the Christian. . . . In our association with each other let it be ever remembered that there are chapters in the experience of others that are sealed from mortal eyes; there are sad histories that are written in the books of heaven but are sacredly guarded from prying eyes. There stand registered long, hard battles with trying circumstances, arising in the very homes, that day by day sap the courage, the faith, the confidence, until the very manhood seems to fall to ruins. But Jesus knows it all, and He never forgets. To such, words of kindness and of affection are welcome as the smile of angels; a strong, helpful grasp of the hand of a true friend is worth more than gold and silver.[75]

The true, honest expression of a sister, or brother, or friend, given in genuine simplicity, has power to open the door of hearts which need the fragrance of Christlike words and the simple, delicate touch of the spirit of Christ's love.[76]

LOVE HEALS MANY WOUNDS

Beloved, let us love one another: for love is of God; and every one that loveth is born of God, and knoweth God.

From the Christian standpoint, love is power. Intellectual and spiritual strength are involved in this principle. Pure love has special efficacy to do good, and can do nothing but good. It prevents discord and misery and brings the truest happiness. Wealth is often an influence to corrupt and destroy; force is strong to do hurt; but truth and goodness are the properties of pure love.[77]

A man at peace with God and his fellow men cannot be made miserable. Envy will not be in his heart; evil surmising will find no room there; hatred cannot exist. The heart in harmony with God is lifted above the annoyances and trials of this life.[78]

That which Satan plants in the heart—envy, jealousy, evil surmising, evil speaking, impatience, prejudice, selfishness, covetousness, and vanity—must be uprooted. If these evil things are allowed to remain in the soul, they will bear fruit by which many shall be defiled. Oh, how many cultivate the poisonous plants, that kill out the precious fruits of love and defile the soul![79]

Only the love that flows from the heart of Christ can heal. Only He in whom that love flows, even as the sap in the tree or the blood in the body, can restore the wounded soul.

Love's agencies have wonderful power, for they are divine. The soft answer that "turneth away wrath," the love that "suffereth long, and is kind," the charity that "covereth a multitude of sins"—would we learn the lesson, with what power for healing would our lives be gifted! How life would be transformed, and the earth become a very likeness and foretaste of heaven![80]

SAY NOTHING THAT WILL WOUND OR GRIEVE

For he that will love life, and see good days, let him refrain his tongue from evil, and his lips that they speak no guile: let him eschew evil, and do good; let him seek peace, and ensue it.

If the lips were constantly guarded so that no guile could corrupt them, what an amount of suffering, degradation, and misery might be prevented. If we would say nothing to wound or grieve, except in necessary reproof of sin, that God might not be dishonored, how much misunderstanding, bitterness, and anguish would be prevented. If we would speak words of good cheer, words of hope and faith in God, how much light we might shed upon the pathway of others, to be reflected in still brighter beams upon our own souls. . . . The plan of salvation, as revealed in the Holy Scriptures, opens up a way whereby man may secure happiness and prolong his days upon the earth, as well as enjoy the favor of Heaven and secure that future life which measures with the life of God.[81]

Many persons complain of Providence because of the discomfort and inconvenience which they suffer, when this is the sure result of their own course. They seem to feel that they are ill-treated of God, when they themselves are alone responsible for the ills which they endure. Our kind and merciful heavenly Father has established laws, which, obeyed, would promote physical, mental, and moral health. . . .

God requires us to yield our own will to His; but He does not ask us to give up anything that it would be for our good to retain. No one can be happy while he devotes his live to selfish gratification. A course of obedience to God is the wisest course for us to pursue; for it brings peace, content, and happiness as a sure result. . . .

If men would place themselves in right relation to God by heeding the counsel of His Word, they would escape innumerable dangers and experience a peace and content that would render life a joy rather than a burden.[82]

PERFECT PEACE

Thou will keep him in perfect peace, whose mind is stayed on thee: because he trusteth in thee.

There are many whose hearts are aching under a load of care because they seek to reach the world's standard. They have chosen its service, accepted its perplexities, adopted its customs. Thus their character is marred and their life made a weariness. In order to gratify ambition and worldly desires, they wound the conscience and bring upon themselves an additional burden of remorse. The continual worry is wearing out the life forces. Our Lord desires them to lay aside this yoke of bondage. He invites them to accept His yoke; He says, "My yoke is easy, and My burden is light." He bids them seek first the kingdom of God and His righteousness, and His promise is that all things needful to them for this life shall be added. Worry is blind, and cannot discern the future; but Jesus sees the end from the beginning. In every difficulty He has His way prepared to bring relief. Our heavenly Father has a thousand ways to provide for us, of which we know nothing. Those who accept the one principle of making the service and honor of God supreme will find perplexities vanish, and a plain path before their feet. . . .

In the heart of Christ, where reigned perfect harmony with God, there was perfect peace. He was never elated by applause or dejected by censure or disappointment. Amid the greatest opposition and the most cruel treatment He was still of good courage.[83]

True happiness is found . . . in learning of Christ. . . . Those who take Christ at His Word and surrender the soul to His keeping, their lives to His ordering, will find peace and quietude. Nothing of the world can make them sad when Jesus makes them glad by His presence.[84]

ຂ⍛ ຂ⍛ ຂ⍛

It is the love of self that brings unrest.[85]

181

TRUST MEANS SECURITY

Surely he shall not be moved for ever: the righteous shall be in everlasting remembrance. He shall not be afraid of evil tidings: his heart is fixed, trusting in the Lord.

God has given in His Word sufficient evidence of its divine character. The great truths which concern our redemption are clearly presented. By the aid of the Holy Spirit, which is promised to all who seek it in sincerity, every man may understand these truths for himself. God has granted to men a strong foundation upon which to rest their faith.

Yet the finite minds of men are inadequate fully to comprehend the plans and purposes of the Infinite One. We can never by searching find out God. We must not attempt to lift with presumptuous hand the curtain behind which He veils His majesty. The apostle exclaims, "How unsearchable are His judgments, and His ways past finding out!" We can so far comprehend His dealings with us and the motives by which He is actuated that we may discern boundless love and mercy united to infinite power. Our Father in heaven orders everything in wisdom and righteousness, and we are not to be dissatisfied and distrustful, but to bow in reverent submission. He will reveal to us as much of His purposes as it is for our good to know, and beyond that we must trust the Hand that is omnipotent, the Heart that is full of love.

While God has given ample evidence for faith, He will never remove all excuse for unbelief. All who look for hooks to hang their doubts upon will find them. . . .

Distrust of God is the natural outgrowth of the unrenewed heart, which is at enmity with Him. But faith is inspired by the Holy Spirit, and it will flourish only as it is cherished. No man can become strong in faith without a determined effort. . . . Only in humble reliance upon God and obedience to all His commandments can we be secure.[86]

WEEP NOT

Why weepest thou?

Often they [the disciples] repeated the words, "We trusted that it had been He which should have redeemed Israel." Lonely and sick at heart they remembered His words, "If they do these things in a green tree, what shall be done in the dry?" They met together in the upper chamber, and closed and fastened the doors, knowing that the fate of their beloved Teacher might at any time be theirs.

And all the time they might have been rejoicing in the knowledge of a risen Saviour. In the garden Mary had stood weeping, when Jesus was close beside her. Her eyes were so blinded by tears that she did not discern Him. And the hearts of the disciples were so full of grief that they did not believe the angels' message or the words of Christ Himself.

How many are still doing what these disciples did. How many echo Mary's despairing cry, "They have taken away the Lord, . . . and we know not where they have laid Him." To how many might the Saviour's words be spoken, "Why weepest thou? whom seekest thou?" He is close beside them, but their tear-blinded eyes do not discern Him. He speaks to them, but they do not understand.

O that the bowed head might be lifted, that the eyes might be opened to behold Him, that the ears might listen to His voice! "Go quickly, and tell His disciples that He is risen." . . . Mourn not as those who are hopeless and helpless. Jesus lives, and because He lives we shall live also. From grateful hearts, from lips touched with holy fire, let the glad song ring out, Christ is risen! He lives to make intercession for us. Grasp this hope, and it will hold the soul like a sure, tried anchor. Believe, and thou shalt see the glory of God.[87]

FEAR NOT

Fear not: for I have redeemed thee, I have called thee by thy name; thou art mine.

Often our trials are such that they seem almost unbearable, and without help from God they are indeed unbearable. Unless we rely upon Him we shall sink under the burden of responsibilities that bring only sadness and grief. But if we make Christ our dependence, we shall not sink under trial. When all seems dark and unexplainable we are to trust in His love; we must repeat the words that Christ has spoken to our souls, "What I do thou knowest not now; but thou shalt know hereafter." . . .

Do not go about as if Jesus were in Joseph's tomb, and a great stone were rolled before the door. . . . In the trial of your faith show that you know you have a risen Saviour, One who is making intercession for you and your loved ones. . . .

The Bible places the responsibility of our happiness upon ourselves. We are to look to the light of life. Our usefulness depends on our own course of action.[88]

We are so anxious, all of us, for happiness, but many rarely find it because of their faulty methods of seeking, in the place of striving. We must strive most earnestly and mingle all our desires with faith. Then happiness steals in upon us almost unsought. . . . When we can, notwithstanding disagreeable circumstances, rest confidingly in His love and shut ourselves in with Him, resting peacefully in His love, the sense of His presence will inspire a deep, tranquil joy. This experience gains for us a faith that enables us not to fret, not to worry, but to depend upon a power that is infinite.[89]

We shall have the power of the Highest with us. . . . Jesus stands by our side. . . . As the trials come, the power of God will come with them.[90]

DOUBT NOT

And we know that all things work together for good to them that love God, to them who are the called according to his purpose.

When trials come, remember that they are sent for your good. . . . When trials and tribulations come to you know that they are sent in order that you may receive from the Lord of glory renewed strength and increased humility, so that He may safely bless and support and uphold you. In faith and with the hope that "maketh not ashamed," lay hold of the promises of God.

O how good the Lord is to us all, and how safely we may trust Him! He calls us His little children. Then let us come to Him as to a loving Father. It is His desire that the bright beams of His righteousness shall shine forth from our faces and in our words and deeds. If we will love one another as Christ has loved us, the barriers that separate us from God and from one another will be broken down, and many obstacles that hinder the Holy Spirit's flowing from heart to heart will be removed. . . . Trust Him with all your heart. He will carry you and your burdens.[91]

The Lord designs that His people shall be happy, and He opens before us one source of consolation after another, that we may be filled with joy and peace in the midst of our present experience. We are not to wait until we shall get into heaven for brightness and comfort and joy. We are to have them right here in this life. . . . We miss very much because we do not grasp the blessings that may be ours in our afflictions. All our sufferings and sorrows, all our temptations and trials, all our sadness and griefs, all our persecutions and privations, and in short all things, work together for our good. . . . All experiences and circumstances are God's workmen whereby good is brought to us. Let us look at the light behind the cloud.[92]

Our happiness comes not from what is around us, but from what is within us; not from what we have, but from what we are.[93]

A SOCIAL LIFE

JESUS AN EXAMPLE IN SOCIAL RELATIONSHIPS

And the third day there was a marriage in Cana of Galilee; and the mother of Jesus was there: and both Jesus was called, and his disciples, to the marriage.

There was to be a marriage in Cana of Galilee. The parties were relatives of Joseph and Mary. Christ knew of this family gathering, and that many influential persons would be brought together there, so, in company with His newly made disciples, He made His way to Cana. As soon as it was known that Jesus had come to the place, a special invitation was sent to Him and His friends. . . .

He had joined the mixed assembly of a festal gathering, and, while no shadow of worldly levity marred His conduct, He had sanctioned the social gathering with His presence.

Here is a lesson for the disciples of Christ through all time, not to exclude themselves from society, renouncing all social communion and seeking a strict seclusion from their fellow beings. In order to reach all classes, we must meet them where they are; for they will seldom seek us of their own accord. Not alone from the pulpit are the hearts of men and women touched by divine truth. Christ awakened their interest by going among them as one who desired their good. He sought them at their daily avocations and manifested an unfeigned interest in their temporal affairs. He carried His instructions into the household of the people, bringing whole families in their own homes under the influence of His divine presence. . . .

Jesus rebuked intemperance, self-indulgence, and folly; yet He was social in His nature. He accepted invitations to dine with the learned and noble, as well as the poor and afflicted. . . . He gave no license to scenes of dissipation and revelry, yet innocent happiness was pleasing to Him. A Jewish marriage was a solemn and impressive occasion, the pleasure and joy of which were not displeasing to the Son of man.[1]

LOVE PEOPLE AS CHRIST LOVED THEM

This is my commandment, That ye love one another, as I have loved you.

Christ carried out in His life His own divine teachings. His zeal never led Him to become passionate. He manifested consistency without obstinacy, benevolence without weakness, tenderness and sympathy without sentimentalism. He was highly social, yet He possessed a reserved dignity that did not encourage undue familiarity. His temperance never led to bigotry or austerity. He was not conformed to this world, yet He was not indifferent to the wants of the least among men. He was awake to the needs of all.[2]

From earliest years to manhood Christ lived a life that was a perfect pattern of humility and industry and obedience. He was always thoughtful and considerate of others, always self-denying. He came bearing the signature of heaven, not to be ministered unto, but to minister. . . .

The unselfish life of Christ is an example to all. His character is a pattern of the characters we may form if we follow on in His footsteps.[3]

Tact and good judgment increase the usefulness of the laborer a hundredfold. If he will speak the right words at the right time and show the right spirit, this will exert a melting power on the heart of the one he is trying to help.[4]

Those who differ with us in faith and doctrine should be treated kindly. They are the property of Christ, and we must meet them in the great day of final account. We shall have to face one another in the judgment, and behold the record of our thoughts, words, and deeds, not as we have viewed them, but as they were in truth. God has enjoined upon us the duty of loving one another as Christ has loved us.[5]

LOVE FRIEND AND FOE ALIKE

Which now of these three, thinkest thou, was neighbour unto him that fell among thieves? And he said, He that shewed mercy on him. Then said Jesus unto him, Go, and do thou likewise.

Christ came to break down every wall of partition. He came to show that His gift of mercy and love is as unconfined as the air, the light, or the showers of rain that refresh the earth. . . . He made no difference between neighbors and strangers, friends and enemies. . . .

He passed by no human being as worthless. . . . In whatever company He found Himself, He presented a lesson appropriate to the time and the circumstances. Every neglect or insult shown by men to their fellow men only made Him more conscious of their need of His divine-human sympathy. He sought to inspire with hope the roughest and most unpromising, setting before them the assurance that they might become blameless and harmless, attaining such a character as would make them manifest as the children of God.

Often He met those who had drifted under Satan's control and who had no power to break from his snare. To such a one, discouraged, sick, tempted, fallen, Jesus would speak words of tenderest pity, words that were needed and could be understood. Others He met who were fighting a hand-to-hand battle with the adversary of souls. These He encouraged to persevere, assuring them that they would win. . . .

At the table of the publicans He sat as an honored guest, by His sympathy and social kindliness showing that He recognized the dignity of humanity; and men longed to become worthy of His confidence. . . .

Though He was a Jew, Jesus mingled freely with the Samaritans. . . . He slept with them under their roofs, ate with them at their tables—partaking of the food prepared and served by their hands—taught in their streets and treated them with the utmost kindness and courtesy. And while He drew their hearts to Him by the tie of human sympathy, His divine grace brought to them the salvation which the Jews rejected.[6]

BE SYMPATHETIC TO ALL MEN

To the weak became I as weak, that I might gain the weak: I am made all things to all men, that I might by all means save some.

All should study carefully how they can themselves become most useful and how they can themselves be a blessing to those with whom they associate.

All who profess to be children of God should unceasingly bear in mind that they are missionaries, in their labors brought in connection with all classes of minds. There will be men who are untrue in their dealing with their fellow men; there will be the aristocrat, the vain, the proud, the frivolous, the independent, the complaining, the desponding, the discouraged, the fanatical, the egotistical, the timid, and the sensitive ones, the elevated in mind, and the courteous in manner, the dissipated, the uncourteous, and the superficial. . . . These varied minds cannot be treated alike; yet all whether they be rich or poor, high or low, dependent or independent, need kindness, sympathy, truth, and love. By mutual contact our minds should receive polish and refinement. We are dependent upon one another, closely bound together by the ties of human brotherhood.

It is through the social relations that Christianity comes in contact with the world. Every man and woman who has tasted of the love of Christ and has received into the heart the divine illumination is required of God to shed light on the pathway of those who are unacquainted with the better way. . . .

We must confess Christ openly and bravely, exhibiting in our characters His meekness, humility, and love, till men shall be charmed with the beauty of holiness.[7]

Social power, sanctified by the Spirit of Christ, must be improved in bringing souls to the Saviour. . . . We are to have Christ in us as a wellspring of water, springing up into everlasting life, refreshing all who come in contact with us.[8]

HOW PLEASANT ARE WORDS FITLY SPOKEN

A word fitly spoken is like apples of gold in pictures of silver.

When at a feast, Christ controlled the conversation, and gave many precious lessons. Those present listened to Him; for had He not healed their sick, comforted their sorrowing, and taken their children in His arms? Publicans and sinners were drawn to Him; and when He spoke, their attention was riveted on Him.

Christ taught His disciples how to conduct themselves when in the company of others. He instructed them in regard to the duties and regulations of true social life, which are the same as the laws of the kingdom of God. He taught the disciples, by example, that when attending any public gathering, they need not want for something to say. His conversation when at a feast differed most decidedly from that which had been listened to at feasts in the past. Every word He uttered was a savor of life unto life. He spoke with clearness and simplicity. His words were as apples of gold in pictures of silver.[9]

Communion with Christ—how unspeakably precious! Such communion it is our privilege to enjoy. . . . When the early disciples heard the words of Christ, they felt their need of Him. They sought, they found, they followed Him. They were with Him in the house, at the table, in the closet, in the field. They were with Him as pupils with a teacher, daily receiving from His lips lessons of holy truth. They looked to Him as servants to their master. . . . They served Him cheerfully, gladly.[10]

Great importance is attached to our associations. We may form many that are pleasant and helpful, but none are so precious as that by which finite man is brought into connection with the infinite God. When thus united, the words of Christ abide in us. . . . The result will be a purified heart, a circumspect life, and a faultless character. But it is only by acquaintance and association with Christ that we can become like Him, the one faultless example.[11]

TRUE REFINEMENT

To speak evil of no man, to be no brawlers, but gentle, shewing all meekness unto all men.

The essence of true politeness is consideration for others. The essential, enduring education is that which broadens the sympathies and encourages universal kindliness. That so-called culture which does not make a youth deferential toward his parents, appreciative of their excellences, forbearing toward their defects, and helpful to their necessities; which does not make him considerate and tender, generous and helpful toward the young, the old, and the unfortunate, and courteous toward all, is a failure.

Real refinement of thought and manner is better learned in the school of the divine Teacher than by any observance of set rules. His love pervading the heart gives to the character those refining touches that fashion it in the semblance of His own. This education imparts a heaven-born dignity and sense of propriety. It gives a sweetness of disposition and a gentleness of manner that can never be equaled by the superficial polish of fashionable society.

The Bible enjoins courtesy, and it presents many illustrations of the unselfish spirit, the gentle grace, the winsome temper, that characterize true politeness. These are but reflections of the character of Christ. All the real tenderness and courtesy in the world, even among those who do not acknowledge His name, is from Him. And He desires these characteristics to be perfectly reflected in His children. It is His purpose that in us men shall behold His beauty.[12]

What rays of softness and beauty shone forth in the daily life of our Saviour! What sweetness flowed from His very presence! . . . Those with whom Christ dwells will be surrounded with a divine atmosphere. Their white robes of purity will be fragrant with perfume from the garden of the Lord.[13]

CHRISTIAN COURTESY

As I have loved you, that ye also love one another.

The value of courtesy is too little appreciated. Many who are kind at heart lack kindliness of manner. Many who command respect by their sincerity and uprightness are sadly deficient in geniality. This lack mars their own happiness and detracts from their service to others. Many of life's sweetest and most helpful experiences are, often for mere want of thought, sacrificed by the uncourteous.[14]

The Holy Scriptures give us marked examples of the exercise of true courtesy. Abraham was a man of God. When he pitched his tent he at once erected his altar for sacrifice and invited God to abide with him. Abraham was a courteous man. His life is not marred with selfishness, so hateful in any character and so offensive in the sight of God. Witness his conduct when about to separate from Lot. Though Lot was his nephew, and much younger than himself, and the first choice of the land belonged to Abraham, courtesy led him to forgo his right, and permit Lot to select for himself that part of the country which seemed to him most desirable. Behold him as he welcomes the three travelers in the heat of the day and hastens to provide for their necessities. Again observe him as he engages in a business transaction with the sons of Heth, to purchase a burying place for Sarah. In his grief he does not forget to be courteous. He bows before them, although he is God's nobleman. Abraham knew what genuine politeness was and what was due from man to his fellow men.[15]

We should be self-forgetful, ever . . . watching for opportunities to cheer others and lighten and relieve their sorrows and burdens by acts of tender kindness and little deeds of love. These thoughtful courtesies, that, commencing in our families, extend outside the family circle, help make up the sum of life's happiness.[16]

THOUGHTFUL OF OTHERS

Finally, be ye all of one mind, having compassion one of another, love as brethren, be pitiful, be courteous.

The great apostle Paul was firm where duty and principle were at stake; he preached Christ with great boldness; but he was never harsh and impolite. He had a tender heart, and was ever kind and thoughtful of others. Courtesy was a marked trait of his character, and this gave him access to the better class of society. . . .

He was zealous for the truth, bold in advocating Christ; but propriety of deportment, the grace of true politeness, marked all his conduct. . . .

Paul attracted warm hearts wherever he went; his soul was linked to the soul of his brethren. When he parted with them, knowing and assuring them that they would never see his face again, they were filled with sorrow, and so earnestly besought him to still remain with them that he exclaimed, "What mean ye to weep and to break mine heart?" His sympathetic heart was breaking as he witnessed and felt their grief at this final separation. They loved him, and felt that they could not give him up. What Christian does not admire the character of Paul? Firm as a rock when standing in defense of the truth, he was affectionate and gentle as a child when surrounded by his friends. . . .

The most Christlike professors are those who are the most kind, pitiful, and courteous; their convictions are firm and their characters strong; nothing can swerve them from their faith or allure them from their duty.

A Christian will cultivate a meek and quiet spirit; he will be calm, considerate of others, and will have a happy temper that sickness will not make irritable or the weather or circumstances disturb. . . . The children of God never forget to do good. . . . Good works are spontaneous with them, for God has transformed their natures by His grace.[17]

HOSPITALITY

Use hospitality one to another without grudging. As every man hath received the gift, even so minister the same one to another, as good stewards of the manifold grace of God.

When the spirit of hospitality dies, the heart becomes palsied with selfishness.[18]

"A lover of hospitality" is among the specifications given by the Holy Spirit as marking one who is to bear responsibility in the church. And to the whole church is given the injunction: "Use hospitality one to another without grudging. . . ." 1 Peter 4:9, 10.

These admonitions have been strangely neglected. Even among those who profess to be Christians, true hospitality is little exercised. Among our own people the opportunity of showing hospitality is not regarded as it should be, as a privilege and blessing. There is altogether too little sociability, too little of a disposition to make room for two or three more at the family board, without embarrassment or parade. Some plead that "it is too much trouble." It would not be if you would say: "We have made no special preparation, but you are welcome to what we have." By the unexpected guest a welcome is appreciated far more than is the most elaborate preparation. . . .

Christ keeps an account of every expense incurred in entertaining for His sake. He supplies all that is necessary for this work. Those who for Christ's sake entertain their brethren, doing their best to make the visit profitable both to their guests and to themselves, are recorded in heaven as worthy of special blessings.[19]

As you open your door to Christ's needy and suffering ones, you are welcoming unseen angels. You invite the companionship of heavenly beings. They bring a sacred atmosphere of joy and peace. They come with praises upon their lips, and an answering strain is heard in heaven. Every deed of mercy makes music there.[20]

CHEERFULNESS

He sheweth mercy, with cheerfulness.

You have a duty to perform, which is to make yourself cheerful and to cultivate unselfishness in your feelings until it will be your greatest pleasure to make all around you happy. . . .

Cheerfulness without levity is one of the Christian graces.[21]

Do not allow the perplexities and worries of everyday life to fret your mind and cloud your brow. If you do, you will always have something to vex and annoy. Life is what we make it, and we shall find what we look for. If we look for sadness and trouble, if we are in a frame of mind to magnify little difficulties, we shall find plenty of them to engross our thoughts and our conversation. But if we look on the bright side of things, we shall find enough to make us cheerful and happy. If we give smiles, they will be returned to us; if we speak pleasant, cheerful words, they will be spoken to us again.[22]

It is Satan's studied plan to push persons from one extreme to the other. As children of the light, God would have us cultivate a cheerful, happy spirit, that we may show forth the praises of Him who hath called us out of darkness into His marvellous light.

Go into a cellar, and you may well talk of darkness, and say, "I cannot see; I cannot see." But come up into the upper chamber, where the light shines, and you need not be in darkness. Come up where Christ is, and you will have light.[23]

Earnest Christians seek to imitate Jesus, for to be Christian is to be Christlike. . . . A hearty, willing service to Jesus produces a sunny religion. . . . In Christ is light and peace and joy forevermore.[24]

KIND SPEECH

The Lord God hath given me the tongue of the learned, that I should know how to speak a word in season to him that is weary: he wakeneth morning by morning, he wakeneth mine ear to hear as the learned.

If we have Christ abiding with us, we shall be Christians at home as well as abroad. He who is a Christian will have kind words for his relatives and associates. He will be kind, courteous, loving, sympathetic, and will be educating himself for an abode with the family above. If he is a member of the royal family, he will represent the kingdom to which he is going. He will speak with gentleness to his children, for he will realize that they too are heirs of God, members of the heavenly court. Among the children of God no spirit of harshness dwells.[25]

Some pride themselves on being outspoken, blunt, and rough, and they call this frankness; but it is not rightly named, it is selfishness of the deepest dye.[26]

Christ is always calm and dignified, and those who labor with Him will use in their work the oil of grace. Their words and actions will be soothing.[27]

We must educate the soul to be pitiful, gentle, tender, full of forgiveness and compassion. While we lay aside all vanity, all foolish talking, jesting, and joking, we are not to become cold, unsympathetic, and unsocial. The Spirit of the Lord is to rest upon you until you shall be like a fragrant flower from the garden of God. You are to keep talking of the light, of Jesus, the Sun of Righteousness, until you shall change from glory to glory, from character to character, going on from strength to strength, and reflecting more and more of the precious image of Jesus.[28]

Christ is ever ready to impart of His riches, and we should gather the jewels that come from Him, that, when we speak, these jewels may drop from our lips.[29]

CHILDREN LOVE MOTHER'S COMPANIONSHIP

Her children arise up, and call her blessed; her husband also, and he praiseth her.

The home should be to the children the most attractive place in the world, and the mother's presence should be its greatest attraction. Children have sensitive, loving natures. They are easily pleased and easily made unhappy. . . .

Young children love companionship, and can seldom enjoy themselves alone. They yearn for sympathy and tenderness. That which they enjoy, they think will please mother also. . . .

Instead of sending her children from her, that she may not be annoyed by their noise or troubled by their little wants, let the mother plan amusement or light work to employ the active hands and minds. By entering into their feelings and directing their amusements and employments, the mother will gain the confidence of her children. . . . By patient, watchful love she can turn the minds of the children in the right direction, cultivating in them beautiful and attractive traits of character.

Mothers should guard against training their children to be dependent and self-absorbed. Never lead them to think that they are the center, and that everything must revolve around them. Some parents give much time and attention to amusing their children, but children should be trained to amuse themselves, to exercise their own ingenuity and skill. Thus they will learn to be content with very simple pleasures. They should be taught to bear bravely their little disappointments and trials. . . . Study to suggest ways by which the children may learn to be thoughtful for others.[30]

In the Word of God we find a beautiful description of a happy home and the woman who presides over it: "Her children arise up, and call her blessed; her husband also, and he praiseth her."[31]

FATHER'S HEART TURNED TO HIS CHILDREN

He shall turn the heart of the fathers to the children, and the heart of the children to their fathers.

The father when he returns from his daily labor will not bring his perplexities to his home. He will feel that home and the family circle are too sacred to be marred with unhappy perplexities. When he left his home he did not leave his Saviour and his religion behind. Both were his companions. The sweet influence of his home, the blessing of his wife, and the love of his children make his burdens light; and he returns with peace in his heart and cheerful, encouraging words for his wife and children, who are waiting joyfully to welcome his coming.[32]

He should find it a pleasant change to spend some time with his children. He may take them into the garden and show them the opening buds and the varied tints of the blooming flowers. . . . He may impress upon their minds the fact that if God cares so much for the trees and flowers, He will care much more for the creatures formed in His image. He may lead them early to understand that God wants children to be lovely, not with artificial adornment, but with beauty of character, the charms of kindness and affection, which will make their hearts bound with joy and happiness.[33]

If the frivolous and pleasure seeking will allow their minds to dwell upon the real and the true, the heart cannot but be filled with reverence, and they will adore the God of nature.[34]

If you would draw your children to Jesus, you must not enter your home with cross words, with a frown upon your brow. If you come from your business weary and worn, just plead with God for His grace, for His restful Spirit, that your heart may be melted with tenderness, that your lips may be filled with words of kindness and comfort. Bind your children to your heart. Recommend your religion to them by its pleasantness.[35]

HAPPY COMPANIONSHIP TOGETHER

We took sweet counsel together, and walked unto the house of God in company.

Throw around your children the charms of home and of your society. If you do this, they will not have so much desire for the society of young associates. . . . Because of the evils now in the world and the restrictions necessary to be placed upon the children, parents should have double care to bind them to their hearts and let them see that they wish to make them happy.[36]

Let parents devote the evenings to their families. Lay off care and perplexity with the labors of the day. . . . Let the evenings be spent as happily as possible.[37]

Form a home reading circle, in which every member of the family shall lay aside the busy cares of the day and unite in study. Fathers, mothers, brothers, sisters, take up this work heartily, and see if the home church will not be greatly improved. . . . Read the literature that will give you true knowledge and that will be a help to the entire family.[38]

If they would gather the children close to them, and show that they love them, and would manifest an interest in all their efforts, and even in their sports, sometimes even being a child among children, they would make the children very happy and would gain their love and win their confidence.[39]

Brought up under the wise and loving guidance of a true home, children will have no desire to wander away in search of pleasure and companionship. Evil will not attract them. The spirit that prevails in the home will mold their characters; they will form habits and principles that will be a strong defense against temptation when they shall leave the home shelter and take their place in the world.[40]

☙ ☙ ☙

The young heart is quick to respond to the touch of sympathy.[41]

HOLD THE FAMILY TOGETHER BY AFFECTION

Shew forth thy lovingkindness in the morning, and thy faithfulness every night.

The religion of Christ will lead us to do all the good possible, to both high and low, rich and poor, happy and oppressed. But especially will it lead to the manifestation of kindness in our own family. It will be manifested by acts of courtesy and love to father and mother, husband, wife, and child. We are to look to Jesus, to catch His Spirit, to live in the light of His goodness and love, and to reflect His glory upon others.[42]

Those who are united by the ties of nature have the strongest claims upon one another. In their dealings with each other they should manifest kindness and the tenderest love.[43]

Gentle manners, cheerful conversation, and loving acts will bind the hearts of children to their parents by the silken cords of affection and will do more to make home attractive than the rarest ornaments that can be bought for gold.[44]

Mutual kindness and forbearance will make home a paradise and attract holy angels into the family circle; but they will flee from a house where there are unpleasant words, fretfulness, and strife.[45]

The most valuable rules for social and family intercourse are to be found in the Bible. . . . Our Saviour's sermon on the mount contains instruction of priceless worth to old and young. It should be often read in the family circle, and its precious teachings exemplified in the daily life. The golden rule, "Whatsoever ye would that men should do to you, do ye even so to them,". . . should be made the law of the family. Those who cherish the spirit of Christ will manifest politeness at home. . . . They will be constantly seeking to make all around them happy, forgetting self in their kind attention to others.[46]

Christian courtesy is the golden clasp which unites the members of the family in bonds of love, becoming closer and stronger every day.[47]

MAKE THE HOME A BLESSING TO OTHERS

When thou makest a feast, call the poor, the maimed, the lame, the blind: . . . for they cannot recompense thee: for thou shalt be recompensed at the resurrection of the just.

God is displeased with the selfish interest so often manifested for "me and my family." Every family that cherishes this spirit needs to be converted by the pure principles exemplified in the life of Christ. Those who shut themselves up within themselves, who are unwilling to be drawn upon to entertain visitors, lose many blessings.[48]

There are many others to whom we might make our homes a blessing. Our social entertainments should not be governed by the dictates of worldly custom, but by the Spirit of Christ and the teaching of His Word. The Israelites, in all their festivities, included the poor, the stranger, and the Levite, who was both the assistant of the priest in the sanctuary and a religious teacher and missionary. These were regarded as the guests of the people, to share their hospitality on all occasions of social and religious rejoicing and to be tenderly cared for in sickness or in need. It is such as these whom we should make welcome to our homes. How much such a welcome might do to cheer and encourage the missionary nurse or the teacher, the care-burdened, hardworking mother, or the feeble and aged, so often without a home, and struggling with poverty and many discouragements. . . .

The warmth of a genial welcome, a place at your fireside, a seat at your home table, the privilege of sharing the blessing of the hour of prayer, would to many of these be like a glimpse of heaven.

Our sympathies are to overflow the boundaries of self and the enclosure of family walls. There are precious opportunities for those who will make their homes a blessing to others. Social influence is a wonderful power. We can use it if we will as a means of helping those about us. . . .

❧ ❧ ❧

Our time here is short. We can pass through this world but once; as we pass along, let us make the most of life.[49]

201

THE HOME SHOULD BE A REFUGE FOR THE YOUTH

Whosoever shall receive one of such children in my name, receiveth me.

Our homes should be a place of refuge for the tempted youth. Many there are who stand at the parting of the ways. Every influence, every impression, is determining the choice that shapes their destiny both here and hereafter.[50]

Do not hold yourselves aloof from them, but come close to them. Bring them to your firesides; invite them to your family altars. There is work that thousands need to have done for them. Every tree in Satan's garden is hung with tempting, poisonous fruit, and a woe is pronounced upon every one who plucks and eats.[51]

Evil invites them. Its resorts are made bright and attractive. They have a welcome for every comer. All about us are youth who have no home and many whose homes have no helpful, uplifting power, and the youth drift into evil. They are going down to ruin within the very shadow of our own doors.

These youth need a hand stretched out to them in sympathy. Kind words simply spoken, little attentions simply bestowed, will sweep away the clouds of temptation which gather over the soul. The true expression of heaven-born sympathy has power to open the door of hearts that need the fragrance of Christlike words and the simple, delicate touch of the spirit of Christ's love. If we would show an interest in the youth, invite them to our homes, and surround them with cheering, helpful influences, there are many who would gladly turn their steps into the upward path.[52]

Remember that happiness will not be found in shutting yourselves up to yourselves, satisfied to pour out all your affection upon each other. Seize upon every opportunity for contributing to the happiness of those around you. . . . True joy can be found only in unselfish service.[53]

LET VISITORS JOIN IN FAMILY WORSHIP

But ye are a chosen generation, a royal priesthood, an holy nation, a peculiar people; that ye should shew forth the praises of him who hath called you out of darkness into his marvellous light.

In a sense the father is the priest of the household, laying upon the family altar the morning and evening sacrifice. But the wife and children should unite in prayer and join in the song of praise. In the morning before he leaves home for his daily labor let the father gather his children about him and, bowing before God, commit them to the care of the Father in heaven. When the cares of the day are past, let the family unite in offering grateful prayer and raising the song of praise, in acknowledgment of divine care during the day. . . . Do not fail to gather your family around God's altar.[54]

In our efforts for the comfort and happiness of guests let us not overlook our obligations to God. The hour of prayer should not be neglected for any consideration. Do not talk and amuse yourselves till all are too weary to enjoy the season of devotion. To do this is to present to God a lame offering. At an early hour of the evening, when we can pray unhurriedly and understandingly, we should present our supplications and raise our voices in happy, grateful praise.

Let all who visit Christians see that the hour of prayer is the most precious, the most sacred, and the happiest hour of the day. These seasons of devotion exert a refining, elevating influence upon all who participate in them. They bring a peace and rest grateful to the spirit.[55]

A lamp, however small, if kept steadily burning, may be the means of lighting many other lamps. . . . Wonderful opportunities are ours through a faithful use of the opportunities of our own homes. If we will open our hearts and homes to the divine principles of life, we shall become channels for currents of life-giving power. From our homes will flow streams of healing, bringing life, and beauty, and fruitfulness where now are barrenness and dearth.[56]

TO HAVE FRIENDS WE MUST BE FRIENDLY

A man that hath friends must shew himself friendly.

In the arrangements for the education of the chosen people it is made manifest that a life centered in God is a life of completeness. Every want He has implanted, He provides to satisfy; every faculty imparted, He seeks to develop.

The Author of all beauty, Himself a lover of the beautiful, God provided to gratify in His children the love of beauty. He made provision also for their social needs, for the kindly and helpful associations that do so much to cultivate sympathy and to brighten and sweeten life.[57]

Christian sociability is altogether too little cultivated by God's people. . . . By social intercourse acquaintances are formed and friendships contracted which result in a unity of heart and an atmosphere of love which is pleasing in the sight of heaven.[58]

Everyone will find companions or make them. And just in proportion to the strength of the friendship, will be the amount of influence which friends will exert over one another for good or for evil. All will have associates, and will influence and be influenced in their turn.

The link is a mysterious one which binds human hearts together, so that the feelings, tastes, and principles of two individuals are closely blended. One catches the spirit and copies the ways and acts of the other. As wax retains the figure of the seal, so the mind retains the impression produced by intercourse and association. The influence may be unconscious, yet it is no less powerful. . . . If choice is made of companions who fear the Lord, the influence will lead to truth, to duty, and to holiness. A truly Christian life is a power for God.[59]

❧ ❧ ❧

The warmth of true friendship . . . is a foretaste of the joys of heaven.[60]

RIGHTEOUSNESS ENRICHES LIFE

He that followeth after righteousness and mercy findeth life, righteousness, and honour.

Gatherings for social intercourse are made in the highest degree profitable and instructive when those who meet together have the love of God glowing in their hearts; when they meet to exchange thoughts in regard to the Word of God or to consider methods for advancing His work and doing good to their fellow men. When the Holy Spirit is regarded as a welcome guest at these gatherings, when nothing is said or done to grieve it away, God is honored, and those who meet together are refreshed and strengthened. . . .

Christ rejoices when the thoughts of the young are occupied by the grand and ennobling themes of salvation. He enters the hearts of all such as an abiding guest, filling them with joy and peace. . . . Those who possess this love will delight to talk of the things that God has prepared for them that love Him.[61]

Young men and young women should not think that their sports, their evening parties, and musical entertainments, as usually conducted, are acceptable to Christ.

Light has been given me, again and again, that all our gatherings should be characterized by a decided religious influence. If our young people would assemble to read and understand the Scriptures, asking, "What shall I do that I may have eternal life?" and then place themselves unitedly upon the side of truth, the Lord would let His blessing come into their hearts. . . .

To all, old and young, the word of the Lord is: Let the truth of God be inwrought in mind and soul. Let your prayer be, "O Lord, preserve my soul, that I shall not dishonor Thee."[62]

TAKE A DAY IN THE COUNTRY

He maketh me to lie down in green pastures: he leadeth me beside the still waters. He restoreth my soul: he leadeth me in the paths of righteousness for his name's sake.

Let several families living in a city or village unite and leave the occupations which have taxed them physically and mentally, and make an excursion into the country to the side of a fine lake or to a nice grove where the scenery of nature is beautiful. They should provide themselves with plain, hygienic food, the very best fruits and grains, and spread their table under the shade of some tree or under the canopy of heaven. The ride, the exercise, and the scenery will quicken the appetite, and they can enjoy a repast which kings might envy.

On such occasions parents and children should feel free from care, labor, and perplexity. Parents should become children with their children, making everything as pleasant for them as possible. Let the whole day be given to recreation. Exercise in the open air for those whose employment has been withindoors and sedentary will be beneficial to health. All who can, should feel it a duty to pursue this course. Nothing will be lost, but much gained. They can return to their occupations with new life and new courage to engage in their labor with zeal, and they are better prepared to resist disease. . . .

But few realize the constant, wearing labor of those who are bearing the responsibilities of the work in the office. They are confined withindoors day after day and week after week, while a constant strain upon the mental powers is surely undermining their constitutions and lessening their hold on life. . . .

They should have a change frequently, should often devote a day wholly to recreation with their families, who are almost entirely deprived of their society.[63]

VISITING WITH ONE ANOTHER

Then they that feared the Lord spake often one to another: and the Lord hearkened, and heard it, and a book of remembrance was written before him for them that feared the Lord, and that thought upon his name. And they shall be mine, saith the Lord of hosts, in that day when I make up my jewels; and I will spare them, as a man spareth his own son that serveth him.

We have an individual accountability to God, an individual work which no one can do for us. It is to make the world better by precept, personal effort, and example. While we should cultivate sociability, let it not be merely for amusement, but for a purpose. There are souls to save. . . . Our intercourse with others should be characterized by sobriety and heavenly-mindedness. Our conversation should be upon heavenly things. . . .

What is more worthy to engross the mind than the plan of redemption? It is a subject that is exhaustless. The love of Jesus, the salvation offered to fallen man through His infinite love, holiness of heart, the precious, saving truth for these last days, the grace of Jesus Christ—these are subjects which may animate the soul and cause the pure in heart to feel that joy that the disciples felt when Jesus came and walked with them as they traveled toward Emmaus. He who has centered his affections upon Christ will relish this kind of hallowed association and will gather divine strength by such intercourse. . . . When the truth of God is an abiding principle in the heart, it will be like a living spring. Attempts may be made to repress it, but it will gush forth in another place; it is there, and cannot be headed off. The truth in the heart is a wellspring of life. It refreshes the weary, restrains the vile thought and utterance, and makes all flourishing. . . . Their happiness will . . . be . . . in Jesus and His love.[64]

JESUS AND HIS FRIENDS AT BETHANY

Jesus loved Martha, and her sister, and Lazarus.

There was one home that He loved to visit—the home of Lazarus, and Mary, and Martha; for in the atmosphere of faith and love His spirit had rest.[65]

Among the most steadfast of Christ's disciples was Lazarus of Bethany. From their first meeting his faith in Christ had been strong; his love for Him was deep, and he was greatly beloved by the Saviour. It was for Lazarus that the greatest of Christ's miracles was performed. The Saviour blessed all who sought His help; He loves all the human family; but to some He is bound by peculiarly tender associations. His heart was knit by a strong bond of affection to the family at Bethany, and for one of them His most wonderful work was wrought.

At the home of Lazarus, Jesus had often found rest. The Saviour had no home of His own; He was dependent on the hospitality of His friends and disciples; and often, when weary, thirsting for human fellowship, He had been glad to escape to this peaceful household, away from the suspicion and jealousy of the angry Pharisees. Here He found a sincere welcome, a pure, holy friendship. Here He could speak with simplicity and perfect freedom, knowing that His words would be understood and treasured.

Our Saviour appreciated a quiet home and interested listeners. He longed for human tenderness, courtesy, and affection. Those who received the heavenly instruction He was always ready to impart were greatly blessed. . . . The multitudes were slow of hearing, and in the home at Bethany Christ found rest from the weary conflict of public life. Here He opened to an appreciative audience the volume of Providence. In these private interviews He unfolded to His hearers that which He did not attempt to tell to the mixed multitude. He needed not to speak to His friends in parables.[66]

THE FRIENDSHIP BETWEEN PAUL AND TIMOTHY

To Timothy, my dearly beloved son: Grace, mercy, and peace, from God the Father and Christ Jesus our Lord. . . . Greatly desiring to see thee, . . . that I may be filled with joy.

From the judgment hall of Caesar, Paul returned to his cell, realizing that he had gained for himself only a brief respite. He knew that his enemies would not rest until they had compassed his death. But he knew also that for a time truth had triumphed. . . .

Sitting day after day in his gloomy cell, knowing that at a word or a nod from Nero his life might be sacrificed, Paul thought of Timothy, and determined to send for him. To Timothy had been committed the care of the church at Ephesus, and he had therefore been left behind when Paul made his last journey to Rome. Paul and Timothy were bound together by an affection unusually deep and strong. Since his conversion Timothy had shared Paul's labors and sufferings, and the friendship between the two had grown stronger, deeper, and more sacred, until all that a son could be to a loved and honored father, Timothy was to the aged, toil-worn apostle. It is little wonder that in his loneliness and solitude Paul longed to see him.

Under the most favorable circumstances several months must pass before Timothy could reach Rome from Asia Minor. Paul knew that his life was uncertain, and he feared that Timothy might arrive too late to see him. He had important counsel and instruction for the young man, to whom so great responsibility had been entrusted; and while urging him to come without delay, he dictated the dying testimony that he might not be spared to utter. His soul filled with loving solicitude for his son in the gospel and for the church under his care, Paul sought to impress Timothy with the importance of fidelity to his sacred trust. . . . Paul closed his letter by commending his beloved Timothy to the guardianship of the Chief Shepherd, who, though the undershepherds might be stricken down, would still care for His flock.[67]

JONATHAN AND DAVID

How are the mighty fallen in the midst of the battle! O Jonathan, thou wast slain in thine high places. I am distressed for thee, my brother Jonathan: very pleasant hast thou been unto me: thy love to me was wonderful, passing the love of women.

The friendship of Jonathan for David was . . . of God's providence, to preserve the life of the future ruler of Israel.[68]

At this time, when there were so few bright spots in the path of David, he was rejoiced to receive an unexpected visit from Jonathan, who had learned the place of his refuge. Precious were the moments which these two friends passed in each other's society. They related their varied experiences, and Jonathan strengthened the heart of David, saying, "Fear not! for the hand of Saul my father shall not find thee; and thou shalt be king over Israel, and I shall be next unto thee; and that also Saul my father knoweth." As they talked of the wonderful dealings of God with David, the hunted fugitive was greatly encouraged. "And they two made a covenant before the Lord: and David abode in the wood, and Jonathan went to his house."

After the visit of Jonathan, David encouraged his soul with songs of praise, accompanying his voice with his harp.[69]

Jonathan, by birth heir to the throne, yet knowing himself set aside by the divine decree; to his rival the most tender and faithful of friends, shielding David's life at the peril of his own; steadfast at his father's side through the dark days of his declining power, and at his side falling at the last—the name of Jonathan is treasured in heaven, and it stands on earth a witness to the existence and the power of unselfish love.[70]

ಜಿ ಜಿ ಜಿ

Connected with Christ, we are connected with our fellow men by the golden links of the chain of love.[71]

RECREATION REFRESHES AND INVIGORATES

Thou wilt shew me the path of life: in thy presence is fulness of joy; at thy right hand there are pleasures for evermore.

It is the privilege and duty of Christians to seek to refresh their spirits and invigorate their bodies by innocent recreation, with the purpose of using their physical and mental powers to the glory of God. Our recreation should not be scenes of senseless mirth, taking the form of the nonsensical. We can conduct them in such a manner as will benefit and elevate those with whom we associate and better qualify us and them to more successfully attend to the duties devolving upon us as Christians. . . . The religion of Christ is cheering and elevating in its influence. It is above everything like foolish jesting and joking, vain and frivolous chitchat. In all our seasons of recreation we may gather from the Divine Source of strength fresh courage and power, that we may the more successfully elevate our lives to purity, true goodness, and holiness.[72]

There are persons with a diseased imagination to whom religion is a tyrant, ruling them as with a rod of iron. Such are constantly mourning over their depravity and groaning over supposed evil. Love does not exist in their hearts; a frown is ever upon their countenances. They are chilled by the innocent laugh from the youth or from anyone. They consider all recreation or amusement a sin and think that the mind must be constantly wrought up to just such a stern, severe pitch. This is one extreme. Others think that the mind must be ever on the stretch to invent new amusements and diversions in order to gain health. They learn to depend on excitement, and are uneasy without it. Such are not true Christians. They go to another extreme. The true principles of Christianity open before all a source of happiness, the height and depth, the length and breadth of which are immeasurable.[73]

211

NO ONE LIVES TO HIMSELF

For none of us liveth to himself.

The young generally conduct themselves as though the precious hours of probation, while mercy lingers, were one grand holiday, and they were placed in this world merely for their own amusement, to be gratified with a continual round of excitement. Satan has been making special efforts to lead them to find happiness in worldly amusements and to justify themselves by endeavoring to show that these amusements are harmless, innocent, and even important to health.[74]

The desire for excitement and pleasing entertainment is a temptation and a snare to God's people, and especially to the young. Satan is constantly preparing inducements to attract minds from the solemn work of preparation for scenes just in the future. Through the agency of worldlings he keeps up a continual excitement to induce the unwary to join in worldly pleasures. There are shows, lectures, and an endless variety of entertainments that are calculated to lead to a love of the world; and through this union with the world faith is weakened.[75]

Worldly pleasures are infatuating; and for their momentary enjoyment many sacrifice the friendship of Heaven, with the peace, love, and joy that it affords.[76]

Christians have many sources of happiness at their command, and they may tell with unerring accuracy what pleasures are lawful and right. They may enjoy such recreations as will not dissipate the mind or debase the soul, such as will not disappoint, and leave a sad after-influence to destroy self-respect or bar the way to usefulness. If they can take Jesus with them, and maintain a prayerful spirit, they are perfectly safe.[77]

In view of their high calling the youth among us should . . . ponder well the paths of their feet, remembering that where they lead the way others will follow.[78]

GOD GIVES US THE GOOD

For God giveth to a man that is good in his sight wisdom, and knowledge, and joy.

Youth cannot be made as sedate and grave as old age, the child as sober as the sire. While sinful amusements are condemned, . . . provide in their stead innocent pleasures, which will not taint or corrupt the morals.[79]

There is a distinction between recreation and amusement. Recreation, when true to its name, re-creation, tends to strengthen and build up. Calling us aside from our ordinary cares and occupations, it affords refreshment for mind and body, and thus enables us to return with new vigor to the earnest work of life. Amusement, on the other hand, is sought for the sake of pleasure, and is often carried to excess; it absorbs the energies that are required for useful work, and thus proves a hindrance to life's true success.[80]

While we shun the false and artificial . . . we must supply sources of pleasure that are pure and noble and elevating.[81]

Our holidays should not be spent in patterning after the world, yet they should not be passed by unnoticed. . . . On these days . . . get something to take the place of more dangerous amusements.[82]

No recreation helpful only to themselves will prove so great a blessing to the children and youth as that which makes them helpful to others.[83]

Would it not be well for us to observe holidays unto God, when we could revive in our minds the memory of His dealing with us? . . .

The world has many holidays, and men become engrossed with games, with horse races, with gambling, smoking, and drunkenness. They show plainly under what banner they are standing. . . . Shall not the people of God more frequently have holy convocations in which to thank God for His rich blessings?[84]

WALK IN THE WAY OF GOOD MEN

Walk in the way of good men, and keep the paths of the righteous.

There are modes of recreation which are highly beneficial to both mind and body. An enlightened, discriminating mind will find abundant means for entertainment and diversion, from sources not only innocent, but instructive. Recreation in the open air, the contemplation of the works of God in nature, will be of the highest benefit.[85]

While we are seeking to refresh our spirits and invigorate our bodies, *we are required of God* to use all our powers at all times to the best purpose. We may associate together as we do here today,* and do all to the glory of God. We can and should conduct our recreations in such a manner that we shall be fitted for the more successful discharge of the duties devolving upon us, and that our influence shall be more beneficial upon those with whom we associate. Especially should it be the case upon an occasion like this, which should be of good cheer to us all. We can return to our homes improved in mind and refreshed in body, and prepared to engage in the work anew, with better hope and better courage.

We believe that it is our privilege every day of our lives to glorify God upon the earth; that we are not to live in this world merely for our own amusement, merely to please ourselves. We are here to benefit humanity, to be a blessing to society. . . .

We here behold the beauties of nature. . . . As we behold these works of nature we should let the mind be carried up higher, to nature's God; let it be elevated to the Creator of the universe, and then adore the Creator who has made all these beautiful things for our benefit and happiness.[86]

We must take periods of rest, periods of recreation, periods for contemplation.[87]

---

* From an address given at an outdoor recreational gathering at Goguac Lake, Michigan

WALK NOT IN THE WAY WITH SINNERS

My son, if sinners entice thee, consent thou not. . . . My son, walk not thou in the way with them; refrain thy foot from their path.

Amusements are doing more to counteract the working of the Holy Spirit than anything else, and the Lord is grieved.[88]

Those who are artificial in character and religious experience too readily gather for pleasure and amusement, and their influence attracts others. Sometimes young men and women who are trying to be Bible Christians are persuaded to join the party. Unwilling to be thought singular, and naturally inclined to follow the example of others, they place themselves under the influence of those who, perhaps, have never felt the divine touch on mind and heart. Had they prayerfully consulted the divine standard, to learn what Christ has said in regard to the fruit to be borne on the Christian tree, they would have discerned that these entertainments were really banquets prepared to keep souls from accepting the invitation to the marriage supper of the Lamb.

It sometimes happens that by frequenting places of amusement, youth who have been carefully instructed in the way of the Lord are carried away by the glamor of human influence, and form attachments for those whose education and training have been of a worldly character. They sell themselves into lifelong bondage by uniting with persons who have not the ornament of a Christlike spirit.[89]

You will be invited to attend places of amusement. . . . If you are true to Christ then, you will not try to form excuses for your nonattendance, but will plainly and modestly declare that you are a child of God, and your principles would not allow you to be in a place, even for one occasion, where you could not invite the presence of your Lord.[90]

God desires His people to show by their lives the advantage of Christianity over worldliness; to show that they are working on a high, holy plane.[91]

ASSOCIATE WITH THOSE WHO LOVE GOD

I am a companion of all them that fear thee, and of them that keep thy precepts.

Between the associations of the followers of Christ for Christian recreation and worldly gatherings for pleasure and amusement, will exist a marked contrast. Instead of prayer and the mentioning of Christ and sacred things, will be heard from the lips of worldlings the silly laugh and the trifling conversation. Their idea is to have a general high time. Their amusements commence in folly and end in vanity. We want in our gatherings to have them so conducted, and to so conduct ourselves, that when we return to our homes we can have a conscience void of offense toward God and man; a consciousness that we have not wounded or injured in any manner those with whom we have associated or had an injurious influence over them.[92]

We are of that class who believe that it is our privilege every day of our lives to glorify God upon the earth; that we are not to live in this world merely for our own amusement, merely to please ourselves. We are here to benefit humanity and to be a blessing to society.[93]

Those who truly love God will not cultivate the society of those who do not love Jesus. They will find that Christian society and conversation is food to the soul, that in the society of those who love God they breathe in the atmosphere of heaven. Christians will exercise love and sympathy one for another. The encouragement given one to another, the esteem manifested one for another, the helps, the instruction, the reproofs, warnings, the Christian counsel that should be found among the followers of Christ will further them in the spiritual life; for Christian fellowship is according to God's plan. . . . They will have tender consideration for all of like precious faith, and will draw toward those who love God. There will be fellowship such as the world knows not of.[94]

A LIFE OF SERVICE

GOD MAKES ME PERFECT IN EVERY GOOD WORK

Now the God of peace, that brought again from the dead our Lord Jesus, that great shepherd of the sheep, through the blood of the everlasting covenant, make you perfect in every good work to do his will, working in you that which is wellpleasing in his sight, through Jesus Christ; to whom be glory for ever and ever.

The religion of Jesus Christ means something more than talk. The righteousness of Christ consists in right actions and good works from pure, unselfish motives. . . . Christ came to do His Father's will. Are we following in His steps? All who have named the name of Christ should be constantly seeking for a more intimate acquaintance with Him, that they may walk even as He walked, and do the works of Christ. . . .

It is the work we do, or do not do, that tells with tremendous power upon our lives and destinies. God requires us to improve every opportunity for usefulness that is offered us. Neglect in doing this is perilous to our spiritual growth. We have a great work to do.[1]

The duties that the Lord places in our way we are to perform, not as a cold, dreary exercise, but as a service of love. Bring into your work your highest powers and sympathies, and you will find that Christ is in it. His presence will make the work light, and your heart will be filled with joy. You will work in harmony with God, and in loyalty and love and fidelity. We are to be sincere, earnest Christians, doing faithfully the work placed in our hands.[2]

Every one who kindles his taper from the divine altar holds his lamp firmly. He does not use common fire upon his censer, but the holy fire, kept burning by the power of God day and night. Those who walk in the footsteps of Jesus, who will surrender their lives to His guidance and to His service, have the golden oil in their vessels with their lamps. They will never be placed in a position for which God has not made provision. The lamp of life is always trimmed by the very hand that lit it.[3]

217

BE ZEALOUS OF GOOD WORKS

Who gave himself for us, that he might redeem us from all iniquity, and purify unto himself a peculiar people, zealous of good works.

Christ's followers have been redeemed for service. Our Lord teaches that the true object of life is ministry. Christ Himself was a worker, and to all His followers He gives the law of service—service to God and to their fellow men. Here Christ has presented to the world a higher conception of life than they had ever known. By living to minister for others man is brought into connection with Christ. The law of service becomes the connecting link which binds us to God and to our fellow men.

To His servants Christ commits "His goods"—something to be put to use for Him. He gives "to every man his work." Each has his place in the eternal plan of Heaven. Each is to work in cooperation with Christ for the salvation of souls. Not more surely is the place prepared for us in the heavenly mansions than is the special place designated on earth where we are to work for God. . . .

And those who would be workers together with God must strive for perfection of every organ of the body and quality of the mind. True education is the preparation of the physical, mental, and moral powers for the performance of every duty; it is the training of body, mind, and soul for divine service. . . .

Of every Christian the Lord requires growth in efficiency and capability in every line. Christ has paid us our wages, even His own blood and suffering, to secure our willing service. He came to our world to give us an example of how we should work and what spirit we should bring into our labor. He desires us to show how we can best advance His work and glorify His name in the world, crowning with honor, with the greatest love and devotion, the Father who "so loved the world, that He gave His only begotten Son, that whosoever believeth in Him should not perish, but have everlasting life."[4]

WORK DILIGENTLY FOR GOD

Whatsoever ye do, do it heartily, as to the Lord, and not unto men.

There is a great work to be done in our world. Men and women are to be converted, not by the gift of tongues nor by the working of miracles, but by the preaching of Christ crucified. Why delay the effort to make the world better? Why wait for some wonderful thing to be done, some costly apparatus to be provided? . . . Into all that we do, whether our work be in the shop, on the farm, or in the office, we are to bring the endeavor to save souls.[5]

This life is full of gracious opportunities, which you can improve in the exercise of your God-given abilities to bless others, and in so doing bless yourself, without considering self in the matter. Trivial circumstances oftentimes prove a decided blessing to the one who acts from principle and has formed the habit of doing right because it is right. Seek for a perfect character, and let all you do, whether seen and appreciated by human eyes or not, be done with an eye single to God's glory, because you belong to God and He has redeemed you at the price of His own life. Be faithful in the least as well as in the greatest; learn to speak the truth, to act at all times the truth. Let the heart be fully submitted to God. If controlled by His grace, you will do little deeds of kindness, take up the duties lying next to you, and bring all the sunshine into your life and character that it is possible to bring, scattering the gifts of love and blessing along the pathway of life. Your works will be far-reaching as eternity. Your lifework will be seen in heaven, and there it will live, through ceaseless ages, because it is found precious in the sight of God.[6]

ð ð ð

Remember that what is worth doing at all is worth doing well.[7]

LET YOUR LIGHT SHINE

Ye are the light of the world. . . . Let your light so shine before men, that they may see your good works, and glorify your Father which is in heaven.

If you walk in the light, you can every one be light bearers to the world. Do not seek to accomplish some great work and neglect the little opportunities close at hand. We can do very much by exemplifying the truth in our daily life. The influence which we may thus exert cannot be easily withstood. Men may combat and defy our logic; they may resist our appeals; but a life of holy purpose, of disinterested love in their behalf, is an argument in favor of the truth that they cannot gainsay. Far more can be accomplished by humble, devoted, virtuous lives than can be affected by preaching when a godly example is lacking. You can labor to build up the church, to encourage your brethren, and to make the social meetings interesting; and you can let your prayers go out, like sharp sickles, with the laborers into the harvest field. Each should have a personal interest, a burden of soul, to watch and pray for the success of the work.

You can also in meekness call the attention of others to the precious truths of God's Word. Young men . . . may never be able to present the truth from the desk, but they could go from house to house and point the people to the Lamb of God that taketh away the sin of the world. The dust and rubbish of error have buried the precious jewels of truth; but the Lord's workers can uncover these treasures, so that many will look upon them with delight and awe.

There is a great variety of work, adapted to different minds and varied capabilities. In the day of God not one will be excused for being shut up to his own selfish interests. And it is by working for others that you will keep your own souls alive. . . . Earnest, unselfish effort will garner sheaves for Jesus. . . . The Lord is a mighty helper.[8]

ABOUND IN LOVE AT HOME AND ABROAD

Now God himself and our Father, and our Lord Jesus Christ, direct our way unto you. And the Lord make you to increase and abound in love one toward another, and toward all men, even as we do toward you.

Missionary work is to be done in the home. Here those who have received Christ are to show what grace has done for them. A divine influence controls the true believer in Christ, and this influence makes itself felt throughout the home and is favorable for the perfection of the characters of all in the home.

The faithful performance of home duties has an influence upon those not in the home. Our spiritual progress in the home is carried into our missionary work abroad. In the father's house is to be given the evidence of a fitness to work for the church. With earnest, humble hearts the members of the family are to seek to know that Christ is abiding in the heart. Then they can go forth fully armed and equipped for service. . . .

The effort to make the home what it should be—a symbol of the home in heaven—prepares us for work in a larger sphere. The education received by showing a tender regard for each other enables us to know how to reach hearts that need to be taught the principles of true religion. The church needs all the cultivated spiritual force which can be obtained, that all, and especially the younger members of the Lord's family, may be carefully guarded. The truth lived at home makes itself felt in disinterested labor abroad. He who lives Christianity in the home will be a bright and shining light everywhere.[9]

The more closely the members of the family are united in their work in the home, the more uplifting and helpful will be the influence that father and mother and sons and daughters will exert outside the home.[10]

A LITTLE MAID WITNESSES FOR GOD

Now Naaman, captain of the host of the king of Syria, was a great man with his master . . . : he was also a mighty man in valour, but he was a leper. And the Syrians had gone out by companies, and had brought away captive out of the land of Israel a little maid; and she waited on Naaman's wife. And she said unto her mistress, Would God my lord were with the prophet that is in Samaria! for he would recover him of his leprosy.

A slave, far from her home, this little maid was nevertheless one of God's witnesses, unconsciously fulfilling the purpose for which God had chosen Israel as His people. As she ministered in that heathen home, her sympathies were aroused in behalf of her master; and, remembering the wonderful miracles of healing wrought through Elisha, she said to her mistress, "Would God my lord were with the prophet that is in Samaria! for he would recover him of his leprosy." She knew that the power of Heaven was with Elisha, and she believed that by this power Naaman could be healed.

The conduct of the captive maid, the way that she bore herself in that heathen home, is a strong witness to the power of early home training. There is no higher trust than that committed to fathers and mothers in the care and training of their children. . . .

We know not in what line our children may be called to serve. They may spend their lives within the circle of the home; they may engage in life's common vocations, or go as teachers of the gospel to heathen lands; but all are alike called to be missionaries for God, ministers of mercy to the world. . . .

The parents of that Hebrew maid, as they taught her of God, did not know the destiny that would be hers. But they were faithful to their trust; and in the home of the captain of the Syrian host, their child bore witness to the God whom she had learned to honor.[11]

GOD SUPPLIES THE RESOURCES

His disciples came to him, saying, . . . Send the multitude away, that they may go into the villages, and buy themselves victuals. But Jesus said unto them, . . . Give ye them to eat. And they say unto him, We have here but five loaves, and two fishes. He said, Bring them hither to me. . . . And looking up to heaven, he blessed, and brake, and gave the loaves to his disciples, and the disciples to the multitude. . . . And they took up of fragments that remained twelve baskets full.

In this parable is wrapped up a deep, spiritual lesson for God's workers. . . . In full reliance upon God, Jesus took the small store of loaves; and although there was but a small supply for His own family of disciples, He did not invite them to eat, but began to distribute to them, bidding them serve the people. The food multiplied in His hands; and the hands of the disciples, reaching out to Christ, Himself the Bread of Life, were never empty. The little store was sufficient for all. After the wants of the people had been supplied, the fragments were gathered up, and Christ and His disciples ate of the precious, Heaven-supplied food.

The disciples were the channel of communication between Christ and the people. This should be a great encouragement to His disciples today. Christ is the great Center, the Source of all strength. His disciples are to receive their supplies from Him. . . . As we continue to impart, we shall continue to receive; and the more we impart, the more we shall receive. . . .

Mark that pool which receives the showers of heaven but has no outlet. It is a blessing to no one, but in stagnant selfishness poisons the air around. Now look at the stream flowing from the mountainside, refreshing the thirsty land through which it passes. What blessing it brings! One would think that in giving so liberally it would exhaust its resources. But not so. It is a part of God's great plan that the stream that gives shall never lack; and day by day and year by year it flows on its way, ever receiving and ever giving.[12]

RESTORE THE OLD PATHS

And they that shall be of thee shall build the old waste places: thou shalt raise up the foundations of many generations; and thou shalt be called, The repairer of the breach, The restorer of paths to dwell in.

The work specified in these words is the work God requires His people to do. It is a work of God's own appointment. With the work of advocating the commandments of God and repairing the breach that has been made in the law of God, we are to mingle compassion for suffering humanity. We are to show supreme love to God; we are to exalt His memorial, which has been trodden down by unholy feet; and with this, we are to manifest mercy, benevolence, and the tenderest pity for the fallen race. "Thou shalt love thy neighbour as thyself." As a people we must take hold of this work. Love revealed for suffering humanity gives significance and power to the truth.[13]

The evangelization of the world is the work that God has given to those who go forth in His name. They are to be colaborers with Christ, revealing to those ready to perish His tender, pitying love. God calls for thousands to work for Him, not by preaching to those who know the truth, going over and over the same ground, but by warning those who have never heard the last message of mercy. Work, with a heart filled with an earnest longing for souls. Do medical missionary work. Thus you will gain access to the hearts of the people. The way will be prepared for more decided proclamation of the truth. You will find that relieving their physical suffering gives you opportunity to minister to their spiritual needs.

The Lord will give you success in this work; for the gospel is the power of God unto salvation when it is interwoven with the practical life, when it is lived and practiced. The union of Christlike work for the body and Christlike work for the soul is the true interpretation of the gospel.[14]

JESUS CAME TO SERVE

Even the Son of man came not to be ministered unto, but to minister.

Many feel that it would be a great privilege to visit the scenes of Christ's life on earth, to walk where He trod, to look upon the lake beside which He loved to teach, and the hills and valleys on which His eyes so often rested. But we need not go to Nazareth, to Capernaum, or to Bethany, in order to walk in the steps of Jesus. We shall find His footprints beside the sickbed, in the hovels of poverty, in the crowded alleys of the great city, and in every place where there are human hearts in need of consolation. In doing as Jesus did when on earth, we shall walk in His steps. . . .

Millions upon millions of human souls ready to perish, bound in chains of ignorance and sin, have never so much as heard of Christ's love for them. Were our condition and theirs to be reversed, what would we desire them to do for us? All this, so far as lies in our power, we are under the most solemn obligation to do for them. Christ's rule of life, by which every one of us must stand or fall in the judgment, is, "Whatsoever ye would that men should do to you, do ye even so to them."

The Saviour has given His precious life in order to establish a church capable of caring for sorrowful, tempted souls. A company of believers may be poor, uneducated, and unknown; yet in Christ they may do a work in the home, the neighborhood, the church, and even in "the regions beyond," whose results shall be as far reaching as eternity.

It is because this work is neglected that so many young disciples never advance beyond the mere alphabet of Christian experience. The light which was glowing in their own hearts when Jesus spoke to them, "Thy sins be forgiven thee," they might have kept alive by helping those in need. The restless energy that is so often a source of danger to the young might be directed into channels through which it would flow out in streams of blessing. Self would be forgotten in earnest work to do others good.[15]

RELIEVE SUFFERING HUMANITY

And he sent them to preach the kingdom of God, and to heal the sick.

Christ established His temporary hospital on the green hill slopes of Galilee and in every other place where the sick and the suffering could be brought to Him. In every city, every town, every village through which He passed, with the tender compassion of a loving Father He laid His hand upon the afflicted ones, and made them whole. This same work Christ has empowered His church to do.[16]

At the close of His earthly ministry, when He charged His disciples with a solemn commission to go "into all the world, and preach the gospel to every creature," He declared that their ministry would receive confirmation through the restoration of the sick to health. Ye "shall lay hands on the sick," He said, "and they shall recover." Mark 16:15, 18. By healing in His name the diseases of the body, they would testify to His power for the healing of the soul.

The Saviour's commission to the disciples includes all believers to the end of time. . . . Never has the world's need for teaching and healing been greater than it is today. The world is full of those who need to be ministered unto—the weak, the helpless, the ignorant, the degraded.[17]

God's people are to be genuine medical missionaries. They are to learn to minister to the needs of soul and body. They should know how to give the simple treatments that do so much to relieve pain and remove disease. They should be familiar with the principles of health reform, that they may show others how, by right habits of eating, drinking, and dressing, disease may be prevented and health regained. . . . The Great Physician . . . will bless every one who will go forward humbly and trustfully, seeking to impart the truth for this time.[18]

≈ ≈ ≈

In a special sense the healing of the sick is our work.[19]

GIVE MEN AND WOMEN THE WATER OF LIFE

Whosoever drinketh of the water that I shall give him shall never thirst; but the water that I shall give him shall be in him a well of water springing up into everlasting life.

In His talk with the Samaritan woman, instead of disparaging Jacob's well, Christ presented something better. . . . He turned the conversation to the treasure He had to bestow, offering the woman something better than she possessed, even living water, the joy and hope of the gospel.[20]

How much interest Christ manifested in this one woman! How earnest and eloquent were His words! When the woman heard them, she left her waterpot and went into the city, saying to those she met, "Come, see a man, which told me all things that ever I did: is not this the Christ?" We read that many of the Samaritans of that city believed on Him. And who can estimate the influence that these words have exerted for the saving of souls in the years that have passed since then![21]

Jesus came in personal contact with men. He did not stand aloof and apart from those who needed His help. He entered the homes of men, comforted the mourner, healed the sick, aroused the careless, and went about doing good. And if we follow in the footsteps of Jesus, we must do as He did. We must give men the same kind of help that He did.[22]

The Lord desires that His word of grace shall be brought home to every soul. To a great degree this must be accomplished by personal labor. This was Christ's method. His work was largely made up of personal interviews. He had a faithful regard for the one-soul audience. Through that one soul the message was often extended to thousands. . . . There are multitudes who will never be reached by the gospel unless it is carried to them.[23]

227

WORK FOR THE CHILDREN

But Jesus said, Suffer little children, and forbid them not, to come unto me: for of such is the kingdom of heaven.

Wherever the Saviour went, the benignity of His countenance and His gentle, kindly manner won the love and confidence of children. . . .

One mother with her child had left her home to find Jesus. On the way she told a neighbor her errand, and the neighbor wanted to have Jesus bless her children. Thus several mothers came together, with their little ones. Some of the children had passed beyond the years of infancy to childhood and youth. . . . But He waited to see how the disciples would treat them. When He saw them send the mothers away, thinking to do Him a favor, He showed them their error, saying, "Suffer the little children to come unto Me, and forbid them not; for of such is the kingdom of God." He took the children in His arms, He laid His hands upon them, and gave them the blessing for which they came.[24]

God wants every child of tender age to be His child, to be adopted into His family. Young though they may be, the youth may be members of the household of faith, and have a most precious experience. . . . Christ will make them little missionaries. The whole current of their thoughts may be changed, so that sin will not appear a thing to be enjoyed but to be hated and shunned. . . . The Lord will give an experience to these children in missionary lines.[25]

We may bring hundreds and thousands of children to Christ if we will work for them.[26]

The children should be so educated that they will sympathize with the aged and afflicted and will seek to alleviate the sufferings of the poor and distressed. They should be taught to be diligent in missionary work; and from their earliest years self-denial and sacrifice for the good of others and the advancement of Christ's cause should be inculcated, that they may be laborers together with God.[27]

WORK FOR PROMINENT MEN AND WOMEN

While he spake . . . unto them, behold, there came a certain ruler, and worshipped him, saying, My daughter is even now dead: but come and lay thy hand upon her, and she shall live. And Jesus arose, and followed him, and so did his disciples.

He [Christ] worked for all who would hear His word—not only the publican and the outcasts, but the rich and cultivated Pharisee, the Jewish nobleman, the centurion, and the Roman ruler. This is the kind of work I have ever seen should be done.[28]

The higher classes have been strangely neglected. In the higher walks of life will be found many who will respond to the truth because it is consistent, because it bears the stamp of the high character of the gospel. Not a few of the men of ability thus won to the cause will enter energetically into the Lord's work.[29]

Rulers and statesmen, men who occupy positions of trust and authority, thinking men and women of all classes, have their attention fixed upon the events taking place about us. They are watching the strained, restless relations that exist among the nations. They observe the intensity that is taking possession of every earthly element, and they recognize that something great and decisive is about to take place—that the world is on the verge of a stupendous crisis.[30]

We are not to forget the . . . lawyers, ministers, senators, and judges, many of whom are slaves to intemperate habits. We are to leave no effort untried to show them that their souls are worth saving, that eternal life is worth striving for.[31]

The greatest men of the earth are not beyond the power of a wonder-working God. . . . When converted to Christ, many will become agencies in the hand of God to work for others of their own class. . . . Only eternity will reveal what has been accomplished by this kind of ministry—how many souls, sick with doubt and tired of worldliness and unrest, have been brought to the great Restorer.[32]

WORK FOR THE NEEDY

And Jesus went about all the cities and villages, teaching in their synagogues, and preaching the gospel of the kingdom, and healing every sickness and every disease among the people.

What a busy life Christ led! Day by day He might be seen entering the humble abodes of want and sorrow, speaking hope to the downcast and peace to the distressed. The poor and suffering received the greatest share of His attention. Children loved Him. They were drawn to Him by His ready sympathy. By His simple, loving words He settled many a difficulty arising among them. Often He took them on His knee and talked with them in a way that won their hearts. . . .

Humble, gracious, tenderhearted, pitiful, He went about doing good, feeding the hungry, lifting up the bowed down, comforting the sorrowing. None who came to Him for aid went away unrelieved. Not a thread of selfishness was woven into the pattern He has left for His children to follow. He lived the life that He would have all live who believe on Him. It was His meat and drink to do the will of His Father. To all who came to Him for help He brought faith and hope and life. Wherever He went He carried blessing.[33]

The tender sympathies of our Saviour were aroused for fallen and suffering humanity. If you would be His followers, you must cultivate compassion and sympathy. Indifference to human woes must give place to lively interest in the sufferings of others. The widow, the orphan, the sick and the dying, will always need help. Here is an opportunity to proclaim the gospel—to hold up Jesus, the hope and consolation of all men. When the suffering body has been relieved, and you have shown a lively interest in the afflicted, the heart is opened, and you can pour in the heavenly balm. If you are looking to Jesus, and drawing from Him knowledge and strength and grace, you can impart His consolation to others because the Comforter is with you.[34]

DO GOOD ON THE SABBATH

It is lawful to do well on the sabbath days.

According to the fourth commandment the Sabbath was dedicated to rest and religious worship. All secular employment was to be suspended, but works of mercy and benevolence were in accordance with the purpose of the Lord. They were not to be limited by time or place. To relieve the afflicted, to comfort the sorrowing, is a labor of love that does honor to God's holy day.[35]

The necessities of life must be attended to, the sick must be cared for, the wants of the needy must be supplied. He will not be held guiltless who neglects to relieve suffering on the Sabbath. God's holy rest day was made for man, and acts of mercy are in perfect harmony with its intent. God does not desire His creatures to suffer an hour's pain that may be relieved upon the Sabbath or any other day. . . .

The Sabbath is not intended to be a period of useless inactivity. The law forbids secular labor on the rest day of the Lord; the toil that gains a livelihood must cease; no labor for worldly pleasure or profit is lawful upon that day; but as God ceased His labor of creating, and rested upon the Sabbath and blessed it, so man is to leave the occupations of his daily life and devote those sacred hours to healthful rest, to worship, and to holy deeds. The work of Christ in healing the sick was in perfect accord with the law. It honored the Sabbath.[36] Labor to relieve the suffering was pronounced by our Saviour a work of mercy and no violation of the Sabbath.[37]

The needs of suffering humanity are never to be neglected. The Saviour, by His example, has shown us that it is right to relieve suffering on the Sabbath.[38]

WHO IS MY NEIGHBOR?

But he . . . said unto Jesus, And who is my neighbour?

Among the Jews the question, "Who is my neighbor?" caused endless dispute. They had no doubt as to the heathen and the Samaritans. These were strangers and enemies. But where should the distinction be made among the people of their own nation, and among the different classes of society? . . . This question Christ answered in the parable of the good Samaritan. He showed that our neighbor does not mean merely one of the church or faith to which we belong. It has no reference to race, color, or class distinction. Our neighbor is every person who needs our help. Our neighbor is every soul who is wounded and bruised by the adversary. Our neighbor is every one who is the property of God.[39]

Every one who is in suffering need is our neighbor. Every straying son and daughter of Adam, who has been ensnared by the enemy of souls and bound in the slavery of wrong habits that blight the God-given manhood or womanhood, is my neighbor.[40]

Our neighbors are not merely our associates and special friends; they are not simply those who belong to our church, or who think as we do. Our neighbors are the whole human family. We are to do good to all men, and especially to those who are of the household of faith. We are to give to the world an exhibition of what it means to carry out the law of God. We are to love God supremely and our neighbor as ourselves.[41]

Today God gives men opportunity to show whether they love their neighbor. He who truly loves God and his fellow man is he who shows mercy to the destitute, the suffering, the wounded, those who are ready to die. God calls upon every man to take up his neglected work, to seek to restore the moral image of the Creator in humanity.[42]

SPEAK THE TRUTH TO MY NEIGHBOR

These are the things that ye shall do; Speak ye every man the truth to his neighbour; execute the judgment of truth and peace in your gates.

To all who are working with Christ I would say, Wherever you can gain access to the people by the fireside, improve your opportunity. Take your Bible, and open before them its great truths. Your success will not depend so much upon your knowledge and accomplishments as upon your ability to find your way to the heart. By being social and coming close to the people, you may turn the current of their thoughts more readily than by the most able discourse.[43]

Take along the publications and ask them to read. When they see that you are sincere they will not despise any of your efforts. There is a way to reach the hardest hearts. Approach in the simplicity and sincerity and humility that will help us to reach the souls of them for whom Christ died.[44]

Allow no opportunity to pass unimproved. Visit those who live near you, and by sympathy and kindness try to reach their hearts. Visit the sick and suffering and show a kindly interest in them. If possible, do something to make them more comfortable. Through this means you can reach their hearts and speak a word for Christ. Eternity alone will reveal how far reaching such a line of labor can be.[45]

Those who do not take up this work, those who act with the indifference that some have manifested, will soon lose their first love and will begin to censure, criticize, and condemn their own brethren.[46]

Those who go forth in the spirit of the Master, seeking to reach souls with the truth, will . . . become more and more vitalized as they give themselves to the service of God. It is a joyous work to open the Scriptures to others.[47]

SAVE MYSELF BY SAVING OTHERS

Take heed unto thyself, and unto the doctrine; continue in them: for in doing this thou shalt both save thyself, and them that hear thee.

I have read of a man who, journeying on a winter's day through deep drifts of snow, became benumbed by the cold, which was almost imperceptibly freezing his vital powers. He was nearly chilled to death, and was about to give up the struggle for life, when he heard the moans of a fellow traveler who was also perishing with cold. His sympathy was aroused, and he determined to rescue him. He chafed the ice-cold limbs of the unfortunate man, and after considerable effort raised him to his feet. As the sufferer could not stand, he bore him in sympathizing arms through the very drifts he had thought he could never get through alone.

When he had carried his fellow traveler to a place of safety, the truth flashed home to him that in saving his neighbor he had also saved himself. His earnest efforts to help another had quickened the blood that was freezing in his own veins and sent a healthy warmth to the extremities of his body.

The lesson that in helping others we ourselves receive help must be urged upon young believers continually, by precept and example, that in their Christian experience they may gain the best results. Let the desponding ones, those disposed to think that the way to eternal life is trying and difficult, go to work to help others. Such efforts, united with prayer for divine light, will cause their own hearts to throb with the quickening influence of the grace of God, their own affections to glow with more divine fervor. Their whole Christian life will be more of a reality, more earnest, more prayerful. . . . The testimonies borne by them in the Sabbath services will be filled with power. With joy they will bear witness to the preciousness of the experience they have gained in working for others.[48]

BE KIND AND TENDERHEARTED

Be ye kind one to another, tenderhearted, forgiving one another, even as God for Christ's sake hath forgiven you.

Let the tenderness and mercy that Jesus has revealed in His own precious life be an example to us of the manner in which we should treat our fellow beings. . . . Many have fainted and become discouraged in the great struggle of life, whom one word of kindly cheer and courage would have strengthened to overcome. . . . We cannot tell how far reaching may be our tender words of kindness, our Christlike efforts to lighten some burden. The erring can be restored in no other way than in the spirit of meekness, gentleness, and tender love.[49]

In all your transactions with your fellow men never forget that you are dealing with God's property. Be kind; be pitiful; be courteous. Respect God's purchased possession. Treat one another with tenderness and courtesy.[50]

If you have enmity, suspicion, envy, and jealousy in your hearts, you have a work to do to make these things right. Confess your sins; come into harmony with your brethren. Speak well of them. Throw out no unfavorable hints, no suggestions that will awaken distrust in the minds of others. Guard their reputation as sacredly as you would have them guard yours; love them as you would be loved of Jesus.[51]

The grace of God leads men to place themselves in all their business transactions in the place of those with whom they are dealing. It leads men to look not only on their own things but also on the things of others. It leads them to reveal tenderness, sympathy, and kindness. Cherishing a right spirit, living a holy life—this is what being Christlike means. . . .

Let your life be controlled by the wide, generous principles of the Bible, the principles of good will, kindness, and courtesy.[52]

HAVE AN UNDERSTANDING HEART

I have given thee a wise and an understanding heart.

Solomon in his youth made David's choice his own. Above every earthly good he asked of God a wise and understanding heart. . . . The power of his understanding, the extent of his knowledge, the glory of his reign, became the wonder of the world.[53]

The name of Jehovah was greatly honored during the first part of Solomon's reign. The wisdom and righteousness revealed by the king bore witness to all nations of the excellency of the attributes of the God whom he served. For a time Israel was as the light of the world, showing forth the greatness of Jehovah. Not in the surpassing wisdom, the fabulous riches, the far-reaching power and fame that were his, lay the real glory of Solomon's early reign; but in the honor that he brought to the name of the God of Israel through a wise use of the gifts of Heaven.

As the years went by and Solomon's fame increased, he sought to honor God by adding to his mental and spiritual strength and by continuing to impart to others the blessings he received. None understood better than he that it was through the favor of Jehovah that he had come into possession of power and wisdom and understanding, and that these gifts were bestowed that he might give to the world a knowledge of the King of kings.[54]

As the man is converted by the truth, the work of transformation of character goes on. He has an increased measure of understanding, in becoming a man of obedience to God. The mind and will of God become His will, and by constantly looking to God for counsel, he becomes a man of increased understanding. There is a general development of the mind that is unreservedly placed under the guidance of the Spirit of God.[55]

BE FULL OF COMPASSION

Unto the upright there ariseth light in the darkness: he is gracious, and full of compassion, and righteous.

Wherever there is an impulse of love and sympathy, wherever the heart reaches out to bless and uplift others, there is revealed the working of God's Holy Spirit. In the depths of heathenism men who have had no knowledge of the written law of God, who have never even heard the name of Christ, have been kind to His servants, protecting them at the risk of their own lives. Their acts show the working of a divine power. The Holy Spirit has implanted the grace of Christ in the heart of the savage, quickening his sympathies contrary to his nature, contrary to his education. . . .

Christ is seeking to uplift all who will be lifted to companionship with Himself, that we may be one with Him as He is one with the Father. He permits us to come in contact with suffering and calamity in order to call us out of our selfishness; He seeks to develop in us the attributes of His character—compassion, tenderness, and love. By accepting this work of ministry we place ourselves in His school, to be fitted for the courts of God. . . .

By cooperating with heavenly beings in their work on earth, we are preparing for their companionship in heaven. "Ministering spirits, sent forth to minister for them who shall be heirs of salvation," angels in heaven will welcome those who on earth have lived "not to be ministered unto, but to minister." In this blessed companionship we shall learn, to our eternal joy, all that is wrapped up in the question, "Who is my neighbor?"[56]

❧ ❧ ❧

Every act of love, every word of kindness, every prayer in behalf of the suffering and oppressed, is reported before the eternal throne and placed on heaven's imperishable record.[57]

SING AND PRAY WITH MY NEIGHBORS

They sang praises with gladness, and they bowed their heads and worshipped.

The presentation of the truth in love and sympathy, from house to house, is in harmony with the instruction that Christ gave to His disciples when He sent them out on their first missionary tour. By songs of praise to God, by humble, heartfelt prayers, by a simple presentation of Bible truth in the family circle, many will be reached. The divine workers will be present to send conviction to hearts. "I am with you alway" is His promise. With the assurance of the abiding presence of such a Helper, we may labor with hope and faith and courage.[58]

Those who have the gift of song are needed. Song is one of the most effective means of impressing spiritual truth upon the heart. Often by the words of sacred songs the springs of penitence and faith have been unsealed. . . . Church members, young and old, should be educated to go forth to proclaim this last message to the world. If they go in humility, angels of God will go with them, teaching them how to lift up the voice in prayer, how to raise the voice in song, and how to proclaim the gospel message for this time.[59]

Learn to sing the simplest of songs. These will help you in house-to-house labor, and hearts will be touched by the influence of the Holy Spirit. Christ was often heard singing hymns of praise. . . . There was joy in His heart. We learn from the Word that there is joy among the angels of heaven over one repentant sinner and that the Lord rejoices over His church with singing.[60]

As, like the disciples, you go from place to place telling the story of the Saviour's love, you will make friends and will see the fruit of your labor.[61]

238

VISIT FATHERLESS AND WIDOWS

Pure religion and undefiled before God and the Father is this, To visit the fatherless and the widows in their affliction, and to keep himself unspotted from the world.

Among all whose needs demand our interest, the widow and the fatherless have the strongest claims upon our tender sympathy and care. . . .

The father who has died in the faith, resting upon the eternal promise of God, left his loved ones in full trust that the Lord would care for them. And how does the Lord provide for these bereaved ones? He does not work a miracle in sending manna from heaven, He does not send ravens to bring them food; but He works a miracle upon human hearts, He expels selfishness from the soul, He unseals the fountain of benevolence. He tests the love of His professed followers by committing to their tender mercies the afflicted and bereaved ones, the poor and the orphan.[62]

Many a widowed mother with her fatherless children is bravely striving to bear her double burden, often toiling far beyond her strength in order to keep her little ones with her and to provide for their needs. Little time has she for their training and instruction, little opportunity to surround them with influences that would brighten their lives. She needs encouragement, sympathy, and tangible help. God calls upon us to supply to these children, so far as we can, the want of a father's care. . . . Seek to aid the careworn mother.[63]

In homes supplied with life's comforts, in bins and granaries filled with the yield of abundant harvests, in warehouses stocked with the products of the loom, and vaults stored with gold and silver, God has supplied means for the sustenance of these needy ones.[64]

Those who have pity for the . . . widows, the orphans, and the needy, Christ represents as commandment keepers, who shall have eternal life.[65]

DEAL MY BREAD TO THE HUNGRY

Is it not to deal thy bread to the hungry, and that thou bring the poor that are cast out to thy house?

What is pure religion? Christ has told us that pure religion is the exercise of pity, sympathy, and love, in the home, in the church, and in the world. . . .

We are to think and care for others who need our love, our tenderness, and care. We should ever remember that we are representatives of Christ, and that we are to share the blessings that He gives, not with those who can recompense us again, but with those who will appreciate the gifts that will supply their temporal and spiritual necessities. Those who give feasts for the purpose of helping those who have but little pleasure, for the purpose of bringing brightness into their dreary lives, for the purpose of relieving their poverty and distress, are acting unselfishly and in harmony with the instruction of Christ.[66]

All around us we see want and suffering. Families are in need of food; little ones are crying for bread. The houses of the poor lack proper furniture and bedding. Many live in mere hovels which are almost destitute of conveniences. The cry of the poor reaches to heaven. God sees; God hears.[67]

The work of gathering in the needy . . . is the very work which every church that believes the truth for this time should long since have been doing. We are to show the tender sympathy of the Samaritan in supplying physical necessities, feeding the hungry, bringing the poor that are cast out to our homes, gathering from God every day grace and strength that will enable us to reach to the very depths of human misery and help those who cannot possibly help themselves. In doing this work we have a favorable opportunity to set forth Christ the crucified One.[68]

CLOTHE THE NAKED

I was . . . naked, and ye clothed me.

Christ . . . says, It was I who was hungry and thirsty. It was I who was a stranger. It was I who was sick. It was I who was in prison. . . . While you crowded your wardrobe with rich apparel, I was destitute. While you pursued your pleasures, I languished in prison.

When you doled out the pittance of bread to the starving poor, when you gave those flimsy garments to shield them from the biting frost, did you remember that you were giving to the Lord of glory? All the days of your life I was near you in the person of these afflicted ones, but you did not seek Me. You would not enter into fellowship with Me.[69]

In the professed Christian world there is enough expended in extravagant display, for jewels and ornaments, to supply the wants of all the hungry and clothe the naked in our towns and cities; and yet these professed followers of the meek and lowly Jesus need not deprive themselves of suitable food or comfortable clothing. What will these church members say when confronted in the day of God by the worthy poor, the afflicted, the widows and fatherless, who have known pinching want for the meager necessities of life, while there was expended by these professed followers of Christ, for superfluous clothing, and needless ornaments expressly forbidden in the Word of God, enough to supply all their wants?[70]

In the fifty-eighth chapter of Isaiah the work that the people of God are to do in Christ's lines is clearly set forth. They are to break every yoke, they are to feed the hungry, to clothe the naked. . . . If they carry out the principles of the law of God in acts of mercy and love, they will represent the character of God to the world, and receive the richest blessings of Heaven.[71]

241

RELIEVE THE OPPRESSED

Learn to do well; seek judgment, relieve the oppressed, judge the fatherless, plead for the widow.

Jesus, the precious Saviour, the pattern man, was firm as a rock where truth and duty were concerned. And His life was a perfect illustration of true courtesy. Kindness and gentleness gave fragrance to His character. He had ever a kind look and a word of comfort and consolation for the needy and oppressed. . . .

When you meet those who are careworn and oppressed, who know not which way to turn to find relief, put your hearts into the work of helping them. It is not God's purpose that His children shall shut themselves up to themselves, taking no interest in the welfare of those less fortunate than themselves. Remember that for them as well as for you Christ has died. Conciliation and kindness will open the way for you to help them, to win their confidence, to inspire them with hope and courage.[72]

Let not men allow their business dealing to rob them of their humaneness. . . . Kind words, pleasant looks, a condescending demeanor, are of great value. There is a charm in the intercourse of men who are truly courteous. . . . How restoring and uplifting the influence of such dealing upon men who are poor and depressed, borne down to the earth by sickness and poverty! Shall we withhold from them the balm that such dealing brings?[73]

Every act of justice, mercy, and benevolence makes melody in heaven. The Father from His throne beholds those who do these acts of mercy, and numbers them with His most precious treasures. "And they shall be Mine, saith the Lord of hosts, in that day when I make up My jewels." Every merciful act to the needy, the suffering, is regarded as though done to Jesus. When you succor the poor, sympathize with the afflicted and oppressed, and befriend the orphan, you bring yourselves into a closer relationship to Jesus.[74]

BE EYES TO THE BLIND; FEET TO THE LAME

I was eyes to the blind, and feet was I to the lame.

Watch carefully, prayerfully, conscientiously, lest the mind become so engrossed with many important business transactions that true godliness is overlooked and love is quenched from the soul, notwithstanding the great and pitiful need of your being God's helping hand to the blind and to all others who are unfortunate. The most friendless demand the most attention. Use your time and strength in learning to be "fervent in spirit," to deal justly, and to love mercy, "serving the Lord." Remember that Christ says, "Inasmuch as ye have done it unto one of the least of these My brethren, ye have done it unto Me."[75]

God requires His people to be far more pitiful and considerate of the unfortunate than they are. . . . God requires that the same consideration which should be given to the widow and fatherless be given to the blind and to those suffering under the affliction of other physical infirmities. Disinterested benevolence is very rare in this age of the world. . . . It is strange that professed Christian men should disregard the plain, positive teachings of the Word of God and feel no compunction of conscience. God places upon them the responsibility of caring for the unfortunate, the blind, the lame, the widow, and the fatherless; but many make no effort to regard it.[76]

There is a great work to be done in our world, and as we approach the close of earth's history, it does not lessen in the least degree; but when the perfect love of God is in the heart, wonderful things will be done.[77]

A FATHER TO THE POOR

I was a father to the poor: and the cause which I knew not I searched out.

This was an evidence that Job had righteousness that was after Christ's order. Through Jesus men may possess a spirit of tender pity toward the needy and distressed. . . . He descended to the lowest humiliation and was obedient unto death, even the death of the cross, that He might exalt us to be joint heirs with Himself. The whole world was in need of that which Christ alone could give them. He did not withdraw Himself from those who called upon Him for help. He did not do as many now do, say, "I wish they would not trouble me with their affairs. I want to hoard up my means, to invest it in houses and lands." Jesus, the Majesty of heaven, turned from the splendor of His heavenly home, and in the gracious purpose of His heart He demonstrated the character of God to men throughout the world.[78]

Take away poverty, and we should have no way of understanding the mercy and love of God, no way of knowing the compassionate and sympathetic heavenly Father.[79]

First meet the temporal necessities of the needy and relieve their physical wants and sufferings, and you will then find an open avenue to the heart, where you may plant the good seeds of virtue and religion.[80]

Never does the gospel put on an aspect of greater loveliness than when it is brought to the most needy and destitute regions. . . . Truth from the Word of God enters the hovel of the peasant and lights up the rude cottages of the poor. . . . Rays from the Sun of Righteousness bring gladness to the sick and suffering. Angels of God are there. . . . Those who have been loathed and abandoned are raised through faith and pardon to the dignity of sons and daughters of God.[81]

ɛa ɛa ɛa

Christianity is the solace of the poor.[82]

REMEMBER ESPECIALLY NEEDY CHURCH MEMBERS

As we have therefore opportunity, let us do good unto all men, especially unto them who are of the household of faith.

In a special sense Christ has laid upon His church the duty of caring for the needy among its own members. He suffers His poor to be in the borders of every church. They are always to be among us, and He places upon the members of the church a personal responsibility to care for them. As the members of a true family care for one another, ministering to the sick, supporting the weak, teaching the ignorant, training the inexperienced, so is the "household of faith" to care for its needy and helpless ones.[83]

It is the duty of each church to make careful, judicious arrangements for the care of its poor and sick.[84]

Any neglect on the part of those who claim to be followers of Christ, a failure to relieve the necessities of a brother or a sister who is bearing the yoke of poverty and oppression, is registered in the books of heaven as shown to Christ in the person of His saints. What a reckoning the Lord will have with many, very many, who present the words of Christ to others but fail to manifest tender sympathy and regard for a brother in the faith who is less fortunate and successful than themselves.[85]

A true Christian is the poor man's friend. He deals with his perplexed and unfortunate brother as one would deal with a delicate, tender, sensitive plant. God wants His workers to move among the sick and suffering as messengers of His love and mercy. He is looking upon us, to see how we are treating one another, whether we are Christlike in our dealing with all, high or low, rich or poor, free or bond.[86]

There is no question in regard to the Lord's poor. They are to be helped in every case where it will be for their benefit.[87]

MY SPIRITUALITY STRENGTHENED AND HEALTH IMPROVES

Then shall thy light break forth as the morning, and thine health shall spring forth speedily: and thy righteousness shall go before thee; the glory of the Lord shall be thy rereward.

Is not this what we all crave? Oh, there is health and peace in doing the will of our Heavenly Father. "Thy righteousness shall go before thee; the glory of the Lord shall be thy rereward. Then shalt thou call, and the Lord shall answer; thou shalt cry, and he shall say, Here I am. If thou take away from the midst of thee the yoke, the putting forth of the finger, and speaking vanity; and if thou draw out thy soul to the hungry, and satisfy the afflicted soul; then shall thy light rise in obscurity, and thy darkness be as the noonday; and the Lord shall guide thee continually, and satisfy thy soul in drought, and make fat thy bones: and thou shalt be like a watered garden, and like a spring of water, whose waters fail not." [88]

If thou clothe the naked, and bring the poor . . . to thy house, and deal thy bread to the hungry, "then shall thy light break forth as the morning, and thine health shall spring forth speedily." Doing good is an excellent remedy for disease. [89]

The pleasure of doing good to others imparts a glow to the feelings which flashes through the nerves, quickens the circulation of the blood, and induces mental and physical health. [90]

Pure and undefiled religion is not a sentiment, but the doing of works of mercy and love. This religion is necessary to health and happiness. It enters the polluted soul temple, and with a scourge drives out the sinful intruders. Taking the throne, it consecrates all by its presence, illuminating the heart. . . . It opens the windows of the soul heavenward, letting in the sunshine of God's love. With it comes serenity and composure. Physical, mental, and moral strength increase, because the atmosphere of heaven, as a living, active agency, fills the soul. [91]

I MAY SHINE AS THE STARS FOR EVER AND EVER

And they that be wise shall shine as the brightness of the firmament; and they that turn many to righteousness as the stars for ever and ever.

He who has appointed "to every man his work," according to his ability, will never let the faithful performance of duty go unrewarded. Every act of loyalty and faith will be crowned with special tokens of God's favor and approbation. To every worker is given the promise: "He that goeth forth and weepeth, bearing precious seed, shall doubtless come again with rejoicing, bringing his sheaves with him."[92]

However short our service or humble our work, if in simple faith we follow Christ, we shall not be disappointed of the reward. That which even the greatest and wisest cannot earn, the weakest and most humble may receive. Heaven's golden gate opens not to the self-exalted. It is not lifted up to the proud in spirit. But the everlasting portals will open wide to the trembling touch of a little child. Blessed will be the recompense of grace to those who have wrought for God in the simplicity of faith and love.[93]

The brows of those who do this work will wear the crown of sacrifice. But they will receive their reward.[94]

To every worker for God this thought should be a stimulus and an encouragement. In this life our work for God often seems to be almost fruitless. Our efforts to do good may be earnest and persevering, yet we may not be permitted to witness their results. To us the effort may seem to be lost. But the Saviour assures us that our work is noted in heaven, and that the recompense cannot fail.[95]

Though his life may be hard and self-denying, . . . in the sight of heaven it will be a success, and he will be ranked as one of God's noblemen. "They that be wise shall shine as the brightest of the firmament; and they that turn many to righteousness as the stars for ever and ever."[96]

A SANCTIFIED LIFE

| September 1 | *Sanctification* | *1 Thess. 5:23* |

WHOLLY SANCTIFIED: BODY, SOUL, AND SPIRIT

The very God of peace sanctify you wholly; and I pray God your whole spirit and soul and body be preserved blameless unto the coming of our Lord Jesus Christ.

The sanctification set forth in the Sacred Scriptures has to do with the entire being—spirit, soul, and body. Here is the true idea of entire consecration. Paul prays that the church at Thessalonica may enjoy this great blessing. "The very God of peace sanctify you wholly; and I pray God your whole spirit and soul and body be preserved blameless unto the coming of our Lord Jesus Christ." 1 Thess. 5:23. . . .

True sanctification is an entire conformity to the will of God. Rebellious thoughts and feelings are overcome, and the voice of Jesus awakens a new life, which pervades the entire being. Those who are truly sanctified will not set up their own opinion as a standard of right and wrong. They are not bigoted or self-righteous; but they are jealous of self, ever fearing, lest a promise being left them, they should come short of complying with the conditions upon which the promises are based. . . .

Bible sanctification does not consist in strong emotion. Here is where many are led into error. They make feelings their criterion. When they feel elated or happy, they claim that they are sanctified. Happy feelings or the absence of joy is no evidence that a person is or is not sanctified. There is no such thing as instantaneous sanctification. True sanctification is a daily work, continuing as long as life shall last. Those who are battling with daily temptations, overcoming their own sinful tendencies, and seeking for holiness of heart and life make no boastful claims of holiness. They are hungering and thirsting for righteousness. Sin appears to them exceedingly sinful.[1]

⁂

Genuine sanctification . . . is nothing less than a daily dying to self and daily conformity to the will of God.[2]

A PRACTICAL EXAMPLE OF SANCTIFICATION

Husbands, love your wives, even as Christ also loved the church, and gave himself for it; that he might sanctify and cleanse it with the washing of water by the word, that he might present it to himself a glorious church, not having spot, or wrinkle, or any such thing; but that it should be holy and without blemish.

Here is Bible sanctification. It is not merely a show or outside work. It is sanctification received through the channel of truth. It is truth received in the heart and practically carried out in the life.

Jesus, considered as a man, was perfect, yet He grew in grace. Luke 2:52: "And Jesus increased in wisdom and stature, and in favour with God and man." Even the most perfect Christian may increase continually in the knowledge and love of God. . . .

"But grow in grace, and in the knowledge of our Lord and Saviour Jesus Christ. To Him be glory both now and forever. Amen."

Sanctification is not the work of a moment, an hour, or a day. It is a continual growth in grace. We know not one day how strong will be our conflict the next. Satan lives, and is active, and every day we need to cry earnestly to God for help and strength to resist him. As long as Satan reigns we shall have self to subdue, besetments to overcome, and there is no stopping place, there is no point to which we can come and say we have fully attained. . . .

The Christian life is constantly an onward march. Jesus sits as a refiner and purifier of His people; and when His image is perfectly reflected in them, they are perfect and holy, and prepared for translation.[3]

Every living Christian will advance daily in the divine life. As he advances toward perfection, he experiences a conversion to God every day; and this conversion is not completed until he attains to perfection of Christian character, a full preparation for the finishing touch of immortality.[4]

SANCTIFIED THROUGH OBEDIENCE

Sanctify yourselves therefore, and be ye holy: for I am the Lord your God. And ye shall keep my statutes, and do them: I am the Lord which sanctify you.

Adam and Eve dared to transgress the Lord's requirements, and the terrible result of their sin should be a warning to us not to follow their example of disobedience. . . . There is no genuine sanctification except through obedience to the truth. Those who love God with all the heart will love all His commandments also. The sanctified heart is in harmony with the precepts of God's law; for they are holy, just, and good.[5]

No one who truly loves and fears God will continue to transgress the law in any particular. When man transgresses he is under the condemnation of the law, and it becomes to him a yoke of bondage. Whatever his profession may be he is not justified, which means pardoned.

"The law of the Lord is perfect, converting the soul." Through obedience comes sanctification of body, soul, and spirit. This sanctification is a progressive work, and an advance from one stage of perfection to another.[6]

Let a living faith run like threads of gold through the performance of even the smallest duties. Then all the daily work will promote Christian growth. There will be a continual looking unto Jesus. Love for Him will give vital force to everything that is undertaken. Thus through the right use of our talents we may link ourselves by a golden chain to the higher world. This is true sanctification, for sanctification consists in the cheerful performance of daily duties in perfect obedience to the will of God.[7]

When it is in the heart to obey God, when efforts are put forth to this end, Jesus accepts this disposition and effort as man's best service, and He makes up for the deficiency with His own divine merit.[8]

THE FRUITS OF SANCTIFICATION

Rejoice in the Lord alway: and again I say, Rejoice.

Through Jesus the fallen sons of Adam become "sons of God." "Both He that sanctifieth and they who are sanctified are all of one: for which cause He is not ashamed to call them brethren." The Christian's life should be one of faith, of victory, and joy in God. "Whatsoever is born of God overcometh the world: and this is the victory that overcometh the world, even our faith." Truly spake God's servant Nehemiah, "The *joy* of the Lord is your strength." And Paul says: "Rejoice in the Lord alway: and again I say, Rejoice." "Rejoice evermore. Pray without ceasing. In everything give thanks: for this is the will of God in Christ Jesus concerning you."

Such are the fruits of Bible conversion and sanctification.[9]

His [the truly righteous man's] nature is so thoroughly imbued with love for God and his fellow men that he works the works of Christ with a willing heart.

All who come within the sphere of his influence perceive the beauty and fragrance of his Christian life, while he himself is unconscious of it, for it is in harmony with his habits and inclinations. He prays for divine light, and loves to walk in that light. It is his meat and drink to do the will of his heavenly Father. His life is hid with Christ in God; yet he does not boast of this, nor seem conscious of it. God smiles upon the humble and lowly ones who follow closely in the footsteps of the Master. Angels are attracted to them and love to linger about their path. They may be passed by as unworthy of notice by those who claim exalted attainments and who delight in making prominent their good works; but heavenly angels bend lovingly over them and are as a wall of fire round about them. . . . To man is granted the privilege of becoming an heir of God and a joint heir with Christ.[10]

CHRIST SANCTIFIED HIMSELF FOR ME

As thou hast sent me into the world, even so have I also sent them into the world. And for their sakes I sanctify myself, that they also might be sanctified through the truth.

Christ declared He sanctified Himself, that we also might be sanctified. He took upon Himself our nature, and became a faultless pattern for men. He made no mistake, that we also might become victors, and enter into His kingdom as overcomers. He prayed that we might be sanctified through the truth. What is truth? He declared, "Thy word is truth." His disciples were to be sanctified through obedience to the truth. He says, "Neither pray I for these alone, but for them also which shall believe on Me through their word." That prayer was for us; we have believed in the testimony of the disciples of Christ. He prays that His disciples may be one, even as He and the Father are one; and this unity of believers is to be as testimony to the world that He has sent us, and that we bear the evidence of His grace.

We are to be brought into a sacred nearness with the world's Redeemer. We are to be one with Christ as He is one with the Father. What a wonderful change the people of God experience in coming into unity with the Son of God! We are to have our tastes, inclinations, ambitions, and passions all subdued, and brought into harmony with the mind and spirit of Christ. This is the very work that the Lord is willing to do for those who believe in Him. Our life and deportment are to have a molding power in the world. The spirit of Christ is to have a controlling influence over the life of His followers, so that they will speak and act like Jesus. Christ says, "The glory which thou gavest Me I have given them." . . .

The grace of Christ is to work a wonderful transformation in the life and character of its receiver; and if we are truly the disciples of Christ, the world will see that divine power has done something for us; for while we are in the world, we shall not be of it.[11]

MEEK MEN AND WOMEN

He will beautify the meek with salvation.

The most precious fruit of sanctification is the grace of meekness. When this grace presides in the soul the disposition is molded by its influence. There is a continual waiting upon God and a submission of the will to His. The understanding grasps every divine truth and the will bows to every divine precept, without doubting or murmuring. True meekness softens and subdues the heart and gives the mind a fitness for the engrafted word. It brings the thoughts into obedience to Jesus Christ. It opens the heart to the Word of God, as Lydia's was opened. It places us with Mary, as learners at the feet of Jesus. "The meek will He guide in judgment, and the meek will He teach His way."

The language of the meek is never that of boasting. Like the child Samuel, they pray, "Speak, Lord, for Thy servant heareth." When Joshua was placed in the highest position of honor, as commander of Israel, he bade defiance to all the enemies of God. His heart was filled with noble thoughts of his great mission. Yet upon the intimation of a message from Heaven, he placed himself in the position of a little child to be directed. "What saith my Lord unto His servant?" was his response. . . .

Meekness in the school of Christ is one of the marked fruits of the Spirit. It is a grace wrought by the Holy Spirit as a sanctifier, and enables its possessor at all times to control a rash and impetuous temper. . . .

Meekness is the inward adorning, which God estimates as of great price. . . . He who garnished the heavens with the orbs of light has by the same Spirit promised that "He will beautify the meek with salvation." Angels of heaven will register as best adorned those who put on the Lord Jesus Christ and walk with Him in meekness and lowliness of mind.[12]

DANIEL'S LIFE OF TEMPERANCE

But Daniel purposed in his heart that he would not defile himself with the portion of the king's meat, nor with the wine which he drank: therefore he requested of the prince of the eunuchs that he might not defile himself.

The life of Daniel is an inspired illustration of what constitutes a sanctified character. It presents a lesson for all, and especially for the young. A strict compliance with the requirements of God is beneficial to the health of body and mind. In order to reach the highest standard of moral and intellectual attainments, it is necessary to seek wisdom and strength from God and to observe strict temperance in all the habits of life. In the experience of Daniel and his companions we have an instance of the triumph of principle over temptation to indulge the appetite. It shows us that through religious principle young men may triumph over the lusts of the flesh, and remain true to God's requirements, even though it cost them a great sacrifice.[13]

Daniel was a devoted servant of the Most High. His long life was filled with noble deeds of service for his Master. His purity of character and unwavering fidelity are equaled only by his humility of heart and his contrition before God. We repeat, The life of Daniel is an inspired illustration of true sanctification.[14]

Wherever they may be, those who are truly sanctified will elevate the moral standards by preserving correct physical habits and, like Daniel, presenting to others an example of temperance and self-denial. . . .

With what care should Christians regulate their habits, that they may preserve the full vigor of every faculty to give to the service of Christit.[15]

❧ ❧ ❧

He who cherishes the light which God has given him upon health reform has an important aid in the work of becoming sanctified through the truth and fitted for immortality.[16]

ENOCH'S LIFE OF HOLINESS

Enoch walked with God . . . three hundred years.

There was a line of holy men who, elevated and ennobled by communion with God, lived as in the companionship of Heaven. They were men of massive intellect, of wonderful attainments. They had a great and holy mission—to develop a character of righteousness, to teach a lesson of godliness, not only to the men of their time, but for future generations. . . .

Of Enoch it is written that he lived sixty-five years, and begat a son. After that he walked with God three hundred years. During these earlier years Enoch had loved and feared God and had kept His commandments. . . . From the lips of Adam he had learned the dark story of the fall and the cheering one of God's grace as seen in the promise, and he relied upon the Redeemer to come. But after the birth of his first son Enoch reached a higher experience; he was drawn into a closer relationship with God. He realized more fully his own obligations and responsibility as a son of God. And as he saw the child's love for its father, its simple trust in his protection; as he felt the deep, yearning tenderness of his own heart for that first-born son, he learned a precious lesson of the wonderful love of God to men in the gift of His Son and the confidence which the children of God may repose in their heavenly Father. The infinite, unfathomable love of God through Christ became the subject of his meditations day and night, and with all the fervor of his soul he sought to reveal that love to the people among whom he dwelt.

Enoch's walk with God was not in a trance or a vision, but in all the duties of his daily life. . . . In the family and in his intercourse with men, as a husband and father, a friend, a citizen, he was the steadfast, unwavering servant of the Lord.[17]

STEADFAST INTEGRITY OF THE THREE HEBREWS

Nebuchadnezzar . . . said unto his counsellors, Did not we cast three men bound into the midst of the fire? They answered and said . . . , True, O king. He answered and said, Lo, I see four men loose, walking in the midst of the fire, and they have no hurt; and the form of the fourth is like the Son of God.

These three Hebrews possessed genuine sanctification. True Christian principle will not stop to weigh consequences. It does not ask, What will people think of me if I do this? or how will it affect my worldly prospects if I do that? With the most intense longing the children of God desire to know what He would have them do, that their works may glorify Him. The Lord has made ample provision that the hearts and lives of all His followers may be controlled by divine grace, that they may be as burning and shining lights in the world.

These faithful Hebrews possessed great natural ability; they had enjoyed the highest intellectual culture, and now occupied a position of honor; but all this did not lead them to forget God. Their powers were yielded to the sanctifying influence of divine grace. By their steadfast integrity they showed forth the praises of Him who had called them out of darkness into His marvelous light. In their wonderful deliverance were displayed, before that vast assembly, the power and majesty of God. Jesus placed Himself by their side in the fiery furnace, and by the glory of His presence convinced the proud king of Babylon that it could be no other than the Son of God. The light of Heaven had been shining forth from Daniel and his companions, until all their associates understood the faith which ennobled their lives and beautified their characters. . . .

What a lesson is here given to the fainthearted, the vacillating, the cowardly in the cause of God! . . . These faithful, steadfast characters exemplify sanctification, while they have no thought of claiming the high honor.[18]

❧ ❧ ❧

Every Christian may enjoy the blessing of sanctification.[19]

JOHN'S LOVE AND LOYALTY

And we have known and believed the love that God hath to us. God is love; and he that dwelleth in love dwelleth in God, and God in him.

The confiding love and unselfish devotion manifested in the life and character of John present lessons of untold value to the Christian church. Some may present him as possessing this love independent of divine grace; but John had, by nature, serious defects of character: he was proud and ambitious and quick to resent slight and injury. . . .

John desired to become like Jesus, and under the transforming influence of the love of Christ, he became meek and lowly of heart. Self was hid in Jesus. He was closely united to the Living Vine, and thus became a partaker of the divine nature. Such will ever be the result of communion with Christ. This is true sanctification.

There may be marked defects in the character of an individual, yet when he becomes a true disciple of Jesus, the power of divine grace makes him a new creature. Christ's love transforms, sanctifies him. But when persons profess to be Christians, and their religion does not make them better men and better women in all the relations of life—living representatives of Christ in disposition and character—they are none of His.[20]

John enjoyed the blessing of true sanctification. But mark, the apostle does not claim to be sinless; he is seeking perfection by walking in the light of God's countenance. He testifies that the man who professes to know God, and yet breaks the divine law, gives the lie to his profession. . . . While we are to love the souls for whom Christ died, and labor for their salvation, we should not make a compromise with sin. We are not to unite with the rebellious, and call this charity. God requires His people in this age of the world to stand, as did John in his time, unflinchingly for the right, in opposition to soul-destroying errors.[21]

LIVES OF JOHN AND JUDAS CONTRASTED

The world passeth away, and the lust thereof: but he that doeth the will of God abideth for ever.

John and his fellow disciples were in a school in which Christ was teacher. . . . John treasured every lesson and constantly sought to bring his life into harmony with the Divine Pattern. The lessons of Jesus, setting forth meekness, humility, and love as essential to growth in grace and a fitness for his work, were of the highest value to John. . . .

An instructive lesson may be drawn from the striking contrast between the character of John and that of Judas. John was a living illustration of sanctification. On the other hand, Judas possessed a form of godliness, while his character was more satanic than divine. He professed to be a disciple of Christ, but in words and in works denied Him.

Judas had the same precious opportunities as had John to study and to imitate the Pattern. He listened to the lessons of Christ, and his character might have been transformed by divine grace. But while John was earnestly warring against his own faults and seeking to assimilate to Christ, Judas was violating his conscience, yielding to temptation, and fastening upon himself habits of dishonesty that would transform him into the image of Satan.

These two disciples represent the Christian world. All profess to be Christ's followers; but while one class walk in humility and meekness, learning of Jesus, the other show that they are not doers of the Word, but hearers only. One class are sanctified through the truth; the other know nothing of the transforming power of divine grace. The former are daily dying to self, and are overcoming sin. The latter are indulging their own lusts, and becoming the servants of Satan.[22]

THE LORD SANCTIFIES SABBATHKEEPERS

Moreover also I gave them my sabbaths, to be a sign between me and them, that they might know that I am the Lord that sanctify them.

The Lord's day mentioned by John was the Sabbath, the day on which Jehovah rested after the great work of creation, and which He blessed and sanctified because He had rested upon it. The Sabbath was as sacredly observed by John upon the Isle of Patmos as when he was among the people, preaching upon that day. By the barren rocks surrounding him, John was reminded of rocky Horeb, and how, when God spoke His law to the people there, He said, "Remember the sabbath day, to keep it holy."

The Son of God spoke to Moses from the mountaintop. God made the rocks His sanctuary. His temple was the everlasting hills. The Divine Legislator descended upon the rocky mountain to speak His law in the hearing of all the people, that they might be impressed by the grand and awful exhibition of His power and glory, and fear to transgress His commandments. . . . The law of Jehovah was unchangeable, and the tablets upon which He wrote that law were solid rock, signifying the immutability of His precepts. Rocky Horeb became a sacred spot to all who loved and revered the law of God.

While John was contemplating the scenes of Horeb, the Spirit of Him who sanctified the seventh day, came upon him. He contemplated the sin of Adam in transgressing the divine law, and the fearful results of that transgression. The infinite love of God, in giving His Son to redeem a lost race, seemed too great for language to express. As he presents it in his epistle, he calls upon the church and the world to behold it.[23]

All who regard the Sabbath as a sign between them and God . . . will represent the principles of His government. They will bring into daily practice the laws of His kingdom. Daily it will be their prayer that the sanctification of the Sabbath may rest upon them.[24]

CHRIST IS THE TRUTH

Jesus saith unto him, I am the way, the truth, and the life: no man cometh unto the Father, but by me.

When Christ bowed on the banks of Jordan, after His baptism, the heavens were opened, and the Spirit descended in the form of a dove, like burnished gold, and encircled Him with its glory; and the voice of God from the highest heaven was heard, saying, "This is My beloved Son, in whom I am well pleased." The prayer of Christ in man's behalf opened the gates of heaven, and the Father had responded, accepting the petition for the fallen race. Jesus prayed as our substitute and surety, and now the human family may find access to the Father through the merits of His well-beloved Son. This earth, because of transgression, had been struck off from the continent of heaven. Communication had ceased between man and his Maker; but the way has been opened so that he may return to the Father's house. Jesus is "the way, the truth, and the life." The gate of heaven has been left ajar, and the radiance from the throne of God shines into the hearts of those who love Him, even though they dwell in this sin-cursed earth. The light that encircled the divine Son of God will fall upon the pathway of all who follow in His footsteps. There is no reason for discouragement. The promises of God are sure and steadfast.

"Come out from among them, and be ye separate, saith the Lord and touch not the unclean thing; and I will receive you, and will be a Father unto you, and ye shall be My sons and daughters, saith the Lord Almighty." Do you desire to become the sons and daughters of the Most High? . . . You may come unto the Father in the name of His Son, and, no matter how broken and feeble your petitions, Jesus will present them before the throne of infinite power, and the light that was shed upon Him will be reflected upon you. You will be "accepted in the Beloved." [25]

TRUTH SANCTIFIES

Sanctify them through thy truth: thy word is truth.

The truth of God is to sanctify the soul. "A new heart will I give you, and a new spirit will I put within you." The sanctifying power of truth is to abide in the soul and be carried with us to our business, there to apply its continual tests to every transaction of life, especially to our dealings with our fellow men. It is to abide in our households, having a subduing power upon the life and character of all its inmates.[26]

I must ever urge upon those who profess to believe the truth the necessity of practicing the truth. This means sanctification, and sanctification means the culture and training of every capability for the Lord's service.[27]

Teach your children to love the truth because it is the truth and because they are to be sanctified through the truth and fitted to stand in the grand review that shall erelong determine whether they are qualified to enter into higher work, and become members of the royal family, children of the heavenly King.[28]

The truth, the precious truth of God's Word, will have a sanctifying effect upon the heart and character. There is work to be done for ourselves and for our children. The natural heart is full of hatred to the truth, as it is to Jesus. Unless parents shall make it the first business of their lives to guide their children's feet into the path of righteousness from their earliest years, the wrong path will be chosen before the right.[29]

The work of sanctification begins in the home. Those who are Christians in the home will be Christians in the church and in the world.[30]

TRUTH ELEVATES

And now, brethren, I commend you to God, and to the word of his grace, which is able to build you up, and to give you an inheritance among all them which are sanctified.

The precious faith inspired of God imparts strength and nobility of character. As His goodness, His mercy, and His love are dwelt upon, clearer and still clearer will be the perception of truth; higher, holier the desire for purity of heart and clearness of thought. The soul dwelling in the atmosphere of holy thought is transformed by intercourse with God through the study of His Word. Truth is so large, so far reaching, so deep, so broad, that self is lost sight of. The heart is softened and subdued into humility, kindness, and love.

The natural powers are enlarged because of holy obedience. From the study of the words of life, students may come forth with minds expanded, elevated, ennobled. . . . Being pure-minded, they will become strong-minded. Every intellectual faculty will be quickened. They may so educate and discipline themselves that all within the sphere of their influence may see what man can be, and what he can do, when connected with the God of wisdom and power.[31]

The truth of God never degrades the receiver. The influence of the truth upon him who accepts it will tend constantly to his elevation. . . .

Those who are sanctified through the truth are living recommendations of its power and representatives of their risen Lord. The religion of Christ will refine the taste, sanctify the judgment, elevate, purify, and ennoble the soul, making the Christian more and more fit for the society of the heavenly angels.[32]

God bids us fill our minds with great thoughts, pure thoughts. . . . No one with a spirit to appreciate its teachings can read a single passage from the Bible without gaining from it some helpful thought.[33]

TRUTH PURIFIES

Seeing ye have purified your souls in obeying the truth through the Spirit unto unfeigned love of the brethren, see that ye love one another with a pure heart fervently.

The lily on the lake strikes its roots down deep beneath the surface of rubbish and slime, and through its porous stem draws those properties that will aid its development and bring to light its spotless blossom to repose in purity on the bosom of the lake.

It refuses all that would tarnish and mar its spotless beauty. . . . Let the youth be found in association with those who fear and love God; for these noble, firm characters are represented by the lily that opens its pure blossom on the bosom of the lake. They refuse to be molded by the influences that would demoralize, and gather to themselves only that which will aid the development of a pure and noble character. They are seeking to be conformed to the divine model.[34]

In the estimation of God a pure heart is more precious than the gold of Ophir. A pure heart is the temple where God dwells, the sanctuary where Christ takes up His abode. A pure heart is above everything that is cheap or low; it is a shining light, a treasure house from which come uplifting, sanctified words. It is a place where the imagery of God is recognized, and where the highest delight is to behold His image. It is a heart that finds its whole and only pleasure and satisfaction in God, and whose thoughts and intents and purposes are alive with godliness. Such a heart is a sacred place; it is a treasury of all virtue. . . .

The very thoughts of those whose hearts are pure are brought into captivity to Christ. They are occupied with thinking how they can best glorify God.[35]

It will then be as natural for us to seek purity and holiness . . . as it is for the angels of glory to execute the mission of love assigned to them.[36]

TRUTH ENLIGHTENS

The eyes of your understanding being enlightened; that ye may know what is the hope of his calling, and what the riches of the glory of his inheritance in the saints.

In a knowledge of God, all true knowledge and real development have their source. Wherever we turn, in the physical, the mental, or the spiritual realm; in whatever we behold, apart from the blight of sin, this knowledge is revealed. Whatever line of investigation we pursue with a sincere purpose to arrive at truth, we are brought in touch with the unseen, mighty Intelligence that is working in and through all. The mind of man is brought into communion with the mind of God, the finite with the Infinite. The effect of such communion on body and mind and soul is beyond estimate.

In this communion is found the highest education. It is God's own method of development. "Acquaint now thyself with Him," is His message to mankind.[37]

As he studies and meditates upon the themes into which "the angels desire to look," he may have their companionship. . . . He may dwell in this world in the atmosphere of heaven, imparting to earth's sorrowing and tempted ones thoughts of hope and longings for holiness; himself coming closer and still closer into fellowship with the Unseen; like him of old who walked with God, drawing nearer and nearer the threshold of the eternal world, until the portals shall open, and he shall enter there. He will find himself no stranger. The voices that will greet him are the voices of the holy ones, who, unseen, were on earth his companions—voices that here he learned to distinguish and to love. He who through the word of God has lived in fellowship with Heaven will find himself at home in heaven's companionship.[38]

Guided by "the Spirit of truth," he will be led into all truth. . . . He will be precious in the sight of heaven.[39]

264

TRUTH TRANSFORMS

Lord, who shall abide in thy tabernacle? who shall dwell in thy holy hill? He that walketh uprightly, and worketh righteousness, and speaketh the truth in his heart.

We must present the principles of truth, and let them work upon the hearts of the people. We may pick the leaves from a tree as often as we please, but this will not cause the tree to die; the next season the leaves will come out again as thick as before. But strike the ax at the root of the tree, and not only will the leaves fall off of themselves, but the tree will die. Those who accept the truth, in the love of it, will die to the world, and will become meek and lowly in heart like their divine Lord. Just as soon as the heart is right, the dress, the conversation, the life, will be in harmony with the Word of God. We all need to humble ourselves under the mighty hand of God. May He help us to plant our feet firmly upon the platform of eternal truth.[40]

The transforming influence of truth sanctifies the soul. He loves the commandments of God. His fear and condemnation are one. The love of Christ, expressed in His great sacrifice to save man, has broken every barrier down. The love of God flows into the soul, and gratitude springs up in the heart that was as cold as a stone. Christ crucified, Christ our righteousness, wins the heart and brings it to repentance. This theme is so simple that children can grasp it, the wise and learned are charmed with it, while they behold it in its depths of wisdom, love, and power which they can never fathom. We want to present this precious truth to the people who are bound in sin. Let all see that Christ was slain for their transgressions, that He desires to save them.[41]

Let us remember that there is need of sanctified pens and sanctified tongues. When we as a people live as God would be pleased to have us live, we shall see the deep movings of His Spirit. Much will then be done for those who have never heard the truth.[42]

We should be pervaded with a deep, abiding sense of the value, sanctity, and the authority of the truth.[43]

TRUTH WILL TRIUMPH GLORIOUSLY

Open ye the gates, that the righteous nation which keepeth the truth may enter in.

The truth of God must be enshrined in the heart, and we must be determined to fight the battles of the Lord, if we would come off conquerors with the final triumph of the truth; for the truth will triumph gloriously. . . . If you are seeking to be a blessing to others, God will bless you. We should bring all the good possible into our lives, that we may glorify God and be a blessing to humanity.[44]

The church is God's agency for the proclamation of truth, empowered by Him to do a special work; and if she is loyal to Him, obedient to all His commandments, there will dwell within her the excellency of divine grace. If she will be true to her allegiance, if she will honor the Lord God of Israel, there is no power that can stand against her.

Zeal for God and His cause moved the disciples to bear witness to the gospel with mighty power. Should not a like zeal fire our hearts with a determination to tell the story of redeeming love, of Christ and Him crucified? It is the privilege of every Christian not only to look for but to hasten the coming of the Saviour.

If the church will put on the robe of Christ's righteousness, withdrawing from all allegiance with the world, there is before her the dawn of a bright and glorious day. God's promise to her will stand fast forever. He will make her an eternal excellency, a joy of many generations. Truth, passing by those who despise and reject it, will triumph. Although at times apparently retarded, its progress has never been checked. When the message of God meets with opposition, He gives it additional force, that it may exert greater influence. Endowed with divine energy, it will cut its way through the strongest barriers, and triumph over every obstacle.[45]

THE WORK OF A LIFETIME

Having therefore these promises, dearly beloved, let us cleanse ourselves from all filthiness of the flesh and spirit, perfecting holiness in the fear of God.

The formation of a right character is the work of a lifetime, and is the outgrowth of prayerful meditation united with a grand purpose. The excellence of character that you possess must be the result of your own effort. Friends may encourage you, but they cannot do the work for you. Wishing, sighing, dreaming, will never make you great or good. You must climb.[46]

The conversation we have by the fireside, the books we read, the business we transact, are all agents in forming our characters, and day by day decide our eternal destiny.[47]

Mental ability and genius are not character, for these are often possessed by those who have the very opposite of a good character. Reputation is not character. True character is a quality of the soul, revealing itself in the conduct.[48]

A character formed according to the divine likeness is the only treasure that we can take from this world to the next. Those who are under the instruction of Christ in this world will take every divine attainment with them to the heavenly mansions. And in heaven we are continually to improve.[49]

A good character is a capital of more value than gold or silver. It is unaffected by panics or failures, and in that day when earthly possessions shall be swept away, it will bring rich returns. Integrity, firmness, and perseverance are qualities that all should seek earnestly to cultivate; for they clothe the possessor with a power which is irresistible—a power which makes him strong to do good, strong to resist evil, strong to bear adversity.[50]

CHARACTERS POLISHED AFTER THE SIMILITUDE OF A PALACE

That our sons may be as plants grown up in their youth; that our daughters may be as corner stones, polished after the similitude of a palace.

If the youth rightly appreciate this important matter of character-building, they will see the necessity of doing their work so that it will stand the test of investigation before God. The humblest and weakest, by persevering effort in resisting temptation and seeking wisdom from above, may reach heights that now seem impossible. These attainments cannot come without a determined purpose to be faithful in the fulfillment of little duties. It requires constant watchfulness that crooked traits shall not be left to strengthen. The young may have moral power; for Jesus came into the world that He might be our example, and give to all youth and those of every age divine help.[51]

This world is God's workshop, and every stone that can be used in the heavenly temple must be hewed and polished until it is a tried and precious stone, fitted for its place in the Lord's building. But if we refuse to be trained and disciplined, we shall be as stones that will not be hewed and polished, and that are cast aside at last as useless.[52]

It may be that much work needs to be done . . . , that you are a rough stone, which must be squared and polished before it can fill a place in God's temple. You need not be surprised if with hammer and chisel God cuts away the sharp corners of your character until you are prepared to fill the place He has for you. No human being can accomplish this work. Only by God can it be done. And be assured that He will not strike one useless blow. His every blow is struck in love, for your eternal happiness. He knows your infirmities and works to restore, not to destroy.[53]

A character polished after the similitude of a palace . . . may shine in the courts of the Lord forever.[54]

RIGHTEOUS SHALL LIVE FOREVER

For the moth shall eat them up like a garment, and the worm shall eat them like wool: but my righteousness shall be for ever, and my salvation from generation to generation.

I found, among the articles of clothing I needed, some woolen goods which at first appeared all right, but when brought to the light and shaken thoroughly, revealed the destructive work of moths. Had we not made close inspection, we should not have discovered their depredations. The moth is so small a creature as to be scarcely observable; but the traces of its existence are apparent, and the destruction that it makes with fur and woolen goods shows that it is a practical worker, although out of sight and unsuspected.

Thinking of the secret but destructive work of these moths reminded us of some human beings we had known. How often our hearts have been pained by some sudden revelation in the outward actions of those for whom we had hoped better things, bringing to light their true character, that had heretofore been hidden from the sight of all! When held up before the light of God's Word, the character is found to be like the moth-eaten garment, which, when shaken out and examined, reveals the destructive work that has been going on secretly for years. . . .

It took time for the moth to do its work of destruction so quietly in the dark; and it takes time, little by little, for a child or youth to be easy and happy and feel secure in a course of prevarication, a course of sin hidden from human eyes. Any one act, either good or evil, does not form the character, but thoughts and feelings indulged prepare the way for acts and deeds of the same kind. . . . Be careful not to let your feet take the first step in any evil way. If you will lay the foundation for your character in a pure, virtuous life, seeking help and strength from God, your character will not be like the moth-eaten garment, but it will be firm and solid.[55]

269

GOD LOVES MOST A BEAUTIFUL CHARACTER

Let the beauty of the Lord our God be upon us.

God is a lover of the beautiful, but that which He most loves is a beautiful character. . . . It is beauty of character that shall not perish, but last through the ceaseless ages of eternity.[56]

The great Master-Artist has taken thought for the lilies, making them so beautiful that they outshine the glory of Solomon. How much more does He care for man, who is the image and glory of God. He longs to see His children reveal a character after His similitude. As the sunbeam imparts to the flowers their varied and delicate tints, so does God impart to the soul the beauty of His own character.

All who choose Christ's kingdom of love and righteousness and peace, making its interest paramount to all other, are linked to the world above, and every blessing needed for this life is theirs. In the book of God's providence, the volume of life, we are each given a page. That page contains every particular of our history, even the hairs of the head are numbered. God's children are never absent from His mind.[57]

Worldly display, however imposing, is of no value in God's sight. Above the seen and temporal He values the unseen and eternal. The former is of worth only as it expresses the latter. The choicest productions of art possess no beauty that can compare with the beauty of character, which is the fruit of the Holy Spirit's working in the soul. . . .

Christ came to the earth and stood before the children of men with the hoarded love of eternity, and this is the treasure that, through our connection with Him, we are to receive, to reveal, and to impart. . . .

We are to be distinguished from the world because God has placed His seal upon us, because He manifests in us His own character of love.[58]

270

PERFECTION, THE GOAL TO BE GAINED

Be ye therefore perfect, even as your Father which is in heaven is perfect.

God will accept only those who are determined to aim high. He places every human agent under obligation to do his best. Moral perfection is required of all. Never should we lower the standard of righteousness in order to accommodate inherited and cultivated tendencies to wrongdoing. We need to understand that imperfection of character is sin. All righteous attributes of character dwell in God as a perfect, harmonious whole, and every one who receives Christ as a personal Saviour is privileged to possess these attributes.

And those who would be workers together with God must strive for perfection of every organ of the body and quality of the mind. True education is the preparation of the physical, mental, and moral powers for the performance of every duty; it is the training of body, mind, and soul for divine service. This is the education that will endure unto eternal life. . . .

But Christ has given us no assurance that to attain perfection of character is an easy matter. A noble, all-round character is not inherited. It does not come to us by accident. A noble character is earned by individual effort through the merits and grace of Christ. God gives the talents, the powers of the mind; we form the character. It is formed by hard, stern battles with self. Conflict after conflict must be waged against hereditary tendencies. We shall have to criticize ourselves closely, and allow not one unfavorable trait to remain uncorrected.

Let no one say, I cannot remedy my defects of character. . . . The real difficulty arises from the corruption of an unsanctified heart and unwillingness to submit to the control of God.[59]

Subjection to the will of Christ means restoration to perfect manhood.[60]

CLOTHED IN THE ROBE OF RIGHTEOUSNESS

And to her was granted that she should be arrayed in fine linen,
clean and white: for the fine linen is the righteousness of saints.

By the wedding garment . . . is represented the pure, spotless
character which Christ's true followers will possess. To the church it
is given "that she should be arrayed in fine linen, clean and white,"
"not having spot, or wrinkle, or any such thing." The fine linen, says
the Scripture, "is the righteousness of saints." It is the righteousness
of Christ, His own unblemished character, that through faith is imparted to all who receive Him as their personal Saviour. . . .

This robe, woven in the loom of heaven, has in it not one thread
of human devising. Christ in His humanity wrought out a perfect
character, and this character He offers to impart to us. . . .

When we submit ourselves to Christ, the heart is united with
His heart, the will is merged in His will, the mind becomes one
with His mind, the thoughts are brought into captivity to Him; we
live His life. This is what it means to be clothed with the garment
of His righteousness. . . .

Righteousness is rightdoing, and it is by their deeds that all will
be judged. Our characters are revealed by what we do.[61]

Let the youth and the little children be taught to choose for
themselves that royal robe woven in heaven's loom—the "fine linen,
clean and white," which all the holy ones of earth will wear. This
robe, Christ's own spotless character, is freely offered to every
human being. But all who receive it will receive and wear it here.[62]

Clothed in the glorious apparel of Christ's righteousness, they
have a place at the King's feast. They have a right to join the blood-
washed throng.[63]

272

SAINTS SHALL POSSESS THE KINGDOM

The saints of the most High shall take the kingdom, and possess the kingdom for ever, even for ever and ever.

God takes none to heaven but those who are first made saints in this world through the grace of Christ, those in whom He can see Christ exemplified. When the love of Christ is an abiding principle in the soul, we shall realize that we are hid with Christ in God. . . .

These only who, by prayer and watchfulness and love, work the works of Christ, can God rejoice over with singing. The more fully the Lord sees the character of His beloved Son revealed in His people, the greater is His satisfaction and delight in them. God Himself and the heavenly angels rejoice over them with singing. The believing sinner is pronounced innocent, while the guilt is placed on Christ. The righteousness of Christ is placed on the debtor's account, and against his name on the balance sheet is written: Pardoned. Eternal Life. . . .

"Ye are God's husbandry." As one takes pleasure in the cultivation of a garden, so God takes pleasure in His believing sons and daughters. A garden demands constant labor. The weeds must be removed; new plants must be set out; branches that are making too rapid development must be pruned back. So the Lord works for His garden, so He tends His plants. He cannot take pleasure in any development that does not reveal the graces of the character of Christ. The blood of Christ has made men and women God's precious charge. . . . Some plants are so feeble that they have hardly any life, and for these the Lord has a special care.[64]

❧ ❧ ❧

Only those will enter heaven who in probationary time have formed a character that breathes a heavenly influence. The saint in heaven must first be a saint upon earth.[65]

PARTAKERS THROUGH GOD'S PROMISES

Whereby are given unto us exceeding great and precious promises: that by these ye might be partakers of the divine nature, having escaped the corruption that is in the world through lust.

Every promise that is in God's book holds out to us the encouragement that we may be partakers of the divine nature. This is the possibility—to rely upon God, to believe His Word, to work His works, and this we can do when we lay hold of the divinity of Christ. This possibility is worth more to us than all the riches in the world. There is nothing on earth that can compare with it. As we lay hold of the power thus placed within our reach, we receive a hope so strong that we can rely wholly upon God's promise; and laying hold of the possibilities there are in Christ, we become the sons and daughters of God. . . .

He who truly believes in Christ is made partaker of the divine nature, and has power that he can appropriate under every temptation. He will not fall under temptation or be left to defeat. In time of trial he will claim the promises, and by these escape the corruptions that are in the world through lust. . . .

To make us partakers of the divine nature, heaven gave its most costly treasure. The Son of God laid aside His royal robe and kingly crown and came to our earth as a little child. He pledged Himself to live from infancy to manhood a perfect life. He engaged to stand in a fallen world as the representative of the Father. And He would die in behalf of a lost race. What a work was this! . . . I hardly know how to present these points; they are so wonderful, wonderful. . . .

By His life of sacrifice and death of shame He has made it possible for us to take hold of His divinity, and to escape the corruption that is in the world through lust. . . . If you are partakers of the divine nature, you will day by day be obtaining a fitting for that life that measures with the life of God. Day by day you will purify your trust in Jesus and follow His example and grow into His likeness until you shall stand before Him perfected.[66]

CHRIST DWELLS IN ME

Jesus said unto them, Verily, verily, I say unto you, Except ye eat the flesh of the Son of man, and drink his blood, ye have no life in you. Whoso eateth my flesh, and drinketh my blood, hath eternal life; and I will raise him up at the last day. For my flesh is meat indeed, and my blood is drink indeed. He that eateth my flesh, and drinketh my blood, dwelleth in me, and I in him.

To eat the flesh and drink the blood of Christ is to receive Him as a personal Saviour, believing that He forgives our sins and that we are complete in Him. It is by beholding His love, by dwelling upon it, by drinking it in, that we are to become partakers of His nature. What food is to the body, Christ must be to the soul. Food cannot benefit us unless we eat it, unless it becomes a part of our being. So Christ is of no value to us if we do not know Him as a personal Saviour. A theoretical knowledge will do us no good. We must feed upon Him, receive Him into the heart, so that His life becomes our life. His love, His grace, must be assimilated.[67]

It is not enough even that we believe on Christ for the forgiveness of sin; we must by faith be constantly receiving spiritual strength and nourishment from Him through His word. . . . "The words that I speak unto you, they are spirit, and they are life." Jesus accepted His Father's law, wrought out its principles in His life, manifested its spirit, and showed its beneficent power in the heart. . . . The followers of Christ must be partakers of His experience. They must receive and assimilate the Word of God so that it shall become the motive power of life and action. By the power of Christ they must be changed into His likeness, and reflect the divine attributes.[68]

It is by receiving the life for us poured out on Calvary's cross that we can live the life of holiness. And this life we receive by receiving His word, by doing those things which He has commanded. Thus we become one with Him.[69]

DWELL TOGETHER IN UNITY

Behold, how good and how pleasant it is for brethren to dwell together in unity!

Christian unity is a mighty agency. It tells in a powerful manner that those who possess it are children of God. It has an irresistible influence upon the world, showing that man in his humanity may be a partaker of the divine nature, having escaped the corruption that is in the world through lust. We are to be one with our fellow men and with Christ, and in Christ one with God. Then of us can be spoken the words, "Ye are complete in Him."

In the plan of redemption a place is allotted to every soul. To each man is given his work. No one can be a member of Christ's body and yet be inactive. . . . The work of God's people may and will be varied, but one Spirit is the mover in it all. All the work done for the Master is to be connected with the great whole. The workers are to labor together in concert, each one controlled by divine power, putting forth undivided effort to draw those around them to Christ. All must move like parts of a well-adjusted machinery, each part dependent on the other part, yet standing distinct in action. And each one is to take the place assigned him and do the work appointed him. God calls upon the members of His church to receive the Holy Spirit, to come together in unity and brotherly sympathy, to bind their interests together in love.

Nothing so manifestly weakens a church as disunion and strife. Nothing so wars against Christ and the truth as this spirit. . . .

He in whose heart Christ abides recognizes Christ abiding in the heart of his brother. Christ never wars against Christ. Christ never exerts an influence against Christ. Christians are to do their work, whatever it may be, in the unity of the Spirit, for the perfecting of the whole body.[70]

STRENGTH FROM ABOVE

But they that wait upon the Lord shall renew their strength; they shall mount up with wings as eagles; they shall run, and not be weary; and they shall walk, and not faint.

Wonderful are the possibilities before the youth to grasp the assurances of God's Word. Scarcely can the human mind comprehend the spiritual attainments which can be reached by them as they become partakers of the divine nature. Daily correcting mistakes and gaining victories, they grow into wise, strong men and women in Christ.[71]

He who has become a partaker of the divine nature knows that his citizenship is above. He catches the inspiration from the Spirit of Christ. His soul is hid with Christ in God. Such a man Satan can no longer employ as his instrumentality to insinuate himself into the very sanctuary of God, to defile the temple of God. He gains victories at every step. He is filled with ennobling thoughts. He regards every human being as precious, because Christ has died for every soul.

"They that wait upon the Lord shall renew their strength; they shall mount up with wings as eagles." The man who waits upon the Lord is strong in his strength, strong enough to hold firm under great pressure. Yet he is easy to be entreated on the side of mercy and compassion, which is the side of Christ. The soul that is submissive to God is ready to do the will of God; he diligently and humbly seeks to know that will. He accepts discipline, and is afraid to walk according to his own finite judgment. He communes with God, and his conversation is in heaven.[72]

Linked to the Infinite One, man is made partaker of the divine nature. Upon him the shafts of evil have no effect; for he is clothed with the panoply of Christ's righteousness.[73]

A REVERENT LIFE

RESPECT FOR PARENTS

Honour thy father and thy mother: that thy days may be long upon the land which the Lord thy God giveth thee.

The best way to educate children to respect their father and mother is to give them the opportunity of seeing the father offering kindly attentions to the mother, and the mother rendering respect and reverence to the father. It is by beholding love in their parents that children are led to obey the fifth commandment. . . .

Our obligation to our parents never ceases. Our love for them, and theirs for us, is not measured by years or distance, and our responsibility can never be set aside. When the nations are gathered before the judgment seat of Christ, but two classes will be represented—those who have identified their interest with Christ and suffering humanity; those who have ignored their God-given obligations, done injury to their fellow men, and dishonor to God. Their eternal destiny will be decided on the ground of what they did and what they did not do to Christ in the person of His saints.[1]

Parents are entitled to a degree of love and respect which is due to no other person. . . . The fifth commandment requires children not only to yield respect, submission, and obedience to their parents, but also to give them love and tenderness, to lighten their cares, to guard their reputation, and to succor and comfort them in old age.[2]

While the parents live it should be the children's joy to honor and respect them. They should bring all the cheerfulness and sunshine into the life of the aged parents that they possibly can. They should smooth their pathway to the grave. There is no better recommendation in this world than that a child has honored his parents, no better record in the books of heaven than that he has loved and honored father and mother.[3]

RESPECT FOR THE AGED

Thou shall rise up before the hoary head, and honour the face of the old man, and fear thy God: I am the Lord.

There are services due to others which we cannot ignore and yet keep the commandments of God. To live, think, and act for self only is to become useless as servants of God. . . .

We have in our ranks too many who are restless, talkative, self-commending, and who take the liberty to put themselves forward, having no reverence for age, experience, or office. The church is suffering today for help of an opposite character—modest, quiet, God-fearing men, who will bear disagreeable burdens when laid upon them, not for the name, but to render service to their Master, who died for them. Persons of this character do not think it detracts from their dignity to rise up before the ancient and to treat gray hairs with respect. . . .

Those who fear and reverence God, He will delight to honor. Man may be so elevated as to form the connecting link between heaven and earth. He came from the hand of his Creator with a symmetrical character, endowed with such capacities for improvement that, combining divine influence with human efforts, he might elevate himself almost to an angel's sphere. Yet, when thus elevated, he will be unconscious of his goodness and greatness.[4]

And God has especially enjoined tender respect toward the aged. He says, "The hoary head is a crown of glory, if it be found in the way of righteousness." It tells of battles fought, and victories gained; of burdens borne, and temptations resisted. It tells of weary feet nearing their rest, of places soon to be vacant. Help the children to think of this, and they will smooth the path of the aged by their courtesy and respect and will bring grace and beauty into their young lives as they heed the command to "rise up before the hoary head, and honour the face of the old man."[5]

RESPECT FOR AUTHORITY

Honour all men. Love the brotherhood. Fear God. Honour the king. Servants, be subject to your masters with all fear; not only to the good and gentle, but also to the froward.

The apostle plainly outlined the attitude that believers should sustain toward the civil authorities: "Submit yourselves to every ordinance of man for the Lord's sake: whether it be to the king, as supreme; or unto governors, as unto them that are sent by him for the punishment of evildoers, and for the praise of them that do well. For so is the will of God, that with welldoing ye may put to silence the ignorance of foolish men: as free, and not using your liberty for a cloke of maliciousness, but as the servants of God. Honour all men. Love the brotherhood. Fear God. Honour the king."[6]

It is our duty in every case to obey the laws of our land, unless they conflict with the higher law which God spoke with an audible voice from Sinai and afterward engraved on stone with His own finger. . . . The ten precepts of Jehovah are the foundation of all righteous and good laws. Those who love God's commandments will conform to every good law of the land.[7]

We are to recognize human government as an ordinance of divine appointment and teach obedience to it as a sacred duty, within its legitimate sphere. But when its claims conflict with the claims of God, we must obey God rather than men. God's Word must be recognized as above all human legislation. A "Thus saith the Lord" is not to be set aside for a "Thus saith the church" or a "Thus saith the state." The crown of Christ is to be lifted above the diadems of earthly potentates.

We are not required to defy authorities. Our words, whether spoken or written, should be carefully considered.[8]

❦ ❦ ❦

Teach the people to conform in all things to the laws of their state when they can do so without conflicting with the law of God.[9]

REVERENCE FOR GOD

God is greatly to be feared in the assembly of the saints, and to be had in reverence of all them that are about him.

Another precious grace that should be carefully cherished is reverence. True reverence for God is inspired by a sense of His infinite greatness and a realization of His presence. With this sense of the Unseen the heart of every child should be deeply impressed. The hour and place of prayer and the services of public worship the child should be taught to regard as sacred because God is there. And as reverence is manifested in attitude and demeanor, the feeling that inspires it will be deepened.

Well would it be for young and old to study and ponder and often repeat those words of Holy Writ that show how the place marked by God's special presence should be regarded.

"Put off thy shoes from off thy feet," He commanded Moses at the burning bush; "for the place whereon thou standest is holy ground."

Jacob, after beholding the vision of the angels, exclaimed, "The Lord is in this place; and I knew it not." [10]

Humility and reverence should characterize the deportment of all who come into the presence of God. In the name of Jesus we may come before Him with confidence, but we must not approach Him with the boldness of presumption, as though He were on a level with ourselves. There are those who address the great and all-powerful and holy God, who dwelleth in light unapproachable, as they would address an equal, or even an inferior. There are those who conduct themselves in His house as they would not presume to do in the audience chamber of an earthly ruler. These should remember that they are in His sight whom seraphim adore, before whom angels veil their faces. God is greatly to be reverenced; all who truly realize His presence will bow in humility before Him. [11]

REVERENCE FOR GOD'S NAME

Holy and reverend is his name.

Reverence should be shown also for the name of God. Never should that name be spoken lightly or thoughtlessly. Even in prayer its frequent or needless repetition should be avoided.[12]

Those who are brought into covenant relation with God are pledged to speak of Him in the most respectful, reverential manner. . . .

Swearing, and all words spoken in the form of an oath, are dishonoring to God. The Lord sees, the Lord hears, and He will not hold the transgressor guiltless. He will not be mocked. Those who take the name of the Lord in vain will find it a fearful thing to fall into the hands of the living God.[13]

By the thoughtless mention of God in common conversation, by appeals to Him in trivial matters, and by the frequent and thoughtless repetition of His name, we dishonor Him.[14]

What faint views some have of the holiness of God, and how much they take His holy and reverend name in vain, without realizing that it is God, the great and terrible God, of whom they are speaking. While praying, many use careless and irreverent expressions, which grieve the tender Spirit of the Lord and cause their petitions to be shut out of heaven.[15]

"Holy and reverend is His name." We are never in any manner to treat lightly the titles or appellations of the Deity. In prayer we enter the audience chamber of the Most High, and we should come before Him with holy awe. The angels veil their faces in His presence. The cherubim and the bright and holy seraphim approach His throne with solemn reverence. How much more should we, finite, sinful beings, come in a reverent manner before the Lord, our Maker![16]

REVERENCE FOR THE WORD OF GOD

Obey my voice, and I will be your God, and ye shall be my people: and walk ye in all the ways that I have commanded you, that it may be well unto you.

You need and I need that the spiritual vision shall be cleared and intensified to behold the scheme of redemption as we have never viewed it before. We want that our hearts should feel the mighty throbs of a Saviour's love. In searching the Scriptures, in feeding upon the words of life, O consider it is the voice of God to the soul. We may be confused sometimes over the voice of our friends; but in the Bible we have the counsel of God upon all important subjects which concern our eternal interests, and in temporal matters we may learn a great deal. Its teachings will be always suited to our peculiar circumstances and calculated to prepare us to endure trial and fit us for our God-given work.[17]

The Bible is God's voice speaking to us, just as surely as if we could hear it with our ears. If we realized this, with what awe we would open God's Word and with what earnestness we would search its precepts. The reading and contemplation of the Scriptures would be regarded as an audience with the Infinite One.[18]

We are to open the Word of God with reverence and with a sincere desire to know the will of God concerning us. Then the heavenly angels will direct our search. God speaks to us in His Word. We are in the audience chamber of the Most High, in the very presence of God. Christ enters the heart.[19]

Show that you reverence your faith, speaking reverently of sacred things. Never allow one expression of lightness and trifling to escape your lips when quoting Scripture. As you take the Bible in your hands, remember that you are on holy ground.[20]

REVERENCE IN THE HOME

Wherefore the Lord God of Israel saith, I said indeed that thy house, and the house of thy father, should walk before me for ever: but now the Lord saith, Be it far from me; for them that honour me I will honour, and they that despise me shall be lightly esteemed.

Make the home life as nearly as possible like heaven.[21]

In the home the foundation is laid for the prosperity of the church. The influences that rule in the home life are carried into the church life; therefore, church duties should first begin in the home.[22]

Those who govern their families in the right way will bring into the church an influence of order and reverence.[23]

Fathers and mothers who make God first in their households, who teach their children that the fear of the Lord is the beginning of wisdom, glorify God before angels and before men. . . . Christ is not a stranger in their homes; His name is a household name, revered and glorified. Angels delight in a home where God reigns supreme and the children are taught to reverence religion, the Bible, and their Creator. Such families can claim the promise, "Them that honour Me, I will honour."[24]

The sacred privilege of communing with God makes distinct and clear the sight of the glorious things prepared for those who love God and reverence His commandments. We need to bring reverence into our daily lives. . . .

We bring too much that is little and common into the daily duties of life, and the result is that we fail to see Him who is invisible. Thus we lose many rich blessings in our religious experience.[25]

True reverence is revealed by obedience. God has commanded nothing that is unessential, and there is no other way of manifesting reverence so pleasing to Him as by obedience to that which He has spoken.[26]

REVERENCE FOR GOD'S REPRESENTATIVES

And the Lord God of their fathers sent to them by his messengers, rising up betimes, and sending; because he had compassion on his people, and on his dwelling place: but they mocked the messengers of God, and despised his words, and misused his prophets, until the wrath of the Lord arose against his people, till there was no remedy.

Reverence should be shown for God's representatives—for ministers, teachers, and parents who are called to speak and act in His stead. In the respect shown to them He is honored.[27]

The education and training of the youth should be of a character that would exalt sacred things and encourage pure devotion for God in His house. Many who profess to be children of the heavenly King have no true appreciation of the sacredness of eternal things. . . .

They are seldom instructed that the minister is God's ambassador, that the message he brings is one of God's appointed agencies in the salvation of souls, and that to all who have the privilege brought within their reach it will be a savor of life unto life or of death unto death. . . .

Many . . . make the service a subject of criticism at home, approving a few things and condemning others. . . . In regard to the service of the sanctuary, if the speaker has a blemish, be afraid to mention it. Talk only of the good work he is doing, of the good ideas he presented, which you should heed as coming through God's agent. . . .

Unless correct ideas of true worship and true reverence are impressed upon the people, there will be a growing tendency to place the sacred and eternal on a level with common things, and those professing the truth will be an offense to God and a disgrace to religion. They can never, with their uncultivated ideas, appreciate a pure and holy heaven, and be prepared to join with the worshipers in the heavenly courts above, where all is purity and perfection, where every being has perfect reverence for God and His holiness.

Paul describes the work of God's ambassadors as that by which every man shall be presented perfect in Christ Jesus.[28]

REVERENCE FOR THE HOUSE OF GOD

Ye shall keep my sabbaths, and reverence my sanctuary: I am the Lord.

God is high and holy; and to the humble, believing soul, His house on earth, the place where His people meet for worship, is as the gate of heaven. The song of praise, the words spoken by Christ's ministers, are God's appointed agencies to prepare a people for the church above, for that loftier worship.[29]

When the worshipers enter the place of meeting, they should do so with decorum, passing quietly to their seats. . . . Common talking, whispering, and laughing should not be permitted in the house of worship, either before or after the service. Ardent, active piety should characterize the worshipers.

If some have to wait a few minutes before the meeting begins, let them maintain a true spirit of devotion by silent meditation, keeping the heart uplifted to God in prayer that the service may be of special benefit to their own hearts and lead to the conviction and conversion of other souls. They should remember that heavenly messengers are in the house. We all lose much sweet communion with God by our restlessness, by not encouraging moments of reflection and prayer. . . .

Elevate the standard of Christianity in the minds of your children; help them to weave Jesus into their experience; teach them to have the highest reverence for the house of God and to understand that when they enter the Lord's house it should be with hearts that are softened and subdued by such thoughts as these: "God is here; this is His house. I must have pure thoughts and holiest motives. . . . This is the place where God meets with and blesses His people." . . .

Parents should not only teach, but command, their children to enter the sanctuary with sobriety and reverence.[30]

Practice reverence until it becomes a part of yourself.[31]

REVERENCE FOR THE SABBATH

Remember the sabbath day, to keep it holy.

"Remember" is placed at the very first of the fourth commandment. Parents, you need to remember the Sabbath day yourselves to keep it holy. And if you do this, you are giving the proper instruction to your children; they will reverence God's holy day. . . . All through the week keep the Lord's holy Sabbath in view, for that day is to be devoted to the service of God. It is a day when the hands are to rest from worldly employment, when the soul's needs are to receive especial attention.[32]

The Sabbath—oh! make it the sweetest, the most blessed day of the whole week. . . . Parents can and should give attention to their children, reading to them the most attractive portions of Bible history, educating them to reverence the Sabbath day, keeping it according to the commandment. . . . They can make the Sabbath a delight if they will take the proper course. The children can be interested in good reading or in conversation about the salvation of their souls.[33]

During a portion of the day all should have an opportunity to be out of doors. . . . Let their young minds be associated with God in the beautiful scenery of nature, let their attention be called to the tokens of His love to man in His created works. . . . As they view the beautiful things which He has created for the happiness of man, they will be led to regard Him as a tender, loving Father. . . . As the character of God puts on the aspect of love, benevolence, beauty, and attraction, they are drawn to love Him.[34]

The Sabbath is the golden clasp that unites God and His people.[35]

It means eternal salvation to keep the Sabbath holy unto the Lord.[36]

HE IS A LIVING GOD

The Lord is the true God, he is the living God, and an everlasting king.

"My presence shall go with thee" (Ex. 33:14), was the promise given during the journey through the wilderness. This assurance was accompanied by a marvelous revelation of Jehovah's character, which enabled Moses to proclaim to all Israel the goodness of God and to instruct them fully concerning the attributes of their invisible King. . . .

Till the close of his long life of patient ministry Moses continued his exhortations to Israel to keep their eyes fixed on their divine Ruler. . . .

With what confidence had Moses assured the Israelites of the merciful attributes of Jehovah! Often during the wilderness sojourn he had pleaded with God in behalf of erring Israel, and the Lord had spared them. . . .

The prophet pleaded the marvelous providences and promises of God in behalf of the chosen nation. And then, as the strongest of all pleas, he urged the love of God for fallen man. . . . "Pardon, I beseech Thee, the iniquity of this people according unto the greatness of Thy mercy, and as thou hast forgiven this people, from Egypt even until now.". . .

Graciously the Lord responded, "I have pardoned according to thy word." And then He imparted to Moses, in the form of a prophecy, a knowledge of His purpose concerning the final triumph of His chosen people. "As truly as I live," He declared, "all the earth shall be filled with the glory of the Lord." . . . God's glory, His character, His merciful kindness and tender love—all that Moses had pleaded in behalf of Israel was to be revealed to all mankind. And this promise of Jehovah was made doubly sure; it was confirmed by an oath. As surely as God lives and reigns, His glory shall be declared "among the heathen, His wonders among all people."[37]

GOD IS MY FATHER

Behold, what manner of love the Father hath bestowed upon us, that we should be called the sons of God.

What love, what matchless love, that, sinners and aliens as we are, we may be brought back to God and adopted into His family! We may address Him by the endearing name, "Our Father," which is a sign of our affection for Him and a pledge of His tender regard and relationship to us. And the Son of God, beholding the heirs of grace, "is not ashamed to call them brethren." They have even a more sacred relationship to God than have the angels who have never fallen.

All the paternal love which has come down from generation to generation through the channel of human hearts, all the springs of tenderness which have opened in the souls of men, are but as a tiny rill to the boundless ocean, when compared with the infinite, exhaustless love of God. Tongue cannot utter it; pen cannot portray it. You may meditate upon it every day of your life; you may search the Scriptures diligently in order to understand it; you may summon every power and capability that God has given you, in the endeavor to comprehend the love and compassion of the heavenly Father; and yet there is an infinity beyond.[38]

In all His children God beholds the image of His only-begotten Son. He looks upon them with a love greater than any language can express. He enfolds them in the arms of His love. The Lord rejoices over His people.[39]

He has redeemed us out of the careless world and has chosen us to become members of the royal family, sons and daughters of the heavenly King. He invites us to trust in Him with a trust deeper and stronger than that of a child in his earthly father.[40]

God is to us a tender, compassionate, heavenly Father.[41]

GOD IS WITH ME

The Lord of hosts is with us; the God of Jacob is our refuge.

"Emmanuel, God with us," this means everything to us. What a broad foundation does it lay for our faith. What a hope big with immortality does it place before the believing soul. God with us in Christ Jesus to accompany us every step of the journey to heaven. The Holy Spirit with us as a comforter, a guide in our perplexities, to soothe our sorrows, and shield us in temptation. "O the depth of the riches both of the wisdom and knowledge of God!"[42]

God commanded Moses for Israel, "Let them make Me a sanctuary, that I may dwell among them," and He abode in the sanctuary, in the midst of His people. Through all their weary wandering in the desert, the symbol of His presence was with them. So Christ set up His tabernacle in the midst of our human encampment. He pitched His tent by the side of the tents of men, that He might dwell among us and make us familiar with His divine character and life. . . .

Since Jesus came to dwell with us, we know that God is acquainted with our trials and sympathizes with our griefs. Every son and daughter of Adam may understand that our Creator is the friend of sinners. . . .

"God with us" is the surety of our deliverance from sin, the assurance of our power to obey the law of heaven.[43]

Christ sought to teach the grand truth so needful for us to learn, that God is always with us, an inmate of every dwelling, that He is acquainted with every action performed on earth. He knows the thoughts that are framed in the mind and endorsed by the soul. He hears every word that falls from the lips of human beings. He is walking and working in the midst of all our transactions in life. He knows every plan, and He measures every method.[44]

GOD SEES ME

Thou God seest me.

God is a vigilant observer of the actions of the children of men. Nothing occurs in earth or heaven without the knowledge of the Creator. Nothing can happen without His permission. He on whom the fate of an empire may depend is watched over with a vigilance which knows no relaxation by Him who "giveth salvation unto kings," to whom belong "the shields of the earth." And the poor man is as tenderly watched over as the monarch upon his throne.

God is constantly at work for the good of His creatures. . . . Times without number God has interposed to avert death, to keep men, women, and children in safety when Satan purposed a result wholly disastrous. . . .

This world has been signally blessed by God. Human beings are the recipients of countless mercies. Providence watches over and shields them. Upon them are poured the choicest gifts in heaven's treasury.[45]

God knows you by name. He knows every action of your life.[46]

God knows every thought, every purpose, every plan, every motive. . . . As the artist transfers to the canvas the features of the face, so the features of each individual character are transferred to the books of heaven. God has a perfect photograph of every man's character.[47]

God wants you to recognize the divine presence. His peace and comfort and grace and joy will change the shadow of death into bright morning and blessed sunshine. . . . A reverential spirit realizes that the heart must be kept by the power of God. Ministering angels open the eyes of the mind and heart to see wonderful things in the divine law, in the natural world, and in the eternal things revealed by the Holy Spirit.[48]

GOD CARES FOR ME

Fear thou not; for I am with thee: be not dismayed; for I am thy God: I will strengthen thee; yea, I will help thee; yea, I will uphold thee with the right hand of my righteousness.

The Lord is in active communication with every part of His vast dominions. He is represented as bending toward the earth and its inhabitants. He is listening to every word that is uttered. He hears every groan; He listens to every prayer; He observes the movements of every one. . . .

God has always had a care for His people. . . . Christ taught His disciples that the amount of divine attention given to any object is proportionate to the rank assigned to it in the creation of God. He called their attention to the birds of the air. Not a sparrow, He said, falls to the ground without the notice of our heavenly Father. And if the little sparrow is regarded by Him, surely the souls of those for whom Christ has died are precious in His sight. The value of man, the estimate God places upon him, is revealed in the cross of Calvary. . . .

God's mercy and love for the fallen race have not ceased to accumulate, nor lost their earthward direction.[49]

It is true that disappointments will come; tribulation we must expect; but we are to commit everything, great and small, to God. He does not become perplexed by the multiplicity of our grievances, nor overpowered by the weight of our burdens. His watchcare extends to every household, and encircles every individual; He is concerned in all our business and our sorrows. He marks every tear; He is touched with the feeling of our infirmities. All the afflictions and trials that befall us here are permitted, to work out His purposes of love toward us—"that we might be partakers of His holiness," and thus become participants in that fullness of joy which is found in His presence.[50]

GOD IS ALL IN ALL

Remember the former things of old: for I am God, and there is none else; I am God, and there is none like me.

In heaven God is all in all. There, holiness reigns supreme; there is nothing to mar the perfect harmony with God. If we are indeed journeying thither, the spirit of heaven will dwell in our hearts here. But if we find no pleasure now in the contemplation of heavenly things; if we have no interest in seeking the knowledge of God, no delight in beholding the character of Christ; if holiness has no attractions for us—then we may be sure that our hope of heaven is vain. Perfect conformity to the will of God is the high aim to be constantly before the Christian. He will love to talk of God, of Jesus, of the home of bliss and purity which Christ has prepared for them that love Him. The contemplation of these themes, when the soul feasts upon the blessed assurances of God, the apostle represents as tasting "the powers of the world to come."[51]

The knowledge of God as revealed in Christ is the knowledge that all who are saved must have. It is the knowledge that works transformation of character. This knowledge, received, will re-create the soul in the image of God. It will impart to the whole being a spiritual power that is divine. . . .

"For this cause," Paul says, "I bow my knees unto the Father of our Lord Jesus Christ, of whom the whole family in heaven and earth is named, that He would grant you, according to the riches of His glory, to be strengthened with might by His Spirit in the inner man; that Christ may dwell in your hearts by faith; that ye, being rooted and grounded in love, may be able to comprehend with all saints what is the breadth, and length, and depth, and height; and to know the love of Christ, which passeth knowledge, that ye might be filled with all the fulness of God."[52]

GOD IN NATURE

The heavens declare the glory of God; and the firmament sheweth his handywork.

God has surrounded us with nature's beautiful scenery to attract and interest the mind. It is His design that we should associate the glories of nature with His character. If we faithfully study the book of nature, we shall find it a fruitful source for contemplating the infinite love and power of God. . . .

The great Master Artist has painted upon heaven's shifting, changing canvas the glories of the setting sun. He has tinted and gilded the heavens with gold, silver, and crimson, as though the portals of high heaven were thrown open, that we might view its gleamings and our imagination take hold of the glory within. Many turn carelessly from this heavenly wrought picture. They fail to trace the infinite love and power of God in the surpassing beauties seen in the heavens, but are almost entranced as they view the imperfect paintings, in imitation of the Master Artist.

The Redeemer of the world chose the open air in which to give His lessons of instruction. . . . He chose the groves and the seaside, where He could have a commanding view of landscape and varied scenery, that He might illustrate important truths of the kingdom of God by the works of God in nature.[53]

Look at the wonderful and beautiful things of nature. Think of their marvelous adaptation to the needs and happiness, not only of man, but of all living creatures. The sunshine and the rain, that gladden and refresh the earth, the hills and seas and plains, all speak to us of the Creator's love. It is God who brings the bud to bloom, the flower to fruit. It is He who supplies the daily needs of all His creatures.[54]

The heart is quickened, and throbs with new and deeper love, mingled with awe and reverence, as we contemplate God in nature.[55]

ABUNDANT LIFE IN CHRIST

I am come that they might have life, and that they might have it more abundantly.

All created beings live by the will and power of God. They are recipients of the life of the Son of God. However able and talented, however large their capacities, they are replenished with life from the source of all life. He is the spring, the fountain, of life. Only He who alone hath immortality, dwelling in light and life, could say, "I have power to lay down My life, and I have power to take it again.". . .

Christ was invested with the right to give immortality. The life which He had laid down in humanity, He again took up and gave to humanity. "I am come," He says, "that they might have life, and that they might have it more abundantly." . . .

All who are one with Christ through faith in Him gain an experience which is life unto eternal life. . . . "Because I live, ye shall live also."

Christ became one with humanity, that humanity might become one in Spirit and life with Him. By virtue of this union in obedience to the Word of God, His life becomes their life. He says to the penitent, "I am the resurrection, and the life." Death is looked upon by Christ as sleep—silence, darkness, sleep. He speaks of it as if it were of little moment. "Whosoever liveth and believeth in Me," He says, "shall never die." . . . And to the believing one, death is but a small matter. With him to die is but to sleep.[56]

The same power that raised Christ from the dead will raise His church, and glorify it with Christ, as His bride, above all principalities, above all powers, above every name that is named, not only in this world, but also in the heavenly courts, the world above. The victory of the sleeping saints will be glorious on the morning of the resurrection.[57]

CHRIST IS MY PERFECT EXAMPLE

For even hereunto were ye called: because Christ also suffered for us, leaving us an example, that ye should follow his steps: who did no sin, neither was guile found in his mouth.

Christ is our example in all things. In the providence of God, His early life was passed in Nazareth, where the inhabitants were of that character that He was continually exposed to temptations, and it was necessary for Him to be guarded in order to remain pure and spotless amid so much sin and wickedness. Christ did not select this place Himself. His heavenly Father chose this place for Him, where His character would be tested and tried in a variety of ways. The early life of Christ was subjected to severe trials, hardships, and conflicts, that He might develop the perfect character which makes Him a perfect example for children, youth, and manhood. . . .

The life of Christ was designed to show that purity, stability, and firmness of principle are not dependent upon a life freed from hardships, poverty, and adversity. The trials and privations of which so many youth complain, Christ endured without murmuring. And this discipline is the very experience the youth need, which will give firmness to their character and make them like Christ, strong in spirit to resist temptation. They will not, if they separate from the influence of those who would lead them astray and corrupt their morals, be overcome by the devices of Satan. Through daily prayer to God they will have wisdom and grace from Him to bear the conflicts and stern realities of life, and come off victorious. Fidelity and serenity of mind can only be retained by watchfulness and prayer. Christ's life was an example of persevering energy, which was not allowed to become weakened by reproach, ridicule, privation, or hardships. . . . And in just that degree that they maintain their integrity of character under discouragements will their fortitude, stability, and power of endurance increase, and they wax strong in spirit.[58]

CHRIST MY ELDER BROTHER

Wherefore in all things it behoved him to be made like unto his brethren, that he might be a merciful and faithful high priest in things pertaining to God, to make reconciliation for the sins of the people.

The Elder Brother of our race is by the eternal throne. He looks upon every soul who is turning his face toward Him as the Saviour. He knows by experience what are the weaknesses of humanity, what are our wants, and where lies the strength of our temptations. . . . He is watching over you, trembling child of God. Are you tempted? He will deliver. Are you weak? He will strengthen. Are you ignorant? He will enlighten. Are you wounded? He will heal. The Lord "telleth the number of the stars"; and yet "He healeth the broken in heart, and bindeth up their wounds."

Whatever your anxieties and trials, spread out your case before the Lord. Your spirit will be braced for endurance. The way will be open for you to disentangle yourself from embarrassment and difficulty. The weaker and more helpless you know yourself to be, the stronger will you become in His strength. The heavier your burdens, the more blessed the rest in casting them upon your Burden Bearer.

Circumstances may separate friends; the restless waters of the wide sea may roll between us and them. But no circumstances, no distance, can separate us from the Saviour. Wherever we may be, He is at our right hand, to support, maintain, uphold, and cheer. Greater than the love of a mother for her child is Christ's love for His redeemed. It is our privilege to rest in His love; to say, "I will trust Him; for He gave His life for me."

Human love may change, but Christ's love knows no change. When we cry to Him for help, His hand is stretched out to save.[59]

He desires us to realize that He has returned to heaven as our Elder Brother and that the measureless power given Him has been placed at our disposal.[60]

JESUS AS A YOUTH

And the child grew, and waxed strong in spirit, filled with wisdom: and the grace of God was upon him.

Wonderful in its significance is the brief record of His early life: "The child grew, and waxed strong in spirit, filled with wisdom; and the grace of God was upon Him." In the sunlight of His Father's countenance Jesus "increased in wisdom and stature, and in favour with God and man." His mind was active and penetrating, with a thoughtfulness and wisdom beyond His years. Yet His character was beautiful in its symmetry. The powers of mind and body developed gradually, in keeping with the laws of childhood.

As a child, Jesus manifested a peculiar loveliness of disposition. His willing hands were ever ready to serve others. He manifested a patience that nothing could disturb and a truthfulness that would never sacrifice integrity. In principle firm as a rock, His life revealed the grace of unselfish courtesy.

With deep earnestness the mother of Jesus watched the unfolding of His powers and beheld the impress of perfection upon His character. With delight she sought to encourage that bright, receptive mind. . . .

From her lips and from the scrolls of the prophets He learned of heavenly things. The very words which He Himself had spoken to Moses for Israel He was now taught at His mother's knee. As He advanced from childhood to youth, He did not seek the schools of the rabbis. He needed not the education to be obtained from such sources; for God was His instructor. . . .

Since He gained knowledge as we may do, His intimate acquaintance with the Scriptures shows how diligently His early years were given to the study of God's Word. . . . From the first dawning of intelligence He was constantly growing in spiritual grace and knowledge of truth.[61]

CHRIST WAS OBEDIENT

And he went down with them, and came to Nazareth, and was subject unto them. . . . And Jesus increased in wisdom and stature, and in favour with God and man.

Notwithstanding the sacred mission of Christ, His exalted relationship with God, of which He was fully aware, He was not above performing the practical duties of life. He was the Creator of the world, and yet He acknowledged His obligation to His earthly parents, and at the call of duty, in compliance with the wishes of His parents, He returned with them from Jerusalem after the Passover, and was subject unto them.

He submitted to restraints of parental authority and acknowledged the obligations of a son, a brother, a friend, and a citizen. He discharged His duties to His earthly parents with respectful courtesy. He was the Majesty of heaven. He had been the great commander in heaven. Angels loved to do His bidding. And now He was a willing servant, a cheerful, obedient son.

Jesus was not turned aside by an influence from the faithful service expected of a son. He did not aim to do anything remarkable to distinguish Himself from other youth or to proclaim His heavenly birth. Even His friends and relatives, in all the years that Christ's life was passed among them, saw no special marks of His divinity. Christ was sedate, self-denying, gentle, cheerful, kind, and ever obedient. . . .

There is an important lesson for parents and children to learn in the silence of the Scriptures in reference to the childhood and youth of Christ. He was our example in all things. In the little notice given of His childhood and youthful life is an example for parents as well as children, that the more quiet and unnoticed the period of childhood and youth is passed, and the more natural and free from artificial excitement, the more safe will it be for the children and the more favorable for the formation of a character of purity, natural simplicity, and true moral worth.[62]

299

CHRIST TEMPTED AS WE ARE

For we have not an high priest which cannot be touched with the feeling of our infirmities; but was in all points tempted like as we are, yet without sin.

The coming of Christ to our world was a great event, not only to this world, but to all the worlds in the universe of God. He came to take upon Him our nature, to be tempted in all points like as we are, and yet to leave before us an example of perfect purity and unblemished character. In that He was tempted in all points like as we are, He knows how to sympathize with us. He knows how to pity and how to aid the children and youth; for He too was a child, and He understands every trial and temptation with which children are beset. . . .

His eyes shone with an expression of that love which led Him to leave the heavenly courts and come to earth to die in the sinner's place. . . . He pitied and loved not only those who sought to be obedient and loving, but those also who were wayward and perverse. Jesus has not changed; He is the same yesterday, today, and forever, and He still loves and pities the erring, seeking to draw them to Himself, that He may give them divine aid. He knows that a demon power is struggling in every soul, striving for the mastery; but Jesus came to break the power of Satan and to set the captives free.

In Christ the character of the Father was revealed. As children looked upon His countenance, they saw purity and goodness shining forth from His eyes. In His countenance gentleness, meekness, love, and conscious power were combined. But though every word, every gesture, every expression of His face, betokened His divine supremacy, humility marked His deportment and bearing. He came but for one purpose, and that was the salvation of the lost.[63]

CHRIST IN ME THE HOPE OF GLORY

To whom God would make known what is the riches of the glory of this mystery among the Gentiles; which is Christ in you, the hope of glory.

"Christ in you, the hope of glory." A knowledge of this mystery furnishes a key to every other. It opens to the soul the treasures of the universe, the possibilities of infinite development.

And this development is gained through the constant unfolding to us of the character of God—the glory and the mystery of the written Word. If it were possible for us to attain to a full understanding of God and His Word, there would be for us no further discovery of truth, no greater knowledge, no further development. God would cease to be supreme, and man would cease to advance. Thank God, it is not so. Since God is infinite, and in Him are all the treasures of wisdom, we may to all eternity be ever searching, ever learning, yet never exhaust the riches of His wisdom, His goodness, or His power.[64]

Let the seeker for the salvation of God possess the same energy and earnestness that he would have for worldly treasure, and the object would be gained. . . .

All who are made partakers of His salvation here, and who hope to share the glories of the kingdom hereafter, must gather with Christ. Each must feel that he is responsible for his own case. . . . If these maintain their Christian walk, Jesus will be in them the hope of glory, and they will love to speak forth His praise that they may be refreshed. The cause of their Master will be near and dear to them. . . . Every Christian must go on from strength to strength, and employ all his powers in the cause of God.[65]

The life of the true believer reveals an indwelling Saviour. . . . His whole life is a testimony to the power of the grace of Christ.[66]

MY GUARDIAN ANGEL

For he shall give his angels charge over thee, to keep thee in all thy ways.

A guardian angel is appointed to every follower of Christ. These heavenly watchers shield the righteous from the power of the wicked one. This Satan himself recognized when he said, "Doth Job fear God for nought? Hast not Thou made a hedge about him, and about his house, and about all that he hath on every side?" The agency by which God protects His people is presented in the words of the psalmist, "The angel of the Lord encampeth round about them that fear Him, and delivereth them."[67]

I have seen the tender love that God has for His people, and it is very great. I saw angels over the saints with their wings spread about them. Each saint had an attending angel. If the saints wept through discouragement, or were in danger, the angels that ever attended them would fly quickly upward to carry the tidings, and the angels in the city would cease to sing. . . . They would bear the tidings upward, and all the angels in the city would weep, and then with a loud voice say, "Amen." But if the saints fixed their eyes upon the prize before them, and glorified God by praising Him, then the angels would bear the glad tidings to the city, and the angels in the city would touch their golden harps and sing with a loud voice, "Alleluia!" and the heavenly arches would ring with their lovely songs.[68]

His angels are appointed to watch over us, and if we put ourselves under their guardianship, then in every time of danger they will be at our right hand. When unconsciously we are in danger of exerting a wrong influence, the angels will be by our side, prompting us to a better course, choosing words for us, and influencing our actions. Thus our influence may be a silent, unconscious, but mighty power in drawing others to Christ and the heavenly world.[69]

ANGELS IN MY DAILY LIFE

The angel of the Lord encampeth round about them that fear him, and delivereth them.

Today . . . heavenly messengers are passing through the length and breadth of the land, seeking to comfort the sorrowing, to protect the impenitent, to win the hearts of men to Christ. We cannot see them personally; nevertheless they are with us, guiding, directing, protecting. . . .

These angels of light create a heavenly atmosphere about the soul, lifting us toward the unseen and the eternal. We cannot behold their forms with our natural sight; only by spiritual vision can we discern heavenly things. The spiritual ear alone can hear the harmony of heavenly voices. . . .

Again and again have angels talked with men as a man speaketh with a friend, and led them to places of security. Again and again have the encouraging words of angels renewed the drooping spirits of the faithful, and carrying their minds above the things of earth, caused them to behold by faith the white robes, the crowns, the palm branches of victory, which overcomers will receive when they surround the great white throne.

It is the work of the angels to come close to the tried, the suffering, the tempted. They labor untiringly in behalf of those for whom Christ died.[70]

Angels are ever present where they are most needed. They are with those who have the hardest battles to fight, with those who must battle against inclination and hereditary tendencies, whose home surroundings are the most discouraging.[71]

Heavenly beings are appointed to do their work of ministry—to guide, guard, and control those who shall be heirs of salvation. . . . Faithful sentinels are on guard to direct souls in right paths.[72]

ANGELS JOIN ME IN SOUL WINNING

Are they not all ministering spirits, sent forth to minister for them who shall be heirs of salvation?

The glad message of Hebrews 1:14 is for all. The entire chapter is a wonderful encouragement for every tried and tempted soul. "But to which of the angels said he at any time, Sit on my right hand, until I make thine enemies thy footstool? Are they not all ministering spirits, sent forth to minister for them who shall be heirs of salvation?" These messages are coming down along the line to our time, to them that shall be heirs of salvation. Angels actually come to our world. Nor are they always invisible. They sometimes veil their angelic appearance, and appearing as men, they converse with and enlighten human beings. . . .

While some are in the valley of decision, angels are uniting with true, wholehearted servants of Christ to help these needy souls.[73]

If angels occupied the place of man in the administration of the gospel, there would not be whole regions left in darkness and the shadow of death. The work would have been as is represented by the angel flying through the midst of heaven proclaiming the everlasting gospel to them that dwell on the earth. But the Lord does nothing without the cooperation of man. Could the intense interest which the angels have for man be put into voice that would be heard by the human agent, what appeals would be heard in burning words to communicate to others that which heaven had communicated to them.[74]

God has manifested His love to men by making them partakers with Himself in the work of salvation. All to whom the heavenly inspiration has come are put in trust with the gospel. "We are labourers together with God," called to represent Him as ambassadors of love. We are to cooperate with the work of the delegates of heaven. . . .

Through the ministration of angels, God sends light to His people, and through His people the light is to be given to the world.[75]

ANGELS EMPLOY MY HANDS TO DO HIS WORK

Bless the Lord, ye his angels, that excel in strength, that do his commandments, hearkening unto the voice of his word. Bless ye the Lord, all ye his hosts; ye ministers of his, that do his pleasure.

Angelic agencies, though invisible, are cooperating with visible human agencies, forming a relief association with men. Is there not something stimulating and inspiring in this thought that the human agent stands as the visible instrument to confer the blessings of angelic agencies? As we are thus laborers together with God, the work bears the inscription of the divine. With what joy and delight all heaven looks upon these blended influences, influences which are acknowledged in the heavenly courts! Human agencies are the hands of heavenly instrumentalities, for heavenly angels employ human hands in practical ministry. Their acts of unselfish ministry make them partakers in the success which is a result of the relief offered. This is Heaven's way of administering saving power. The knowledge and actions of the heavenly order of workers, united with the knowledge and power which are imparted to human agencies, relieve the oppressed and distressed.

The very angels who when Satan was seeking the supremacy fought the battle in the heavenly courts, and triumphed on the side of God; the very angels who from their exalted position shouted for joy over the creation of our world, and over the creation of our first parents, who were to inhabit the earth . . . are most intensely interested to work in union with the fallen, redeemed race in the development of that power which God gives to help every man who will unite with heavenly intelligences to seek and save human beings who are perishing in their sins. . . .

Human agencies are called to be hand helpers, to work out the knowledge and use the facilities of heavenly angels. By uniting with these powers that are omnipotent, we shall be benefited by their higher education and experience. . . . Such a cooperation will accomplish a work which will give honor and glory and majesty to God.[76]

305

PETER DELIVERED BY AN ANGEL

And when Peter was come to himself, he said, Now I know of a surety, that the Lord hath sent his angel, and hath delivered me out of the hand of Herod.

Peter was confined in a rock-hewn cell, the doors of which were strongly bolted and barred. . . . But the bolts and bars and the Roman guard, which effectually cut off all possibility of human aid, were but to make more complete the triumph of God in the deliverance of Peter. . . .

It is the last night before the proposed execution. A mighty angel is sent from heaven to rescue Peter. . . . He enters the cell, and there lies Peter, sleeping the peaceful sleep of perfect trust. . . .

Not until he feels the touch of the angel's hand and hears a voice saying, "Arise up quickly," does he awaken sufficiently to see his cell illuminated by the light of heaven and an angel of great glory standing before him. Mechanically he obeys the word spoken to him, and as in rising he lifts his hands, he is dimly conscious that the chains have fallen from his wrists. . . .

He [the angel] moves toward the door, followed by the usually talkative Peter, now dumb from amazement. They step over the guard, and reach the heavily bolted door, which of its own accord swings open, and closes again immediately. . . .

The second door . . . is reached. It opens . . . with no creaking of hinges or rattling of iron bolts. . . . In the same way they pass through the third gateway, and find themselves in the open street. . . . The angel glides on in front, encircled by a light of dazzling brightness. . . . Thus they pass on through one street, and then, the mission of the angel being accomplished, he suddenly disappears.

Today, as verily as in the days of the apostles, heavenly messengers are passing through the length and breadth of the land. . . . We cannot see them personally; nevertheless they are with us, guiding, directing, protecting.[77]

ANGELS ARE PREPARING ME FOR ETERNITY

Behold, I send an Angel before thee, to keep thee in the way, and to bring thee into the place which I have prepared.

All heaven is engaged in the work of preparing a people to stand in the day of the Lord's preparation. The connection of heaven with earth seems very close. . . .

The heavenly intelligences are waiting with almost impatient earnestness to make Him known to the human agents, that they may be laborers together with these heavenly angels in presenting Jesus—the world's Redeemer, full of grace and truth. . . .

The first tear of penitence for sins creates joy among the heavenly angels in the courts of heaven. The heavenly messengers are ready to be on the wing to minister to the soul who is seeking Jesus. . . .

Grand and glorious things hath God prepared for those who love Him. Angels are looking forward with earnest expectation to the final triumph of the people of God, when seraphim and cherubim and the "ten thousand times ten thousand, and thousands of thousands" shall swell the anthems of the blessed and celebrate the triumphs of the mediatorial achievements in the recovery of man.[78]

Jesus counted the cost of the salvation of every son and daughter of Adam. He provided abundant means that, if they would but comply with the conditions, none need perish, but might have everlasting life. . . . Every heavenly intelligence works as His agent to win man to God.[79]

The angels of glory find their joy in . . . giving love and tireless watchcare to souls that are fallen and unholy. Heavenly beings woo the hearts of men; they bring to this dark world light from the courts above; by gentle and patient ministry they move upon the human spirit, to bring the lost into a fellowship with Christ which is even closer than they themselves can know.[80]

ANGELS HOLDING THE FOUR WINDS

I saw another angel ascending from the east, having the seal of the living God: and he cried with a loud voice to the four angels, . . . saying, Hurt not the earth, neither the sea, nor the trees, till we have sealed the servants of our God in their foreheads.

Four mighty angels are still holding the four winds of the earth. Terrible destruction is forbidden to come in full. The accidents by land and by sea; the loss of life, steadily increasing, by storm, by tempest, by railroad disaster, by conflagration; the terrible floods, the earthquakes, and the winds will be the stirring up of the nations to one deadly combat, while the angels hold the four winds, forbidding the terrible power of Satan to be exercised in its fury until the servants of God are sealed in their foreheads.[81]

Angels are holding the four winds, which are represented as an angry horse seeking to break loose and rush over the face of the whole earth, bearing destruction and death in its path.[82]

A terrible conflict is before us. We are nearing the battle, of the great day of God Almighty. That which has been held in control is to be let loose. The angel of mercy is folding her wings, preparing to step down from the throne and leave the world to the control of Satan. The principalities and powers of earth are in bitter revolt against the God of heaven. They are filled with hatred against those who serve Him, and soon, very soon, will be fought the last great battle between good and evil. The earth is to be the battlefield—the scene of the final contest and the final victory.[83]

While their hands were loosening, and the four winds were about to blow, the merciful eye of Jesus gazed on the remnant that were not sealed, and He raised His hands to the Father and pleaded with Him that He had spilled His blood for them. Then another angel was commissioned to fly swiftly to the four angels and bid them hold until the servants of God were sealed with the seal of the living God in their foreheads.[84]

A VICTORIOUS LIFE

November 1   *Equipped for Victory*   Eph. 6:11, 12

PUT ON THE WHOLE ARMOR OF GOD

Put on the whole armour of God, that ye may be able to stand against the wiles of the devil. For we wrestle not against flesh and blood, but against principalities, against powers, against the rulers of the darkness of this world, against spiritual wickedness in high places.

It is not safe for us, when going into battle, to cast away our weapons. It is then that we need to be equipped with the whole armor of God. Every piece is essential.[1]

While Satan is constantly seeking to blind their minds to the fact, let Christians never forget that they "wrestle not against flesh and blood, but against principalities, against powers, against the rulers of the darkness of this world, against wicked spirits [margin] in high places." The inspired warning is sounding down the centuries to our time: "Be sober, be vigilant; because your adversary the devil, as a roaring lion, walketh about, seeking whom he may devour.". . .

From the days of Adam to our own time our great enemy has been exercising his power to oppress and destroy. He is now preparing for his last campaign against the church. All who seek to follow Jesus will be brought into conflict with this relentless foe. The more nearly the Christian imitates the divine Pattern, the more surely will he make himself a mark for the attacks of Satan.[2]

We must have on the whole armor of God, and be ready at any moment for a conflict with the powers of darkness. When temptations and trials rush in upon us, let us go to God, and agonize with Him in prayer. He will not turn us away empty, but will give us grace and strength to overcome, and to break the power of the enemy. Oh, that all could see these things in their true light, and endure hardness as good soldiers of Jesus! Then would Israel move forward, strong in God, and in the power of His might.[3]

LOINS GIRT ABOUT WITH TRUTH

Wherefore take unto you the whole armour of God, that ye may be able to withstand in the evil day, and having done all, to stand. Stand therefore, having your loins girt about with truth.

It is when we walk in the light that shines upon us, obeying the truth that is open to our understanding, that we receive greater light. We cannot be excusable in accepting only the light which our fathers had one hundred years ago. . . . We want the truth on every point, and we are to put it in practice daily.[4]

The whole mind and soul should become imbued with the truth, that you may be a living representation of Christ. . . . God would have you filled with His Holy Spirit, endowed with power from on high. Labor not to become great men; but labor rather to become good and perfect men, showing forth the praises of Him who hath called you out of darkness into His marvelous light. God calls for Calebs and Joshuas, fearless, singlehearted men, who will work with faith and courage.[5]

If the truth of God be not deep rooted in the heart, you cannot stand the test of temptation. There is only one power that can keep us steadfast under the most trying circumstances—the grace of God in truth. The ungodly are lynx-eyed to mark every inconsistency, and prompt to pour contempt on the weak and halting ones. Let the youth make their mark high. Let them seek in humble prayer for that help which Christ has promised, that they may exert an influence upon others that they will not be ashamed to meet in the great day of final settlement and rewards. Those who have exemplified the loftiest Christian principles in every department of business and religious life will have the inexpressible advantage, for they will enter the Paradise of God as conquerors.[6]

THE BREASTPLATE OF RIGHTEOUSNESS

Having on the breastplate of righteousness.

Clad in the armor of Christ's righteousness, the church is to enter upon her final conflict. "Fair as the moon, clear as the sun, and terrible as an army with banners," she is to go forth into all the world, conquering and to conquer.[7]

Only the covering which Christ Himself has provided can make us meet to appear in God's presence. This covering, the robe of His own righteousness, Christ will put upon every repenting, believing soul. "I counsel thee," He says, "to buy of Me . . . white raiment, that thou mayest be clothed, and that the shame of thy nakedness do not appear." . . .

"All our righteousnesses are as filthy rags." Everything that we of ourselves can do is defiled by sin. But the Son of God was "manifested to take away our sins; and in Him is no sin." Sin is defined to be "the transgression of the law." But Christ was obedient to every requirement of the law. . . . When on earth He said to His disciples, "I have kept My Father's commandments." By His perfect obedience He has made it possible for every human being to obey God's commandments. When we submit ourselves to Christ . . . we live His life. This is what it means to be clothed with the garment of His righteousness. Then, as the Lord looks upon us, He sees, not the figleaf garment, not the nakedness and deformity of sin, but His own robe of righteousness, which is perfect obedience to the law of Jehovah.[8]

To every one God has made an offer that will help to brace every nerve and spiritual muscle for the time of test that is to come to us all. I am charged with the message, Clothe yourself with the whole armor of Christ's righteousness. . . . And, having done all you can do on your part, you have the assurance of victory. To every soul is granted the gracious opportunity of standing on the Rock of Ages.[9]

FEET SHOD WITH GOSPEL OF PEACE

And your feet shod with the preparation of the gospel of peace.

The Lord is soon coming. Talk it, pray it, believe it. Make it a part of the life. You will have to meet a doubting, objecting spirit, but this will give way before firm, consistent trust in God. When perplexities or hindrances present themselves, lift the soul to God in songs of thanksgiving. Gird on the Christian armor, and be sure that your feet are "shod with the preparation of the gospel of peace." [10]

We are living in the midst of an "epidemic of crime," at which thoughtful, God-fearing men everywhere stand aghast. The corruption that prevails, it is beyond the power of the human pen to describe. Every day brings fresh revelations of political strife, bribery, and fraud. Every day brings its heart-sickening record of violence and lawlessness, of indifference to human suffering, of brutal, fiendish destruction of human life. Every day testifies to the increase of insanity, murder, and suicide. Who can doubt that satanic agencies are at work among men with increasing activity to distract and corrupt the mind and defile and destroy the body? . . .

Everywhere there are hearts crying out for something which they have not. They long for a power that will give them mastery over sin, a power that will deliver them from the bondage of evil, a power that will give health and life and peace. Many who once knew the power of God's Word have dwelt where there is no recognition of God, and they long for the divine presence.

The world needs today what it needed nineteen hundred years ago—a revelation of Christ. [11]

For earth's sin and misery the gospel is the only antidote. [12]

THE SHIELD OF FAITH

Above all, taking the shield of faith, wherewith ye shall be able to quench all the fiery darts of the wicked.

Faith in God's Word, prayerfully studied and practically applied, will be our shield from Satan's power and will bring us off conquerors through the blood of Christ.[13]

When souls are converted their salvation is not yet accomplished. They then have the race to run; the arduous struggle is before them to do, what? "To fight the good *fight of faith,*" to press forward to the mark for the prize of the high calling which is in Christ Jesus. There is no release in this warfare; the battle is lifelong, and must be carried forward with determined energy proportionate to the value of the object you are in pursuit of, which is eternal life. Immense interests are here involved. We are made partakers of Christ's self-sacrifice here in this life, and then we are assured that we shall be partakers of all its benefits in the future immortal life, if we hold the beginning of our confidence steadfast unto the end. Think of this.

The promise is, "God is faithful, who will not suffer you to be tempted above that ye are able; but will with the temptation also make a way to escape." Maintain to the last your Christian integrity, and do not murmur against God. . . . Consider that eternal interests are here involved. You cannot afford to become discouraged and cast away your confidence. The Lord loves you, trust in the Lord. The Lord Jesus is your only hope. Make sure work for eternity. You must not murmur or complain or condemn yourself. Neglect no means of grace. Encourage your soul to *believe* and to *trust* in God.[14]

In the Lord we have righteousness and strength. Lean upon Him, and through His power you may quench all the fiery darts of the adversary and come off more than conqueror.[15]

THE HELMET OF SALVATION

For he put on righteousness as a breastplate, and an helmet of salvation upon his head; and he put on the garments of vengeance for clothing, and was clad with zeal as a cloke.

Many have confused ideas in regard to conversion. They have often heard the words repeated from the pulpit, "Ye must be born again." "You must have a new heart." These expressions have perplexed them. They could not comprehend the plan of salvation.

Many have stumbled to ruin because of the erroneous doctrines taught by some ministers concerning the change that takes place at conversion. Some have lived in sadness for years, waiting for some marked evidence that they were accepted by God. They have separated themselves in a large measure from the world, and find pleasure in associating with the people of God; yet they dare not profess Christ, because they fear it would be presumption to say that they are children of God. They are waiting for that peculiar change that they have been led to believe is connected with conversion.

After a time some of these do receive evidence of their acceptance with God, and are then led to identify themselves with His people. And they date their conversion from this time. But . . . they were adopted into the family of God before that time. God accepted them when they became weary of sin, and having lost their desire for worldly pleasures, resolved to seek God earnestly. But, failing to understand the simplicity of the plan of salvation, they lost many privileges and blessings which they might have claimed had they only believed, when they first turned to God, that He had accepted them.

Others fall into a more dangerous error. They are governed by impulse. Their sympathies are stirred, and they regard this flight of feeling as an evidence that they are accepted by God and are converted. But the principles of their life are not changed. The evidences of a genuine work of grace on the heart are to be found not in feeling, but in the life.[16]

THE SWORD OF THE SPIRIT

And take the helmet of salvation, and the sword of the Spirit, which is the word of God.

We know the dangers and temptations that beset the youth at the present time are not few or small. . . . We live in an age when to resist evil calls for constant watchfulness and prayer. God's precious Word is the standard for youth who would be loyal to the King of heaven. Let them study the Scriptures. Let them commit text after text to memory, and acquire a knowledge of what the Lord has said. . . . And in trial let the youth spread out the Word of God before them, and with humble hearts, and in faith, seek the Lord for wisdom to find out His way, and for strength to walk in it. . . .

Let our young men institute a warfare against every habit that has the least danger of leading the soul from duty and devotion. Let them have stated seasons for prayer, never neglecting them if it can possibly be avoided. If they go out to battle with their vicious habits indulged as before they professed fellowship with Christ, they will soon fall an easy prey to Satan's devices. But armed with the Word of God, having it treasured in heart and mind, they will come forth unharmed by all the assaults of the foes of God or man. . . .

In the name of God lift your banner for truth and righteousness— the commandments of God and the faith of Jesus. You need the perfect armor of truth now, the sword of the Spirit, whose edge will never be blunted, but will cut its way through sin and unrighteousness.[17]

Let them take the Word of truth as the man of their counsel, and become skillful in the use of "the sword of the Spirit." Satan is a wise general; but the humble, devoted soldier of Jesus Christ may overcome him.[18]

IN CHRIST THERE IS STRENGTH

Let him take hold of my strength, that he may make peace with me; and he shall make peace with me.

The enemy cannot overcome the humble learner of Christ, the one who walks prayerfully before the Lord. Christ interposes Himself as a shelter, a retreat, from the assaults of the wicked one. The promise is given, "When the enemy shall come in like a flood, the Spirit of the Lord shall lift up a standard against him." . . .

Satan was permitted to tempt the too-confident Peter, as he had been permitted to tempt Job; but when that work was done he had to retire. Had Satan been suffered to have his way, there would have been no hope for Peter. He would have made complete shipwreck of faith. But the enemy dare not go one hairbreadth beyond his appointed sphere. There is no power in the whole satanic force that can disable the soul that trusts, in simple confidence, in the wisdom that comes from God.[19]

Christ is our tower of strength, and Satan can have no power over the soul that walks with God in humility of mind. The promise, "Let him take hold of My strength, that he may make peace with Me; and he shall make peace with Me." In Christ there is perfect and complete help for every tempted soul. Dangers beset every path, but the whole universe of heaven is standing on guard, that none may be tempted above that which he is able to bear. Some have strong traits of character, that will need to be constantly repressed. If kept under the control of the Spirit of God, these traits will be a blessing; but if not, they will prove a curse. . . . If we will give ourselves unselfishly to the work, never swerving in the least from principle, the Lord will throw about us the everlasting arms, and will prove a mighty helper. If we will look to Jesus as the One in whom we may trust, He will never fail us in any emergency.[20]

THROUGH CHRIST THERE IS VICTORY

Thanks be to God, which giveth us the victory through our Lord Jesus Christ.

Christ has power from His Father to give His divine grace and strength to man, making it possible for him through His name to overcome. . . .

All are personally exposed to the temptations that Christ overcame, but strength is provided for them in the all-powerful name of the great Conqueror. And all must, for themselves, individually overcome.[21]

He knows every trial and sorrow of childhood and youth. He was once just your age. The temptations and trials which come to you came also to Him. The sorrows which come to you came to Him. But He was never overcome by temptation. His life held nothing that was not pure and noble. He is your helper, your Redeemer.[22]

His heart of divine love and sympathy is drawn out most of all for the one who is the most hopelessly entangled in the snares of the enemy. With His own blood He has signed the emancipation papers of the race.

Jesus does not desire those who have been purchased at such a cost to become the sport of the enemy's temptations. He does not desire us to be overcome and perish. He who curbed the lions in their den and walked with His faithful witnesses amid the fiery flames is just as ready to work in our behalf, to subdue every evil in our nature. Today He is standing at the altar of mercy, presenting before God the prayers of those who desire His help. He turns no weeping, contrite one away. . . . The souls that turn to Him for refuge, Jesus lifts above the accusing and the strife of tongues. No man or evil angel can impeach these souls. Christ unites them to His own divine-human nature.[23]

THE WILL IS THE DECIDING POWER

Be not conformed to this world: but be ye transformed by the renewing of your mind, that ye may prove what is that good, and acceptable, and perfect, will of God.

There is nothing that can keep you away from God but a rebellious will.[24]

The will is the governing power in the nature of man. If the will is set right, all the rest of the being will come under its sway. The will is not the taste or the inclination, but it is the choice, the deciding power, the kingly power, which works in the children of men unto obedience to God or to disobedience.

You will be in constant peril until you understand the true force of the will. You may believe and promise all things, but your promises and your faith are of no account until you put your will on the right side. If you will fight the fight of faith with your will power, there is no doubt that you will conquer.

Your part is to put your will on the side of Christ. When you yield your will to His, He immediately takes possession of you, and works in you to will and to do of His good pleasure. Your nature is brought under the control of His Spirit. Even your thoughts are subject to Him. If you cannot control your impulses, your emotions, as you may desire, you can control the will, and thus an entire change will be wrought in your life. When you yield up your will to Christ, your life is hid with Christ in God. It is allied to the power which is above all principalities and powers. You have a strength from God that holds you fast to His strength; and a new life, even the life of faith, is possible to you.

You can never be successful in elevating yourself, unless your will is on the side of Christ, cooperating with the Spirit of God. Do not feel that you cannot; but say, "I can, I will." And God has pledged His Holy Spirit to help you in every decided effort.[25]

318

FIRST VICTORIES WON IN THE HOME

*Thou therefore, my son, be strong in the grace that is in Christ Jesus.
. . . Thou therefore endure hardness, as a good soldier of Jesus Christ.*

In all that pertains to the success of God's work, the very first victories are to be won in the home life.[26]

Beyond the discipline of the home and the school, all have to meet the stern discipline of life. How to meet this wisely is a lesson that should be made plain to every child and to every youth. It is true that God loves us, that He is working for our happiness, and that, if His law had always been obeyed, we should never have known suffering; and it is no less true that, in this world, as the result of sin, suffering, trouble, burdens, come to every life. We may do the children and the youth a lifelong good by teaching them to meet bravely these troubles and burdens. While we should give them sympathy, let it never be such as to foster self-pity. What they need is that which stimulates and strengthens rather than weakens.

They should be taught that this world is not a parade ground, but a battlefield. All are called to endure hardness, as good soldiers. They are to be strong, and quit themselves like men. Let them be taught that the true test of character is found in the willingness to bear burdens, to take the hard place, to do the work that needs to be done, though it bring no earthly recognition or reward.[27]

There is no greater curse upon households than to allow the youth to have their own way.[28]

Temptation once resisted will give power to more firmly resist the second time; every new victory gained over self will smooth the way for higher and nobler triumphs. Every victory is a seed sown to eternal life.[29]

BE STEADFAST, UNMOVABLE

Therefore, my beloved brethren, be ye stedfast, unmovable, always abounding in the work of the Lord, forasmuch as ye know that your labour is not in vain in the Lord.

Those who stand in defense of the honor of God, and maintain the purity of truth at any cost, will have manifold trials, as did our Saviour in the wilderness of temptation. The yielding temperaments, who have not courage to condemn wrong, but keep silent when their influence is needed to stand in the defense of right against any pressure, may avoid many heartaches and escape many perplexities, and lose a very rich reward, if not their own souls.

Those who in harmony with God, and through faith in Him, receive strength to resist wrong, and stand in defense of the right, will always have severe conflicts and will frequently have to stand almost alone. But precious victories will be theirs while they make God their dependence. His grace will be their strength. Their moral sense will be keen, clear, and sensitive. Their moral powers will be equal to withstand wrong influences. Their integrity, like that of Moses, of the purest character.[30]

It will require moral courage to do God's work unflinchingly. Those who do this can give no place to self-love, to selfish considerations, ambition, love of ease, or desire to shun the cross. . . . Shall we obey His voice, or shall we listen to the soothing voice of the evil one, and be rocked to a fatal slumber just on the eve of eternal realities?[31]

Our Saviour longs to save the young. . . . He is waiting to place upon their heads the crown of life and hear their happy voices join in ascribing honor and glory and majesty to God and the Lamb in the song of victory that shall echo and re-echo throughout the courts of heaven.[32]

WALK IN THE LIGHT

O send out thy light and thy truth: let them lead me; let them bring me unto thy holy hill, and to thy tabernacles.

In these days of peril we should be exceedingly careful not to reject the rays of light which Heaven in mercy sends us, for it is by these that we are to discern the devices of the enemy. We need light from Heaven every hour, that we may distinguish between the sacred and the common, the eternal and the temporal. If left to ourselves, we shall blunder at every step; we shall incline to the world, we shall shun self-denial, and see no necessity for constant watchfulness and prayer, and we shall be taken captive by Satan at his will. Some are today in this position. Having refused the light which God has sent them, they know not at what they stumble.

All whose names shall at last be found written in the Lamb's book of life will fight manfully the battles of the Lord. They will labor most earnestly to discern and put away temptations and every evil thing. They will feel that the eye of God is upon them and that the strictest fidelity is required. As faithful sentinels they will keep the passage barred, that Satan may not pass them disguised as an angel of light to work his work of death in their midst. . . .

The white-robed ones who surround the throne of God are not composed of that company who were lovers of pleasures more than lovers of God, and who choose to drift with the current rather than to breast the waves of opposition. All who remain pure and uncorrupted from the spirit and influence prevailing at this time will have stern conflicts. They will come through great tribulation; they will wash their robes of character and make them white in the blood of the Lamb. These will sing the song of triumph in the kingdom of glory.[33]

HOLD FAST

Hold that fast which thou hast, that no man take thy crown.

Decisions may be made in a moment that fix one's condition forever. . . . But remember, it would take the work of a lifetime to recover what a moment of yielding to temptation and thoughtlessness throws away. . . .

By a momentary act of will you may place yourself in the power of Satan, but it will require more than a momentary act of will to break his fetters and reach for a higher, holier life. The purpose may be formed, the work begun, but its accomplishment will require toil, time, and perseverance, patience, and sacrifice. The man who deliberately wanders from God in the full blaze of light will find, when he wishes to set his face to return, that briars and thorns have grown up in his path, and he must not be surprised or discouraged if he is compelled to travel long with torn and bleeding feet. The most fearful and most to be dreaded evidence of man's fall from a better state is the fact that it costs so much to get back. The way of return can be gained only by hard fighting, inch by inch, every hour. . . .

Those who win heaven will put forth their noblest efforts and will labor with all long-suffering, that they may reap the fruit of toil. There is a hand that will open wide the gates of Paradise to those who have stood the test of temptation and kept a good conscience by giving up the world, its honors, its applause, for the love of Christ, thus confessing Him before men and waiting with all patience for Him to confess them before His Father and the holy angels.[34]

Keep the conscience tender, that you may hear the faintest whisper of the voice that spake as never man spake.[35]

CHRIST'S VICTORY AS COMPLETE AS ADAM'S FAILURE

For as by one man's disobedience many were made sinners, so by the obedience of one shall many be made righteous.

Christ is called the second Adam. In purity and holiness, connected with God and beloved by God, He began where the first Adam began. Willingly He passed over the ground where Adam fell, and redeemed Adam's failure.

But the first Adam was in every way more favorably situated than was Christ. The wonderful provision made for man in Eden was made by a God who loved him. Everything in nature was pure and undefiled. . . . Not a shadow interposed between them [Adam and Eve] and their Creator. They knew God as their beneficent Father, and in all things their will was conformed to the will of God. . . .

But Satan came to the dwellers in Eden and insinuated doubts of God's wisdom. He accused Him, their Heavenly Father and Sovereign, of selfishness, because, to test their loyalty, He had prohibited them from eating of the tree of knowledge. . . .

Christ was tempted by Satan in a hundredfold severer manner than was Adam, and under circumstances in every way more trying. The deceiver presented himself as an angel of light, but Christ withstood his temptations. He redeemed Adam's disgraceful fall, and saved the world. . . .

In His human nature He maintained the purity of His divine character. He lived the law of God, and honored it in a world of transgression, revealing to the heavenly universe, to Satan, and to all the fallen sons and daughters of Adam that through His grace humanity can keep the law of God. He came to impart His own divine nature, His own image, to the repentant, believing soul.[36]

Christ's victory was as complete as had been Adam's failure. So we may resist temptation, and force Satan to depart from us.[37]

CHRIST OVERCAME THE WORLD

These things I have spoken unto you, that in me ye might have peace. In the world ye shall have tribulation: but be of good cheer; I have overcome the world.

When the last steps of Christ's humiliation were to be taken, when the deepest sorrow was closing about His soul, He said to His disciples, "The prince of this world cometh, and hath nothing in Me." "The prince of this world is judged." Now shall he be cast out. With prophetic eye Christ traced the scenes to take place in His last great conflict. He knew that when He should exclaim, "It is finished," all heaven would triumph. His ear caught the distant music and the shouts of victory in the heavenly courts. He knew that the knell of Satan's empire would then be sounded, and the name of Christ would be heralded from world to world throughout the universe.

Christ rejoiced that He could do more for His followers than they could ask or think. He spoke with assurance, knowing that an almighty decree had been given before the world was made. He knew that truth, armed with the omnipotence of the Holy Spirit, would conquer in the contest with evil; and that the bloodstained banner would wave triumphantly over His followers. He knew that the life of His trusting disciples would be like His, a series of uninterrupted victories, not seen to be such here, but recognized as such in the great hereafter. . . .

"In the world ye shall have tribulation: but be of good cheer; I have overcome the world." Christ did not fail, neither was He discouraged, and His followers are to manifest a faith of the same enduring nature. . . . Though apparent impossibilities obstruct their way, by His grace they are to go forward. . . . They are to have power to resist evil, power that neither earth, nor death, nor hell can master, power that will enable them to overcome as Christ overcame.[38]

ᨀ ᨀ ᨀ

Satan trembles and flees before the weakest soul who finds refuge in that mighty name.[39]

324

CHRISTIANS IN ALL AGES HAVE OVERCOME

For whatsoever is born of God overcometh the world: and this is the victory that overcometh the world, even our faith.

The apostles built upon a sure foundation, even the Rock of Ages. To this foundation they brought the stones that they quarried from the world. Not without hindrance did the builders labor. Their work was made exceedingly difficult by the opposition of the enemies of Christ. They had to contend against the bigotry, prejudice, and hatred of those who were building upon a false foundation. . . .

Kings and governors, priests and rulers, sought to destroy the temple of God. But in the face of imprisonment, torture, and death, faithful men carried the work forward; and the structure grew, beautiful and symmetrical. . . .

Centuries of fierce persecution followed the establishment of the Christian church, but there were never wanting men who counted the work of building God's temple dearer than life itself. . . .

The enemy of righteousness left nothing undone in his effort to stop the work committed to the Lord's builders. But God "left not Himself without witness." Workers were raised up who ably defended the faith once delivered to the saints. History bears record to the fortitude and heroism of these men. Like the apostles, many of them fell at their post, but the building of the temple went steadily forward. The workmen were slain, but the work advanced. The Waldenses, John Wycliffe, Huss and Jerome, Martin Luther and Zwingli, Cranmer, Latimer, and Knox, the Huguenots, John and Charles Wesley, and a host of others brought to the foundation material that will endure throughout eternity. . . . We may look back through the centuries and see the living stones of which it is composed gleaming like jets of light through the darkness of error and superstition. Throughout eternity these precious jewels will shine with increasing luster, testifying to the power of the truth of God.[40]

PAUL'S SHOUT OF VICTORY

Who shall separate us from the love of Christ? shall tribulation, or distress, or persecution, or famine, or nakedness, or peril, or sword? . . . Nay, in all these things we are more than conquerors through him that loved us.

Paul suffered for the truth's sake, and yet we hear no complaints from his lips. As he reviews his life of toil and care and sacrifice, he says, "I reckon that the sufferings of this present time are not worthy to be compared with the glory which shall be revealed in us." The shout of victory from God's faithful servant comes down the line to our time: "Who shall separate us from the love of Christ? shall tribulation, or distress, or persecution, or famine, or nakedness, or peril, or sword? . . . Nay, in all these things we are more than conquerors through Him that loved us. For I am persuaded, that neither death, nor life, nor angels, nor principalities, nor powers, nor things present, nor things to come, nor height, nor depth, nor any other creature, shall be able to separate us from the love of God, which is in Christ Jesus our Lord."

Though Paul was at last confined in a Roman prison—shut away from the light and air of heaven, cut off from his active labors in the gospel, and momentarily expecting to be condemned to death—yet he did not yield to doubt or despondency. From that gloomy dungeon came his dying testimony, full of sublime faith and courage that has inspired the hearts of saints and martyrs in all succeeding ages. His words fitly describe the results of . . . sanctification. . . . "I am now ready to be offered, and the time of my departure is at hand. I have fought a good fight, I have finished my course, I have kept the faith: henceforth there is laid up for me a crown of righteousness, which the Lord, the righteous judge, shall give me at that day: and not to me only, but unto all them also that love His appearing."[41]

The wounds and scars of our warfare will be to us, as to Paul, the trophies of victory.[42]

JEREMIAH'S DECLARATION OF THANKSGIVING

It is of the Lord's mercies that we are not consumed, because his compassions fail not. They are new every morning: great is thy faithfulness.

The faithful prophet was daily strengthened to endure. "The Lord is with me as a mighty terrible one," he declared in faith; "therefore my persecutors shall stumble, and they shall not prevail: they shall be greatly ashamed; for they shall not prosper: their everlasting confusion shall never be forgotten." "Sing unto the Lord, praise ye the Lord: for He hath delivered the soul of the poor from the hand of the evildoers." The experiences through which Jeremiah passed in the days of his youth and also in the later years of his ministry taught him the lesson that "the way of man is not in himself: it is not in man that walketh to direct his steps." He learned to pray, "O Lord, correct me, but with judgment; not in Thine anger, lest Thou bring me to nothing."

When called to drink of the cup of tribulation and sorrow, and when tempted in his misery to say, "My strength and my hope is perished from the Lord," he recalled the providences of God in his behalf, and triumphantly exclaimed, "It is of the Lord's mercies that we are not consumed, because His compassions fail not. They are new every morning: great is Thy faithfulness."[43]

Many professed Christians dwell too much on the dark side of life, when they might rejoice in the sunshine; they repine when they should be glad; they talk of trials when they should offer praise for the rich blessings they enjoy. They look at the unpleasant things, hoard up the disappointments, and sigh over the griefs, and, as a consequence, grow heavyhearted and sad, when, should they count up their blessings, they would find them so numerous that they would forget to mention their annoyances. If they would every day take note of the favors that are done them; if they would store their minds with the precious memory of kindnesses received, how much occasion they would find to render thanks and praise to the Giver of all good.[44]

JOB KNEW THAT HIS REDEEMER LIVED

I know that my redeemer liveth, that he shall stand at the latter day upon the earth: and though after my skin worms destroy this body, yet in my flesh shall I see God.

Into the experience of all there come times of keen disappointment and utter discouragement—days when sorrow is the portion, and it is hard to believe that God is still the kind benefactor of His earth-born children; days when troubles harass the soul, till death seems preferable to life. It is then that many lose their hold on God and are brought into the slavery of doubt, the bondage of unbelief. Could we at such times discern with spiritual insight the meaning of God's providences, we should see angels seeking to save us from ourselves, striving to plant our feet upon a foundation more firm than the everlasting hills; and new faith, new life, would spring into being.

The faithful Job, in the day of his affliction and darkness, declared: . . .

"My soul chooseth . . . death rather than my life.

I loathe it;

I would not live alway:

Let me alone;

For my days are vanity."

But though weary of life, Job was not allowed to die. To him were pointed out the possibilities of the future, and there was given him the message of hope:

"Thou shalt be steadfast, and shalt not fear:

Because thou shalt forget thy misery,

And remember it as waters that pass away. . . ."

From the depths of discouragement and despondency Job rose to the heights of implicit trust in the mercy and the saving power of God. Triumphantly he declared: "Though He slay me, yet will I trust in Him." [45]

NONE GREATER THAN JOHN THE BAPTIST

Verily I say unto you, Among them that are born of women there hath not risen a greater than John the Baptist.

The tall reeds that grew beside the Jordan, bending before every breeze, were fitting representatives of the rabbis who had stood as critics and judges of the Baptist's mission. They were swayed this way and that by the winds of popular opinion. They would not humble themselves to receive the heart-searching message of the Baptist, yet for fear of the people they dared not openly oppose his work. But God's messenger was of no such craven spirit. The multitudes who were gathered about Christ had been witnesses to the work of John. They had heard his fearless rebuke of sin. To the self-righteous Pharisees, the priestly Sadducees, King Herod and his court, princes and soldiers, publicans and peasants, John had spoken with equal plainness. He was no trembling reed, swayed by the winds of human praise or prejudice. In the prison he was the same in his loyalty to God and his zeal for righteousness as when he preached God's message in the wilderness. In his faithfulness to principle he was as firm as a rock. . . .

In the announcement to Zacharias before the birth of John, the angel had declared, "He shall be great in the sight of the Lord." In the estimation of Heaven, what is it that constitutes greatness?—Not that which the world accounts greatness. . . . It is moral worth that God values. Love and purity are the attributes He prizes most. John was great in the sight of the Lord, when before the messengers from the Sanhedrim, before the people, and before his own disciples he refrained from seeking honor for himself, but pointed all to Jesus as the Promised One. His unselfish joy in the ministry of Christ presents the highest type of nobility ever revealed in man.[46]

WITH HONESTY

Recompense to no man evil for evil. Provide things honest in the sight of all men.

In every business transaction a Christian will be just what he wants his brethren to think he is. His course of action is guided by underlying principles. He does not scheme; therefore he has nothing to conceal, nothing to gloss over. He may be criticized, he may be tested, but his unbending integrity will shine forth like pure gold. He is a blessing to all connected with him, for his word is trustworthy. He is a man who will not take an advantage of his neighbor. He is a friend and benefactor to all, and his fellow men put confidence in his counsel. . . . A truly honest man will never take advantage of weakness or incompetency in order to fill his own purse. He accepts a fair equivalent for that which he sells. If there are defects in the articles sold, he frankly tells his brother or his neighbor, although by so doing he may work against his own pecuniary interests.

In all the details of life the strictest principles of honesty are to be maintained. These are not the principles which govern our world, for Satan, deceiver, liar, and oppressor is the master, and his subjects follow him and carry out his purposes. But Christians serve under a different Master, and their actions must be wrought in God, irrespective of all selfish gain. Deviation from perfect fairness in business deal may appear as a small thing in the estimation of some, but our Saviour did not thus regard it. . . .

A man may not have a pleasant exterior, he may be deficient in many respects, but if he has a reputation for straightforward honesty, he will be respected. . . . A man who steadfastly adheres to truth will win the confidence of all. Not only will his brethren in the faith trust him, but unbelievers will be constrained to acknowledge him as a man of honor.[47]

WITH TRUTHFULNESS

The remnant of Israel shall not do iniquity, nor speak lies; neither shall a deceitful tongue be found in their mouth: for they shall feed and lie down, and none shall make them afraid.

Truthfulness and integrity are attributes of God, and he who possesses these qualities possesses a power that is invincible.[48]

Never prevaricate; never tell an untruth in precept or in example. . . . Be straight and undeviating. Even a slight prevarication should not be allowed.[49]

The Saviour has a deep contempt for all deception. The stern punishment meted out to Ananias and Sapphira shows this.[50]

Lying lips are an abomination to Him. He declares that into the holy city "there shall in no wise enter . . . any thing that defileth, neither whatsoever worketh abomination, or maketh a lie." Let truth telling be held with no loose hand or uncertain grasp. Let it become a part of the life. Playing fast and loose with truth, and dissembling to suit one's own selfish plans, means shipwreck of faith. . . . He who utters untruths sells his soul in a cheap market. His falsehoods may seem to serve in emergencies; he may thus seem to make business advancement that he could not gain by fair dealing; but he finally reaches the place where he can trust no one. Himself a falsifier, he has no confidence in the word of others.[51]

No man can pride himself on his truthfulness, for unless he has overcome he does not know what truthfulness is. No one can know the strength of his truthfulness and honesty until he has passed the fiery ordeal of the temptation to acquire means in questionable ways.[52]

He whose heart is filled with the love that proceeds from God does not allow self-exaltation or dishonesty to find place in his life. He who is "born again," of the Spirit, reveals Christ in the daily life. He is upright in all his dealings. He does no sly, cunning, underhand work. The good fruit that appears in his life testifies to the condition of his heart.[53]

WITH HUMILITY

A man's pride shall bring him low: but honour shall uphold the humble in spirit.

Man may lift himself up in pride and boast of his power, but in an instant God can bring him to nothingness. It is Satan's work to lead men to glorify themselves with their entrusted talents. Every man through whom God works will have to learn that the living, ever-present, ever-acting God is supreme, and has lent him talents to use—an intellect to originate; a heart to be the seat of his throne; affections to flow out in blessing to all with whom he shall come in contact; a conscience through which the Holy Spirit can convict him of sin, of righteousness, and of judgment.[54]

Pride, ignorance, and folly are constant companions. The Lord is displeased with the pride manifested among His professed people.[55]

Parents, . . . it is easier for you to teach your children a lesson of pride than a lesson of humility.[56]

Before honor is humility. To fill a high place before men, Heaven chooses the worker who . . . takes a lowly place before God. The most childlike disciple is the most efficient in labor for God. The heavenly intelligences can cooperate with him who is seeking, not to exalt self, but to save souls. . . . From communion with Christ he will go forth to work for those who are perishing in their sins. He is anointed for his mission, and he succeeds where many of the learned and intellectually wise would fail. . . .

The simplicity, the self-forgetfulness, and the confiding love of a little child are the attributes that Heaven values. These are the characteristics of real greatness.[57]

Solomon was never so rich or so wise or so truly great as when he confessed, "I am but a little child: I know not how to go out or come in."[58]

WITH LIBERALITY

There is that scattereth, and yet increaseth; and there is that withholdeth more than is meet, but it tendeth to poverty. The liberal soul shall be made fat; and he that watereth shall be watered also himself.

It is God who blesses men with property, and He does this that they may be able to give toward the advancement of His cause. He sends the sunshine and the rain. He causes vegetation to flourish. He gives health and the ability to acquire means. All our blessings come from His bountiful hand. In turn, He would have men and women show their gratitude by returning Him a portion in tithes and offerings—in thank offerings, in freewill offerings, in trespass offerings. Should means flow into the treasury in accordance with this divinely appointed plan—a tenth of all the increase, and liberal offerings—there would be an abundance for the advancement of the Lord's work.

But the hearts of men become hardened through selfishness, and like Ananias and Sapphira, they are tempted to withhold part of the price, while pretending to fulfill God's requirements. Many spend money lavishly in self-gratification. Men and women consult their pleasure and gratify their taste, while they bring to God, almost unwillingly, a stinted offering. They forget that God will one day demand a strict account of how His goods have been used.[59]

Constant, self-denying benevolence is God's remedy for the cankering sins of selfishness and covetousness. God has arranged systematic benevolence to sustain His cause and relieve the necessities of the suffering and needy. He has ordained that giving should become a habit, that it may counteract the dangerous and deceitful sin of covetousness. Continual giving starves covetousness to death. . . . He requires the constant exercise of benevolence, that the force of habit in good works may break the force of habit in an opposite direction.[60]

WITH LOVE

Charity suffereth long, and is kind; charity envieth not; charity vaunteth not itself, is not puffed up.

Those who open their hearts and homes to invite Jesus to abide with them should keep the moral atmosphere unclouded by strife, bitterness, wrath, malice, or even an unkind word. Jesus will not abide in a home where are contention, envy, and bitterness. . . .

Paul had a healthful religious experience. The love of Christ was his grand theme and the constraining power that governed him.

When in most discouraging circumstances, which would have had a depressing influence upon halfway Christians, he is firm of heart, full of courage and hope and cheer, exclaiming, "Rejoice in the Lord alway, and again I say, Rejoice." The same hope and cheerfulness is seen when he is upon the deck of the ship, the tempest beating about him, the ship going to pieces. He gives orders to the commander of the ship and preserves the lives of all on board. Although a prisoner, he is really the master of the ship, the freest and happiest man on board. When wrecked and driven to a barbarous island, he is the most self-possessed, the most helpful in saving his fellow men from a watery grave. His hands brought the wood to kindle the fire for the benefit of the chilled, shipwrecked passengers. When they saw the deadly viper fasten upon his hand, they were filled with terror; but Paul calmly shook it into the fire, knowing it could not harm him; for he implicitly trusted in God.

When before kings and dignitaries of the earth, who held his life in their hands, he quailed not; for he had given his life to God. . . . Grace, like an angel of mercy, makes his voice heard sweet and clear, repeating the story of the cross, the matchless love of Jesus.[61]

Love's agencies have wonderful power, for they are divine.[62]

WITH CHRISTLIKE WORDS AND DEEDS

By thy words thou shalt be justified, and by thy words thou shalt be condemned.

When you do your appointed work without contention or criticism of others, a freedom, a light, and a power will attend it that will give character and influence to the institutions and enterprises with which you are connected.

Remember that you are never on vantage ground when you are ruffled and when you carry the burden of setting right every soul who comes near you. If you yield to the temptation to criticize others, to point out their faults, to tear down what they are doing, you may be sure that you will fail to act your own part nobly and well.

This is a time when every man in a responsible position and every member of the church should bring every feature of his work into close accord with the teachings of the Word of God. By untiring vigilance, by fervent prayer, by Christlike words and deeds, we are to show the world what God desires His church to be. . . .

Christ humbled Himself to stand at the head of humanity, to meet the temptations and endure the trials that humanity must meet and endure. He must know what humanity has to meet from the fallen foe, that He might know how to succor those who are tempted.

And Christ has been made our judge. The Father is not the judge. The angels are not. He who took humanity upon Himself, and in this world lived a perfect life, is to judge us. He only can be our judge. . . . No one of you has been appointed to be judge of others. It is all that you can do to discipline yourselves. . . .

We have a character to maintain, but it is the character of Christ. . . . May the Lord help us to die to self, and be born again, that Christ may live in us, a living, active principle, a power that will keep us holy.[63]

WITH PEACE

Acquaint now thyself with him, and be at peace: thereby good shall come unto thee.

We embarked in a small boat which was to convey us across the channel to the coast of Denmark. Here I was provided with a state-room containing two sofas, and shut in by heavy curtains—accommodations which we then thought hardly necessary for a day journey of only six hours. We had occasion, however, to change this opinion before reaching land. The first hour we spent on deck in the cheerful and well-furnished ladies' cabin. The weather was pleasant, the sea smooth, and we anticipated an enjoyable trip. But soon the captain, passing through the cabin, advised us to go below and lie down at once, for we were coming into rough water. We complied, though rather unwillingly. In a short time the boat began to rock violently; we could hardly keep our position upon the sofas. I became very ill, now in a profuse perspiration, as if every organ was struggling against the terrible malady, and then overcome by deathly seasickness. . . .

Death seemed very near; but I felt that I could cling, with the firm grasp of faith, to the hand of Jesus. He who holds the waters in the hollow of His hand could keep us in the tempest. The waves of the great deep obey His voice, "Hitherto shalt thou come, but no further: and here shall thy proud waves be stayed." I thought how Jesus calmed the fears of His disciples as He stilled the stormy Galilee; and should I be afraid to trust to His protection who had given me my work? My heart was kept in perfect peace because it was stayed on Him. The lesson of trust I learned during these few hours was very precious. I have found that every trial of life is given to teach me a new lesson of my own dependence, and of trust in my heavenly Father. We may believe that God is with us in every place, and in every trying hour we may hold fast that hand which has all power.[64]

336

NOT ONE WORD OF HIS PROMISE HAS FAILED

Blessed be the Lord, that hath given rest unto his people Israel, according to all that he promised: there hath not failed one word of all his good promise, which he promised by the hand of Moses his servant.

We were favored with a sight of the most glorious sunset it was ever my privilege to behold. Language is inadequate to picture its beauty. The last beams of the setting sun, silver and gold, purple, amber, and crimson, shed their glories athwart the sky, growing brighter and brighter, rising higher and higher in the heavens, until it seemed that the gates of the city of God had been left ajar and gleams of the inner glory were flashing through. For two hours the wondrous splendor continued to light up the cold northern sky—a picture painted by the great Master-Artist upon the shifting canvas of the heavens. Like the smile of God it seemed, above all earthly homes, above the rock-bound plains, the rugged mountains, the lonely forests, through which our journey lay.

Angels of mercy seemed whispering, "Look up. This glory is but a gleam of the light which flows from the throne of God. Live not for earth alone. Look up, and behold by faith the mansions of the heavenly home." This scene was to me as the bow of promise to Noah, enabling me to grasp the assurance of God's unfailing care and to look forward to the haven of rest awaiting the faithful worker. Ever since that time I have felt that God granted us this token of His love for our encouragement. Never while memory lingers can I forget that vision of beauty and the comfort and peace it brought.[65]

It is impossible for any mind to comprehend all the richness and greatness of even one promise of God. One catches the glory of one point of view, another the beauty and grace from another point, and the soul is filled with the heavenly light.[66]

In them He is speaking to us individually. . . . It is in these promises that Christ communicates to us His grace and power.[67]

337

GOD'S PROMISES ARE FOR ME

Sing unto the Lord, O ye saints of his, and give thanks at the remembrance of his holiness. For his anger endureth but a moment; in his favour is life: weeping may endure for a night, but joy cometh in the morning.

To blot the promises of God from the Word would be like blotting the sun from the sky. There would then be nothing to gladden our experience. God has placed the promises in His Word to lead us to have faith in Him. In these promises He draws back the veil from eternity, giving us a glimpse of the far more exceeding and eternal weight of glory which awaits the overcomer. Let us, then, rest in God. Let us praise Him for giving us such a glorious revelation of His purposes.

All along our pathway God places the flowers of promise to brighten our journey. But many refuse to gather these flowers, choosing instead the thorns and thistles. At every step they weep and mourn, when they might rejoice in the Lord because He has made the road to heaven so pleasant.

As we look at the promises of God we find comfort and hope and joy, for they speak to us the words of the Infinite One. Properly to appreciate these precious promises we should study them carefully, examining them in detail. How much joy we might bring into life, how much goodness into the character, if we would but make these promises our own! As we journey in the upward way, let us talk of the blessings strewn along the path. As we think of the mansions Christ is preparing for us, we forget the petty annoyances which we meet day by day. We seem to breathe the atmosphere of the heavenly country to which we are journeying, and we are soothed and comforted. . . . Let us honor God by weaving more of Jesus and heaven into our lives.[68]

The unfailing promises of God will keep your heart in perfect peace.[69]

AN ETERNAL LIFE

December 1   *Preparing for Eternal Life*   *2 Peter 1:10, 11*

MAKE YOUR CALLING AND ELECTION SURE

Wherefore the rather, brethren, give diligence to make your calling and election sure: for if ye do these things, ye shall never fall: for so an entrance shall be ministered unto you abundantly into the everlasting kingdom of our Lord and Saviour Jesus Christ.

Here a life insurance policy is offered us which insures for us eternal life in the kingdom of God. I ask you to study these words of the apostle Peter. There is understanding and intelligence in every sentence. By taking hold upon the Lifegiver, who gave His life for us, we receive eternal life.[1]

We are each deciding our eternal destiny, and it rests wholly with us whether we shall gain eternal life. Will we live the lessons given in the Word of God, Christ's great lesson book? It is the grandest, and yet the most simply arranged and easily understood book ever prepared for giving an education in proper behaviour, in speech, in manners, in affection. It is the only book that will prepare human beings for the life that measures with the life of God. And those who make this Word their daily study are the only ones who are worthy of receiving a diploma entitling them to educate and train the children for entrance into the higher school, to be crowned as victorious overcomers.

Christ Jesus is the only judge of the fitness of human agents to receive eternal life. The gates of the holy city will open to those who have been humble, meek, lowly followers of His, having learned their lessons from Him, and received from Him their life insurance policy, forming characters after the divine similitude.[2]

When the ransomed are redeemed from the earth, the city of God will be opened to you. . . . Then the harp will be placed in your hand, and your voice will be raised in songs of praise to God and to the Lamb, by whose great sacrifice you are made partakers of His nature and given an immortal inheritance in the kingdom of God.[3]

KEEP THE COMMANDMENTS

Blessed are they that do his commandments, that they may have right to the tree of life, and may enter in through the gates into the city.

The conflict is before us. The only safety for any one of us now is to be one with Christ in God. We are to strive to enter in at the strait gate. But this gate does not swing loosely on its hinges. It will not admit doubtful characters. We must now strive for eternal life with an intensity that is proportionate to the value of the prize before us. It is not money or lands or position, but the possession of a Christlike character, that will open to us the gates of Paradise. It is not dignity, it is not intellectual attainments, that will win for us the crown of immortality. Only the meek and lowly ones, who have made God their sufficiency, will receive this gift. . . .

To create the soul anew, to bring light out of darkness, love out of enmity, holiness out of impurity, is the work of Omnipotence alone. The work of the Infinite, as He engages, by the consent of the human being, to make the life complete in Christ, to bring perfection to the character, is the science of eternity.

What is the honor conferred upon Christ? Without employing any compulsion, without using any violence, He blends the will of the human subject to the will of God. This is the science of all true science; for by it a mighty change is wrought in mind and character—the change that must be wrought in the life of every one who passes through the gates of the city of God.[4]

Then they that have kept God's commandments shall breathe in immortal vigor beneath the tree of life; and through unending ages the inhabitants of sinless worlds shall behold, in that garden [Eden] of delight, a sample of the perfect work of God's creation, untouched by the curse of sin—a sample of what the whole earth would have become, had man but fulfilled the Creator's glorious plan.[5]

WALK WITH GOD CONTINUALLY

And Enoch walked with God: and he was not; for God took him.

When God takes the members of His church to heaven, it will be because they have walked with Him here on this earth, receiving from above strength and wisdom which enables them to serve Him aright. Those who are taken to God will be men and women who now pray in humility and contrition, whose hearts are not lifted up unto vanity. In their dealing with believers and unbelievers they represent Christ.[6]

Those who have no pleasure in thinking and talking of God in this life will not enjoy the life that is to come, where God is ever present, dwelling among His people. But those who love to think of God will be in their element, breathing in the atmosphere of heaven. Those who on earth love the thought of heaven will be happy in its holy associations and pleasures. . . .

When in the world they did not claim to be their own, and God set to His seal that they were His. Heaven will be for those who desire it with intense desire, who put forth efforts in proportion to the value of the object which they seek. The thoughts of those who will obtain heaven will be upon heavenly things.[7]

"Blessed are the pure in heart; for they shall see God." For three hundred years Enoch had been seeking purity of soul, that he might be in harmony with Heaven. For three centuries he had walked with God. Day by day he had longed for a closer union; nearer and nearer had grown the communion, until God took him to Himself. He had stood at the threshold of the eternal world, only a step between him and the land of the blest; and now the portals opened, the walk with God, so long pursued on earth, continued, and he passed through the gates of the Holy City—the first from among men to enter there.[8]

WALK BY FAITH

For we walk by faith, not by sight.

We are to live, not to elevate ourselves, but that we may, as God's little children, do to the very best of our ability the work that He has committed to us. It is our business to give a right impression to others. We are preparing for eternity, for the sanitarium above, where the Great Physician shall wipe away the tears from every eye, and where the leaves of the tree of life are for the healing of the nation.

Let us all take hold of Christ Jesus by a living faith, and walk in humility of mind. Then the grace of God will be revealed in us, and we shall see of His salvation. We shall greet the holy family of the redeemed. . . . We shall touch our golden harps, and heaven will ring with rich music. We shall cast our glittering crowns at His feet and give glory to Him who has overcome in our behalf.

There may be some things here that we do not understand. Some things in the Bible may appear to us mysterious, because they are beyond our finite comprehension. But as our Saviour leads us by the living waters, He will make clear to our minds that which was not before clearly understood.

As I think of the future glory of heaven, I feel an intense desire that every living soul may know about it. . . . I long to hold Him up as the mighty Healer. . . .

It means much to us whether we are in pursuit of the heavenly things or of the earthly. The earthly will soon pass away. In these days there is great destruction of earthly treasures. There are "earthquakes in divers places," and trouble and difficulties are seen on every hand. But it is our privilege to be preparing to become members of the heavenly family, children of the heavenly King.[9]

BE READY AND WAITING

And it shall be said in that day, Lo, this is our God; we have waited for him, and he will save us: this is the Lord, we have waited for him, we will be glad and rejoice in his salvation.

As I hear of the terrible calamities that from week to week are taking place, I ask myself: What do these things mean? The most awful disasters are following one another in quick succession. How frequently we hear of earthquakes and tornadoes, of destruction by fire and flood, with great loss of life and property! Apparently these calamities are capricious outbreaks of seemingly disorganized, unregulated forces, but in them God's purpose may be read. They are one of the means by which He seeks to arouse men and women to a sense of their danger. . . .

The judgments of God are in the land. They speak in solemn warning, saying: "Be ye also ready: for in such an hour as ye think not the Son of man cometh." . . .

We are living in the closing scenes of this earth's history. . . . We have no time—not a moment—to lose. Let us not be found sleeping on guard. . . . Let us persuade men and women everywhere to repent and flee from the wrath to come. Let us arouse them to immediate preparation, for we little know what is before us. . . .

He [the Lord] is soon coming, and we must be ready and waiting for His appearing. Oh, how glorious it will be to see Him and be welcomed as His redeemed ones! . . . If we can but see the King in His beauty we shall be forever blessed. I feel as if I must cry aloud: "Homeward bound!" We are nearing the time when Christ will come in power and great glory to take His ransomed ones to their eternal home. . . .

In the great closing work we shall meet with perplexities that we know not how to deal with; but let us not forget that the three great powers of heaven are working, that a divine hand is on the wheel, and that God will bring His promises to pass. He will gather from the world a people who will serve Him in righteousness.[10]

GOD'S PEOPLE DELIVERED

And the ransomed of the Lord shall return, and come to Zion with songs and everlasting joy upon their heads: they shall obtain joy and gladness, and sorrow and sighing shall flee away.

It is at midnight that God manifests His power for the deliverance of His people. The sun appears, shining in its strength. Signs and wonders follow in quick succession. The wicked look with terror and amazement upon the scene, while the righteous behold with solemn joy the tokens of their deliverance. Everything in nature seems turned out of its course. . . . Dark, heavy clouds come up, and clash against each other. In the midst of the angry heavens is one clear space of indescribable glory, whence comes the voice of God like the sound of many waters, saying, "It is done."

That voice shakes the heavens and the earth. There is a mighty earthquake, "such as was not since men were upon the earth, so mighty an earthquake, and so great." The firmament appears to open and shut. The glory from the throne of God seems flashing through. The mountains shake like a reed in the wind, and ragged rocks are scattered on every side. . . .

Graves are opened, and "many of them that sleep in the dust of the earth . . . awake, some to everlasting life, and some to shame and everlasting contempt." All who have died in the faith of the third angel's message come forth from the tomb glorified, to hear God's covenant of peace with those who have kept His law. . . .

The voice of God is heard from heaven, declaring the day and hour of Jesus' coming and delivering the everlasting covenant to His people. Like peals of loudest thunder, His words roll through the earth. The Israel of God stand listening, with their eyes fixed upward. Their countenances are lighted up with His glory, and shine as did the face of Moses when he came down from Sinai. The wicked cannot look upon them. And when the blessing is pronounced on those who have honored God by keeping His Sabbath holy, there is a mighty shout of victory.[11]

CHRIST HIMSELF COMES FOR US

For the Lord himself shall descend from heaven with a shout, with the voice of the archangel, and with the trump of God: and the dead in Christ shall rise first: then we which are alive and remain shall be caught up together with them in the clouds, to meet the Lord in the air: and so shall we ever be with the Lord. Wherefore comfort one another with these words.

Jesus is coming, coming with clouds and great glory. A multitude of shining angels will attend Him. He will come to honor those who have loved Him and kept His commandments, and to take them to Himself. He has not forgotten them or His promise.[12]

There appears in the East a small black cloud. . . . The people of God know this to be the sign of the Son of man. In solemn silence they gaze upon it as it draws nearer the earth, . . . until it is a great white cloud, its base a glory like consuming fire, and above it the rainbow of the covenant. Jesus rides forth as a mighty conqueror. . . .

As the living cloud comes still nearer, every eye beholds the Prince of life. No crown of thorns now mars that sacred head, but a diadem of glory rests on His holy brow. His countenance outshines the dazzling brightness of the noonday sun. "And He hath on His vesture and on His thigh a name written, King of kings, and Lord of lords." . . . The heavens are rolled together as a scroll, the earth trembles before Him, and every mountain and island is moved out of its place. . . .

Amid the reeling of the earth, the flash of lightning, and the roar of thunder, the voice of the Son of God calls forth the sleeping saints. . . . Throughout the length and breadth of the earth the dead shall hear that voice, and they that hear shall live. . . . All arise with the freshness and vigor of eternal youth. . . .

The living righteous are changed "in a moment, in the twinkling of an eye." At the voice of God they were glorified; now they are made immortal, and with the risen saints are caught up to meet their Lord in the air.[13] Oh, what a glorious meeting![14]

CHRIST'S CORONATION DAY

Great and marvellous are thy works, Lord God Almighty; just and true are thy ways, thou King of saints.

In that day the redeemed will shine forth in the glory of the Father and His Son. The angels of heaven, touching their golden harps, will welcome the King and those who are the trophies of His victory—those who have been washed and made white in the blood of the Lamb. A song of triumph will peal forth, filling all heaven. Christ has conquered. He enters the heavenly courts accompanied by His redeemed ones, the witnesses that His mission of suffering and sacrifice has not been in vain.[15]

Far above the city, upon a foundation of burnished gold, is a throne, high and lifted up. Upon this throne sits the Son of God, and around Him are the subjects of His kingdom. The power and majesty of Christ no language can describe, no pen portray. The glory of the Eternal Father is enshrouding His Son. The brightness of His presence fills the city of God and flows out beyond the gates, flooding the whole earth with its radiance.

Nearest the throne are those who were once zealous in the cause of Satan, but who, plucked as brands from the burning, have followed their Saviour with deep, intense devotion. Next are those who perfected Christian characters in the midst of falsehood and infidelity, those who honored the law of God when the Christian world declared it void, and the millions of all ages who were martyred for their faith. And beyond is the "great multitude, which no man could number, of all nations, and kindreds, and people, and tongues, . . . before the throne, and before the Lamb, clothed with white robes, and palms in their hands." Their warfare is ended, their victory won. They have run the race and reached the prize. . . .

In the presence of the assembled inhabitants of earth and heaven the final coronation of the Son of God takes place.[16]

CHRIST PRESENTS ME WITH A CROWN AND HARP

Henceforth there is laid up for me a crown of righteousness, which the Lord, the righteous judge, shall give me at that day: and not to me only, but unto all them also that love his appearing.

Before entering the city of God the Saviour bestows upon His followers the emblems of victory and invests them with the insignia of their royal state. The glittering ranks are drawn up in the form of a hollow square about their King, whose form rises in majesty high above saint and angel, whose countenance beams upon them full of benignant love. Throughout the unnumbered host of the redeemed every glance is fixed upon Him, every eye beholds His glory whose "visage was so marred more than any man, and His form more than the sons of men." Upon the heads of the overcomers Jesus with His own right hand places the crown of glory. For each there is a crown, bearing his own "new name," and the inscription, "Holiness to the Lord." In every hand are placed the victor's palm and the shining harp. Then, as the commanding angels strike the note, every hand sweeps the harp strings with skillful touch, awaking sweet music in rich, melodious strains. Rapture unutterable thrills every heart, and each voice is raised in grateful praise: "Unto Him that loved us, and washed us from our sins in His own blood, and hath made us kings and priests unto God and His Father; to Him be glory and dominion for ever and ever." [17]

Oh, what joy unspeakable, to see Him whom we loved—to see Him in His glory who so loved us that He gave Himself for us—to behold those hands once pierced for our redemption stretched out to us in blessing and welcome! [18]

Those who . . . place themselves in God's hands . . . will see the King in His beauty. They will behold His matchless charms, and touching their golden harps, they will fill all heaven with rich music and with songs to the Lamb. [19]

GIVEN A WHITE ROBE OF RIGHTEOUSNESS

These are they which came out of great tribulation, and have washed their robes, and made them white in the blood of the Lamb.

Glorious will be the reward bestowed when the faithful workers gather about the throne of God and of the Lamb. . . . They will stand before the throne, accepted in the Beloved. All their sins have been blotted out, all their transgressions borne away. Now they can look upon the undimmed glory of the throne of God. . . . In that day the redeemed will shine forth in the glory of the Father and the Son. The angels, touching their golden harps, will welcome the King and His trophies of victory—those who have been washed and made white in the blood of the Lamb.[20]

All will be a happy, united family, clothed with the garments of praise and thanksgiving—the robe of Christ's righteousness. All nature in its surpassing loveliness will offer to God a constant tribute of praise and adoration. The world will be bathed in the light of heaven. The years will move on in gladness. The light of the moon will be as the light of the sun, and the light of the sun will be sevenfold greater than it is now. Over the scene the morning stars will sing together, and the sons of God will shout for joy, while God and Christ will unite in proclaiming, "There shall be no more sin, neither shall there be any more death." . . .

The conflict is over. All tribulation and strife are at an end. Songs of victory fill all heaven as the redeemed stand around the throne of God. All take up the joyful strain, "Worthy, worthy is the Lamb that was slain, and lives again, a triumphant conqueror."

"I beheld, and, lo, a great multitude, which no man could number, of all nations, and kindreds, and people, and tongues, stood before the throne, and before the Lamb, clothed with white robes, and palms in their hands; and cried with a loud voice, saying, Salvation to our God which sitteth upon the throne, and unto the Lamb."[21]

VICTORY OVER DEATH

And God shall wipe away all tears from their eyes; and there shall be no more death, neither sorrow, nor crying, neither shall there be any more pain: for the former things are passed away.

We have a living, risen Saviour. He burst the fetters of the tomb after He had lain there three days, and in triumph He proclaimed over the rent sepulcher of Joseph, "I am the resurrection, and the life." And He is coming. Are we getting ready for Him? Are we ready so that if we shall fall asleep, we can do so with hope in Jesus Christ? . . .

The Life-giver is soon to come . . . to break the fetters of the tomb. He is to bring forth the captives. . . . The last thoughts they had were of the grave and the tomb, but now they proclaim, "O death, where is thy sting? O grave, where is thy victory?" The pangs of death were the last things they felt. . . . When they awake the pain is all gone. "O grave, where is thy victory?" Here they stand, and the finishing touch of immortality is put upon them, and they go up to meet their Lord in the air. The gates of the city of God swing back upon their hinges, . . . and the ransomed of God walk in through the cherubims and seraphims. Christ bids them welcome and puts upon them His benediction. "Well done, thou good and faithful servant: . . . enter thou into the joy of thy Lord." What is that joy? He sees of the travail of his soul, and is satisfied. . . . Here is one who in the night season we pleaded with God on his behalf. There is one that we talked with on his dying bed, and he hung his helpless soul upon Jesus. Here is one who was a poor drunkard. We tried to get his eyes fixed upon Him who is mighty to save, and we told him that Christ could give him the victory. There are the crowns of immortal glory upon their heads.[22]

There, there is no disappointment, no sorrow, no sin, no one who shall say, "I am sick." There, there is no burial train, no mourning, no death, no parting, no broken hearts; and Jesus is there, peace is there. . . . In His presence is fullness of joy, at His right hand there are pleasures forevermore![23]

NO MORE SIN

And there shall be no more curse: but the throne of God and of the Lamb shall be in it; and his servants shall serve him: and they shall see his face; and his name shall be in their foreheads.

Every trace of the curse is swept away. . . . One reminder alone remains: our Redeemer will ever bear the marks of His crucifixion. Upon His wounded head, upon His side, His hands and feet, are the only traces of the cruel work that sin has wrought. Says the prophet, beholding Christ in His glory, "He had bright beams [margin] coming out of His side: and there was the hiding of His power." That pierced side whence flowed the crimson stream that reconciled man to God—there is the Saviour's glory, there "the hiding of His power." "Mighty to save," through the sacrifice of redemption, He was therefore strong to execute justice upon them that despised God's mercy. And the tokens of His humiliation are His highest honor; through the eternal ages the wounds of Calvary will show forth His praise and declare His power. . . .

The time has come to which holy men have looked with longing since the flaming sword barred the first pair from Eden—the time for "the redemption of the purchased possession." The earth originally given to man as his kingdom, betrayed by him into the hands of Satan, and so long held by the mighty foe, has been brought back by the great plan of redemption. All that was lost by sin has been restored. . . . God's original purpose in the creation of the earth is fulfilled as it is made the eternal abode of the redeemed. "The righteous shall inherit the land, and dwell therein forever." [24]

Then we shall enjoy with Him all the glories of the world to come throughout the ceaseless ages of eternity. . . . There is nothing in the kingdom of God to disturb or annoy. This is the life that is promised to the overcomer—a life of happiness and peace, a life of love and beauty. . . . There is no sin, no distracting care, nothing to mar the peace of the inhabitant. [25]

AS HEIRS, WE INHERIT THE KINGDOM

Come, ye blessed of my Father, inherit the kingdom prepared for you from the foundation of the world.

Before the ransomed throng is the holy city. Jesus opens wide the pearly gates, and the nations that have kept the truth enter in. There they behold the Paradise of God, the home of Adam in his innocency. Then that voice, richer than any music that ever fell on mortal ear, is heard, saying, "Your conflict is ended." "Come, ye blessed of My Father, inherit the kingdom prepared for you from the foundation of the world."

Now is fulfilled the Saviour's prayer for His disciples, "I will that they also, whom Thou hast given Me, be with Me where I am." "Faultless before the presence of His glory with exceeding joy," Christ presents to the Father the purchase of His blood, declaring, "Here am I, and the children whom Thou hast given Me." "Those that Thou gavest Me I have kept." Oh, the wonders of redeeming love! the rapture of that hour when the infinite Father, looking upon the ransomed, shall behold His image, sin's discord banished, its blight removed, the human once more in harmony with the divine![26]

Then the redeemed will be welcomed to the home that Jesus is preparing for them. . . . They will associate with those who have overcome Satan and through divine grace have formed perfect characters. Every sinful tendency, every imperfection, that afflicts them here, has been removed by the blood of Christ, and the excellence and brightness of His glory, far exceeding the brightness of the sun, is imparted to them. And the moral beauty, the perfection of His character, shines through them in worth far exceeding this outward splendor. They are without fault before the great white throne, sharing the dignity and the privileges of the angels.[27]

FAMILIES WILL BE REUNITED

Refrain thy voice from weeping, and thine eyes from tears: for thy work shall be rewarded, saith the Lord; and they shall come again from the land of the enemy. And there is hope in thine end, saith the Lord, that thy children shall come again to their own border.

Christ is coming with clouds and with great glory. . . . He will come to raise the dead, and to change the living saints from glory to glory. . . . There will be a re-linking of the family chain.[28]

Oh, wonderful redemption! long talked of, long hoped for, contemplated with eager anticipation. . . .

The living righteous are changed "in a moment, in the twinkling of an eye." At the voice of God they were glorified; now they are made immortal, and with the risen saints are caught up to meet their Lord in the air. Angels "gather together the elect from the four winds, from one end of heaven to the other." Little children are borne by holy angels to their mothers' arms. Friends long separated by death are united, nevermore to part, and with songs of gladness ascend together to the city of God.[29]

With joy unutterable parents see the crown, the robe, the harp, given to their children. The days of hope and fear are ended. . . . Their children have been redeemed.[30]

There we shall see on every hand the beautiful trees of Paradise, in the midst of them the tree of life. There we shall behold with undimmed vision the beauties of Eden restored. There we shall cast at the feet of our Redeemer the crowns that He has placed on our heads, and touching our golden harps, we shall offer praise and thanksgiving to Him that sitteth on the throne. . . . May you all be among those who shall enter through the gates of pearl into the city of our God. May you, as unbroken families, dwell forever in that haven of rest. To this end may God help you now to strive for the crown of life.[31]

WE SHALL RECOGNIZE EACH OTHER

Now I know in part; but then I shall know even as also I am known.

In the mansions above we shall meet to part no more. We shall know each other in our heavenly home.[32]

The redeemed will meet and recognize those whose attention they have directed to the uplifted Saviour. What blessed converse they have with these souls! "I was a sinner," it will be said, "without God and without hope in the world, and you came to me and drew my attention to the precious Saviour as my only hope. . . ." Others will say, "I was a heathen in heathen lands. You left your friends and comfortable home and came to teach me how to find Jesus and believe in Him as the only true God. I demolished my idols and worshiped God, and now I see Him face to face. I am saved, eternally saved, ever to behold Him whom I love. . . ."

Others will express their gratitude to those who fed the hungry and clothed the naked. "When despair bound my soul in unbelief, the Lord sent you to me," they say, "to speak words of hope and comfort. You brought me food for my physical necessities, and you opened to me the Word of God, awakening me to my spiritual needs. You treated me as a brother. You sympathized with me in my sorrows, and restored my bruised and wounded soul, so that I could grasp the hand of Christ that was reached out to save me. In my ignorance you taught me patiently that I had a Father in heaven who cared for me. You read to me the precious promises of God's Word. You inspired in me the faith that He would save me. My heart was softened, subdued, broken, as I contemplated the sacrifice which Christ had made for me. . . . I am here, saved, eternally saved, ever to live in His presence and to praise Him who gave His life for me."

What rejoicing there will be as these redeemed ones meet and greet those who have had a burden in their behalf! And those who have lived, not to please themselves, but to be a blessing to the unfortunate who have so few blessings—how their hearts will thrill with satisfaction![33]

A BEAUTIFUL COUNTRY

And truly, if they had been mindful of that country from whence they came out, they might have had opportunity to have returned. But now they desire a better country, that is, an heavenly: wherefore God is not ashamed to be called their God: for he hath prepared for them a city.

A fear of making the future inheritance seem too material has led many to spiritualize away the very truths which lead us to look upon it as our home. Christ assured His disciples that He went to prepare mansions for them in the Father's house. Those who accept the teachings of God's Word will not be wholly ignorant concerning the heavenly abode. And yet "eye hath not seen, nor ear heard, neither have entered into the heart of man, the things which God hath prepared for them that love Him." Human language is inadequate to describe the reward of the righteous. It will be known only to those who behold it. No finite mind can comprehend the glory of the Paradise of God.

In the Bible the inheritance of the saved is called a country. There the heavenly Shepherd leads His flock to fountains of living waters. The tree of life yields its fruit every month, and the leaves of the tree are for the service of the nations. There are ever-flowing streams, clear as crystal, and beside them waving trees cast their shadows upon the paths prepared for the ransomed of the Lord.[34]

The grass will be a living green, and will never wither. There will be roses and lilies and all kinds of flowers there. They will never blight or fade or lose their beauty and fragrance.

The lion, we should much dread and fear here, will then lie down with the lamb, and everything in the New Earth will be peace and harmony. The trees of the New Earth will be straight and lofty, without deformity.[35]

In the New Earth there are no chilling winds, no disagreeable changes. The atmosphere is ever right and healthful.[36]

354

EAT OF THE TREE OF LIFE

In the midst of the street of it, and on either side of the river, was there the tree of life, which bare twelve manner of fruits, and yielded her fruit every month: and the leaves of the tree were for the healing of the nations.

Out of the throne came a pure river of water, and on either side of the river was the tree of life. . . . The fruit was glorious; it looked like gold mixed with silver.[37]

The fruit of the tree of life in the Garden of Eden possessed supernatural virtue. To eat of it was to live forever. Its fruit was the antidote of death. Its leaves were for the sustaining of life and immortality. . . . After the entrance of sin the heavenly Husbandman transplanted the tree of life to the Paradise above.[38]

The redeemed saints, who have loved God and kept His commandments here, will enter in through the gates of the city, and have right to the tree of life. They will eat freely of it as our first parents did before their fall. The leaves of that immortal widespread tree will be for the healing of the nations. All their woes will then be gone. Sickness, sorrow, and death they will never again feel, for the leaves of the tree of life have healed them. Jesus will then see of the travail of His soul and be satisfied, when the redeemed, who have been subject to sorrow, toil, and afflictions, who have groaned beneath the curse, are gathered up around that tree of life to eat of its immortal fruit, that our first parents forfeited all right to, by breaking God's commands. There will be no danger of their ever losing right to the tree of life again, for he that tempted our first parents to sin will be destroyed by the second death.[39]

Upon the tree of life was most beautiful fruit, of which the saints could partake freely. . . . The most exalted language fails to describe the glory of heaven or the matchless depths of a Saviour's love.[40]

AT THE MARRIAGE SUPPER

Blessed are they which are called unto the marriage supper of the Lamb.

In both the Old and the New Testament the marriage relation is employed to represent the tender and sacred union that exists between Christ and His people. To the mind of Jesus the gladness of the wedding festivities pointed forward to the rejoicing of that day when He shall bring home His bride to the Father's house, and the redeemed with the Redeemer shall sit down to the marriage supper of the Lamb. He says, "As the bridegroom rejoiceth over the bride, so shall thy God rejoice over thee." "Thou shalt no more be termed Forsaken; . . . but thou shalt be called My Delight [margin]; . . . for the Lord delighteth in thee." "He will rejoice over thee with joy; He will rest in His love, He will joy over thee with singing." When the vision of heavenly things was granted to John the apostle, he wrote: "I heard as it were the voice of a great multitude, and as the voice of many waters, and as the voice of mighty thunderings, saying, Alleluia: for the Lord God omnipotent reigneth. Let us be glad and rejoice, and give honour to Him: for the marriage of the Lamb is come, and His wife hath made herself ready." "Blessed are they which are called unto the marriage supper of the Lamb."

Jesus saw in every soul one to whom must be given the call to His kingdom.[41] Having received the kingdom, He will come in His glory, as King of kings and Lord of lords, for the redemption of His people, who are to "sit down with Abraham, and Isaac, and Jacob" at His table in His kingdom, to partake of the marriage supper of the Lamb.[42]

THE GLORIES OF OUR HEAVENLY HOME

And the building of the wall of it was of jasper: and the city was pure gold, like unto clear glass. And the foundations of the wall of the city were garnished with all manner of precious stones.

The glorious city of God has twelve gates, set with pearls most glorious. It also has twelve foundations of various colors. The streets of the city are of pure gold. In this city is the throne of God, and a pure, beautiful river proceeding out of it, as clear as crystal. Its sparkling purity and beauty make glad the city of God. The saints will drink freely of the healing waters of the river of life. . . .

All faces will reflect the image of their Redeemer. There will then be no anxious, troubled countenances, but all will be bright, and smiling in spotless purity. The angels will be there, also the resurrected saints with the martyrs, and the best of all, and what will cause us the most joy, our lovely Saviour, who suffered and died that we might enjoy that happiness and freedom, will be there. His glorious face will shine brighter than the sun, and light up the beautiful city and reflect glory all around.

Children will be there. They will never be engaged in strife or discord. Their love will be fervent and holy. They will also have a crown of gold upon their heads and a harp in their hands. And their little countenances, that we here see so often troubled and perplexed, will beam with holy joy, expressive of their perfect freedom and happiness. . . .

The saints will have crowns of glory upon their heads and harps of gold in their hands. They will play upon the golden harp and sing redeeming love, and make melody unto God. Their former trials and suffering in this world will be forgotten and lost amid the glories of the New Earth. And they will ever have the approving smiles of Jesus upon them, and their happiness will be complete. . . . The future abode of the saints will be all glorious.[43]

LABOR FOR PLEASURE AND ENJOYMENT

And they shall build houses, and inhabit them; and they shall plant vineyards, and eat the fruit of them. They shall not build, and another inhabit; they shall not plant, and another eat: for as the days of a tree are the days of my people, and mine elect shall long enjoy the work of their hands.

There the wide-spreading plains swell into hills of beauty, and the mountains of God rear their lofty summits. On those peaceful plains, beside those living streams, God's people, so long pilgrims and wanderers, shall find a home.

"My people shall dwell in a peaceable habitation, and in sure dwellings, and in quiet resting places." [44]

In the earth made new the redeemed will engage in the occupations and pleasure that brought happiness to Adam and Eve in the beginning. The Eden life will be lived, the life in garden and field. "They shall build houses, and inhabit them; and they shall plant vineyards, and eat the fruit of them. . . ."

There every power will be developed, every capability increased. The grandest enterprises will be carried forward, the loftiest aspirations will be reached, the highest ambitions realized. And there will appear new heights to surmount, new wonders to admire, new truths to comprehend, fresh objects of study to call forth the powers of body and mind and soul. [45]

There certainly is and ever will be employment in heaven. The whole family of the redeemed will not live in a state of dreamy idleness. There remaineth a rest to the people of God. In heaven activity will not be wearing and burdensome; it will be rest. The whole family of the redeemed will find their delight in serving Him whose they are by creation and by redemption. [46]

To the weary and heavy laden, to those who have fought the good fight of faith, it will be a glorious rest; for the youth and vigor of immortality will be theirs, and against sin and Satan they will no longer have to contend. [47]

HARMONIOUS SOCIAL LIFE

The lines are fallen unto me in pleasant places; yea, I have a goodly heritage.

The loves and sympathies which God Himself has planted in the soul shall there find truest and sweetest exercise. The pure communion with holy beings, the harmonious social life with the blessed angels and with the faithful ones of all ages, who have washed their robes and made them white in the blood of the Lamb, the sacred ties that bind together "the whole family in heaven and earth"— these help to constitute the happiness of the redeemed.[48]

Amid the ransomed throng are the apostles of Christ, the heroic Paul, the ardent Peter, the loved and loving John, and their true-hearted brethren, and with them the vast host of martyrs.[49]

Heaven is full of joy. It resounds with the praise of Him who made so wonderful a sacrifice for the redemption of the human race. Should not the church on earth be full of praise? Should not Christians publish throughout the world the joy of serving Christ? Those who in heaven join with the angelic choir in their anthem of praise must learn on earth the song of heaven, the keynote of which is thanksgiving.[50]

Everything in heaven is noble and elevated. All seek the interest and happiness of others. No one devotes himself to looking out and caring for self. It is the chief joy of all holy beings to witness the joy and happiness of those around them.[51]

If you have trials here, and feel lonesome, look away from this dark world to the bright glories of heaven. Set your affections upon heavenly joys, and then you will not feel so deeply the trials and disappointments of this life, for you will feel that you have a home in glory, a crown, a harp, and a lovely Saviour there. Strive for that blest inheritance which God has promised to those that love Him and keep His commandments.[52]

STUDY GOD'S WISDOM THROUGHOUT ETERNITY

The God of our Lord Jesus Christ, the Father of glory, may give unto you the spirit of wisdom and revelation in the knowledge of him: the eyes of your understanding being enlightened.

The science of redemption is the science of all sciences, the science that is the study of the angels and of all the intelligences of the unfallen worlds, the science that engages the attention of our Lord and Saviour, the science that enters into the purpose brooded in the mind of the Infinite—"kept in silence through times eternal," the science that will be the study of God's redeemed throughout the endless ages. This is the highest study in which it is possible for man to engage. As no other study can, it will quicken the mind and uplift the soul. . . .

The theme of redemption is one that angels desire to look into; it will be the science and the song of the redeemed throughout the ceaseless ages of eternity. Is it not worthy of careful thought and study now? . . .

The subject is inexhaustible. The study of the incarnation of Christ, His atoning sacrifice, and mediatorial work will employ the mind of the diligent student as long as time shall last; and looking to heaven with its unnumbered years, he will exclaim, "Great is the mystery of godliness."

In eternity we shall learn that which, had we received the enlightenment that it was possible to obtain here, would have opened our understanding. The themes of redemption will employ the hearts and minds and tongues of the redeemed through the everlasting ages. They will understand the truths which Christ longed to open to His disciples, but which they did not have faith to grasp. Forever and forever new views of the perfection and glory of Christ will appear. Through endless ages the faithful Householder will bring forth from His treasures things new and old.[53]

Since God is infinite, and in Him are all the treasures of wisdom, we may to all eternity be ever searching, ever learning, yet never exhaust the riches of His wisdom, His goodness, or His power.[54]

CHRIST WILL TEACH THE REDEEMED

And they shall be all taught of God.

In the school of Christ students never graduate. Among the pupils are both the old and the young. Those who give heed to the instructions of the Divine Teacher constantly advance in wisdom, refinement, and nobility of soul, and thus they are prepared to enter that higher school, where advancement will continue throughout eternity. . . .

To dwell forever in this home of the blest, to bear in soul, body, and spirit, not the dark traces of sin and the curse, but the perfect likeness of our Creator, and through ceaseless ages to advance in wisdom, in knowledge and holiness, ever exploring new fields of thought, ever finding new wonders and new glories, ever increasing in capacity to know and to enjoy and to love, and knowing that there is still beyond us joy and love and wisdom infinite—such is the object to which the Christian hope is pointing.[55]

In the world to come Christ will lead the redeemed beside the river of life and will teach them wonderful lessons of truth. He will unfold to them the mysteries of nature. They will see that a master hand holds the world in position. They will behold the skill displayed by the great Artist in coloring the flowers of the field, and will learn of the purposes of the merciful Father, who dispenses every ray of light, and with the holy angels the redeemed will acknowledge in songs of grateful praise God's supreme love to an unthankful world. Then it will be understood that "God so loved the world, that He gave His only begotten Son, that whosoever believeth in Him should not perish, but have everlasting life."[56]

He [Christ] will impart rich stores of knowledge. He will unravel mysteries in the providences of God which in this life we are unable to understand.[57]

We must get an education here that will enable us to live with God through the eternal ages. The education we begin here will be perfected in heaven. We will only just enter a higher grade.[58]

TRAVEL TO WORLDS AFAR

These are they which follow the Lamb whithersoever he goeth. These were redeemed from among men, being the firstfruits unto God and to the Lamb.

All the treasures of the universe will be open to the study of God's redeemed. Unfettered by mortality, they wing their tireless flight to worlds afar—worlds that thrilled with sorrow at the spectacle of human woe and rang with songs of gladness at the tidings of a ransomed soul. With unutterable delight the children of earth enter into the joy and the wisdom of unfallen beings. They share the treasures of knowledge and understanding gained through ages upon ages in contemplation of God's handiwork. With undimmed vision they gaze upon the glory of creation—suns and stars and systems, all in their appointed order circling the throne of Deity. Upon all things, from the least to the greatest, the Creator's name is written, and in all are the riches of His power displayed.

And the years of eternity, as they roll, will bring richer and still more glorious revelations of God and of Christ. As knowledge is progressive, so will love, reverence, and happiness increase. The more men learn of God, the greater will be their admiration of His character. As Jesus opens before them the riches of redemption, and the amazing achievements in the great controversy with Satan, the hearts of the ransomed thrill with more fervent devotion, and with more rapturous joy they sweep the harps of gold; and ten thousand times ten thousand and thousands of thousands of voices unite to swell the mighty chorus of praise. . . .

The great controversy is ended. Sin and sinners are no more. The entire universe is clean. One pulse of harmony and gladness beats through the vast creation. From Him who created all, flow life and light and gladness throughout the realms of illimitable space. From the minutest atom to the greatest world, all things, . . . in their unshadowed beauty and perfect joy declare that God is love.[59]

LISTEN TO THE ANGEL CHOIR

And suddenly there was with the angel a multitude of the heavenly host praising God, and saying, Glory to God in the highest, and on earth peace, good will toward men.

No one born into the world, not even the most gifted of God's children, has ever been accorded such demonstration of joy as greeted the Babe born in Bethlehem.[60]

The angels . . . appeared to the humble shepherds, guarding their flocks by night, upon Bethlehem's plains. . . . The angel of the Lord came to them, and said, "Fear not; for, behold, I bring you good tidings of great joy, which shall be to all people. For unto you is born this day in the city of David a Saviour, which is Christ the Lord. And this shall be a sign unto you; Ye shall find the babe wrapped in swaddling clothes, lying in a manger." No sooner had their eyes become accustomed to the glorious presence of the one angel than, lo! the whole plain was lighted up with the wondrous glory of the multitude of angels that peopled the plains of Bethlehem . . . , all praising God, and saying, "Glory to God in the highest; and on earth, peace, good will toward men."

Then was the melody of heaven heard by mortal ears, and the heavenly choir swept back to heaven as they closed their ever memorable anthem. The light faded away . . . ; but there remained in the hearts of the shepherds the brightest picture mortal man had ever looked upon, and the blessed promise and assurance of the advent to our world of the Saviour of men, which filled their hearts with joy and gladness, mingled with faith and wondrous love to God.[61]

O that today the human family could recognize that song! The declaration then made, the note then struck, will swell to the close of and resound to the ends of the earth. When the Sun of Righteousness shall arise, with healing in His wings, that song will be reechoed by the voice of a great multitude, as the voice of many waters, saying, "Alleluia, for the Lord God omnipotent reigneth."[62]

WORSHIP TOGETHER

For as the new heavens and the new earth, which I will make, shall remain before me, saith the Lord, so shall your seed and your name remain. And it shall come to pass, that from one new moon to another, and from one sabbath to another, shall all flesh come to worship before me, saith the Lord.

In the beginning the Father and the Son had rested upon the Sabbath after their work of creation. When "the heavens and the earth were finished, and all the host of them," the Creator and all heavenly beings rejoiced in contemplation of the glorious scene. "The morning stars sang together, and all the sons of God shouted for joy." . . .

When there shall be a "restitution of all things, which God hath spoken by the mouth of all His holy prophets since the world began," the creation Sabbath, the day on which Jesus lay at rest in Joseph's tomb, will still be a day of rest and rejoicing. Heaven and earth will unite in praise, as "from one sabbath to another" the nations of the saved shall bow in joyful worship to God and the Lamb.[63]

The nations of the saved will know no other law than the law of heaven. All will be a happy, united family, clothed with the garments of praise and thanksgiving. Over the scene the morning stars will sing together, and the sons of God will shout for joy. . . .

"And it shall come to pass, that from one new moon to another, and from one sabbath to another, shall all flesh come to worship before Me, saith the Lord." "The glory of the Lord shall be revealed, and all flesh shall see it together." "The Lord God will cause righteousness and praise to spring forth before all the nations." "In that day shall the Lord of hosts be for a crown of glory, and for a diadem of beauty, unto the residue His people."[64]

So long as the heavens and the earth endure, the Sabbath will continue as a sign of the Creator's power. And when Eden shall bloom on earth again, God's holy rest day will be honored by all beneath the sun.[65]

PRIVILEGE OF OPEN COMMUNION WITH GOD

I saw no temple therein: for the Lord God Almighty and the Lamb are the temple of it.

The people of God are privileged to hold open communion with the Father and the Son. "Now we see through a glass, darkly." We behold the image of God reflected, as in a mirror, in the works of nature and in His dealings with men; but then we shall see Him face to face, without a dimming veil between. We shall stand in His presence and behold the glory of His countenance.[66]

We may address Him by the endearing name, "Our Father," which is a sign of our affection for Him and a pledge of His tender regard and relationship to us. And the Son of God, beholding the heirs of grace, "is not ashamed to call them brethren." They have even a more sacred relationship to God than have the angels who have never fallen.

All the paternal love which has come down from generation to generation through the channel of human hearts, all the springs of tenderness which have opened in the souls of men, are but as a tiny rill to the boundless ocean when compared with the infinite, exhaustless love of God.[67]

Heaven is a ceaseless approaching to God through Christ. The longer we are in the heaven of bliss, the more and still more of glory will be opened to us; and the more we know of God, the more intense will be our happiness.[68]

And what is the happiness of heaven but to see God? What greater joy could come to the sinner saved by the grace of Christ than to look upon the face of God and know Him as Father?[69]

How much comfort it gives to behold Him here by the eye of faith, that we may by beholding be made like Him, but what will it be to behold Him as He is, without one dimming veil between?[70]

THE VEIL WILL BE DRAWN ASIDE

Now we see through a glass, darkly; but then face to face.

There, when the veil that darkens our vision shall be removed, and our eyes shall behold that world of beauty of which we now catch glimpses through the microscope; when we look on the glories of the heavens, now scanned afar through the telescope; when, the blight of sin removed, the whole earth shall appear "in the beauty of the Lord our God," what a field will be open to our study! There the student of science may read the records of creation, and discern no reminders of the law of evil. He may listen to the music of nature's voices, and detect no note of wailing or undertone of sorrow. In all created things he may trace one handwriting—in the vast universe behold "God's name writ large," and not in earth or sea or sky one sign of ill remaining. . . .

There will be open to the student history of infinite scope and of wealth inexpressible. Here, from the vantage ground of God's Word, the student is afforded a view of the vast field of history, and may gain some knowledge of the principles that govern the course of human events. But his vision is still clouded and his knowledge incomplete. Not until he stands in the light of eternity will he see all things clearly. . . .

The veil that interposes between the visible and the invisible world will be drawn aside, and wonderful things will be revealed. . . .

There all who have wrought with unselfish spirit will behold the fruit of their labors. The outworking of every right principle and noble deed will be seen. . . . How little of the result of the world's noblest work is in this life manifest to the doer! . . . Parents and teachers lie down in their last sleep, their lifework seeming to have been wrought in vain; they know not that their faithfulness has unsealed springs of blessing that can never cease to flow . . . , and the influence repeat itself a thousandfold. . . . In the hereafter the action and reaction of all these will be seen.[71]

I SHALL MEET MY GUARDIAN ANGEL

Take heed that ye despise not one of these little ones; for I say unto you, That in heaven their angels do always behold the face of my Father which is in heaven.

Not until the providences of God are seen in the light of eternity shall we understand what we owe to the care and interposition of His angels. Celestial beings have taken an active part in the affairs of men. They have appeared in garments that shone as the lightning; they have come as men, in the garb of wayfarers. They have accepted the hospitalities of human homes; they have acted as guides to benighted travelers. They have thwarted the spoiler's purpose, and turned aside the stroke of the destroyer.

Though the rulers of this world know it not, yet often in their councils angels have been spokesmen. Human eyes have looked upon them. Human ears have listened to their appeals. In the council hall and the court of justice heavenly messengers have pleaded the cause of the persecuted and oppressed. They have defeated purposes and arrested evils that would have brought wrong and suffering to God's children. . . .

Every redeemed one will understand the ministry of angels in his own life. The angel who was his guardian from his earliest moment; the angel who watched his steps, and covered his head in the day of peril; the angel who was with him in the valley of the shadow of death, who marked his resting place, who was the first to greet him in the resurrection morning—what will it be to hold converse with him, and to learn the history of divine interposition in the individual life, of heavenly cooperation in every work for humanity!

All the perplexities of life's experience will then be made plain. Where to us have appeared only confusion and disappointment, broken purposes and thwarted plans, will be seen a grand, overruling, victorious purpose, a divine harmony.[72]

WHY THE GREAT CONTROVERSY WAS PERMITTED

And to make all men see what is the fellowship of the mystery, which from the beginning of the world hath been hid in God, who created all things by Jesus Christ: to the intent that now unto the principalities and powers in heavenly places might be known by the church the manifold wisdom of God.

For what was the great controversy permitted to continue throughout the ages? Why was it that Satan's existence was not cut short at the outset of his rebellion?—It was that the universe might be convinced of God's justice in His dealing with evil, that sin might receive eternal condemnation. In the plan of redemption there are heights and depths that eternity itself can never exhaust, marvels into which the angels desire to look. The redeemed only, of all created beings, have in their own experience known the actual conflict with sin; they have wrought with Christ, and, as even the angels could not do, have entered into the fellowship of His sufferings. . . .

He "hath raised us up together, and made us sit together in heavenly places: . . . that in the ages to come He might shew the exceeding riches of His grace in His kindness toward us through Christ Jesus."[73]

As the nations of the saved look upon their Redeemer, and behold the eternal glory of the Father shining in His countenance; as they behold His throne, which is from everlasting to everlasting, and know that His kingdom is to have no end, they break forth in rapturous song. . . .

Mercy, tenderness, and parental love are seen to blend with holiness, justice, and power. While we behold the majesty of His throne, high and lifted up, we see His character in its gracious manifestations, and comprehend, as never before, the significance of that endearing title, "Our Father." . . .

The result of the Saviour's conflict with the powers of darkness is joy to the redeemed, redounding to the glory of God throughout eternity.[74]

I PRESS TOWARD THE MARK

This one thing I do, forgetting those things which are behind, and reaching forth unto those things which are before, I press toward the mark for the prize of the high calling of God in Christ Jesus.

Another year of your life closes today. How can you look back upon it? Have you made advancement in the divine life? Have you increased in spirituality? Have you crucified self, with the affections and lusts? Have you an increased interest in the study of God's Word? Have you gained decided victories over your own feelings and waywardness? Oh, what has been the record of your life for the year which has now passed into eternity, never to be recalled?

As you enter upon a new year, let it be with an earnest resolve to have your course onward and upward. Let your life be more elevated and exalted than it has hitherto been. Make it your aim not to seek your own interest and pleasure, but to advance the cause of your Redeemer. Remain not in a position where you ever need help yourself, and where others have to guard you to keep you in the narrow way. You may be strong to exert a sanctifying influence upon others. You may be where your soul's interest will be awakened to do good to others, to comfort the sorrowful, strengthen the weak, and to bear your testimony for Christ whenever opportunity offers. Aim to honor God in everything, always and everywhere. Carry your religion into everything.[75]

Prepare for eternity with such a zeal as you have not yet manifested. Educate your mind to love the Bible, to love the prayer meeting, to love the hour of meditation, and, above all, the hour when the soul communes with God. Become heavenly-minded if you would unite with the heavenly choir in the mansions above. . . .

A new page is turned in the book of the recording angel. . . . Let a record be stamped there which you will not be ashamed to have revealed to the gaze of men and angels.[76]

SOURCE REFERENCES

On the following pages are listed the source references for the excerpts appearing in this volume. The key below indicates the abbreviations used for the various books, pamphlets, and periodicals.

AA	*The Acts of the Apostles*	Letter	Ellen G. White letter
AUCR	*The Australasian Union Conference Record*	LS	*Life Sketches of Ellen G. White*
BE	*Bible Echo*	MB	*Thoughts From the Mount of Blessing*
BTS	*Bible Training School*		
CE	*Colporteur Evangelist*	MH	*The Ministry of Healing*
CDF	*Counsels on Diet and Foods*	MM	*Medical Ministry*
CH	*Counsels on Health*	Med. Miss.	*Medical Missionary*
Ch. Ed.	*Christian Education*	MS	Ellen G. White manuscript
COL	*Christ's Object Lessons*	MYP	*Messages to Young People*
CPT	*Counsels to Parents, Teachers, and Students*	NL	Notebook Leaflet
		PHJ	*Pacific Health Journal*
CTBH	*Christian Temperance and Bible Hygiene*	PK	*Prophets and Kings*
		PP	*Patriarchs and Prophets*
DA	*The Desire of Ages*	PUR	*Pacific Union Recorder*
Ed.	*Education*	R&H	*Review and Herald*
Ev.	*Evangelism*	Signs	*Signs of the Times*
EW	*Early Writings*	SC	*Steps to Christ*
FE	*Fundamentals of Christian Education*	SL	*The Sanctified Life*
		SR	*The Story of Redemption*
GC	*The Great Controversy*	Sp. T	*Special Testimonies*
GCB	*General Conference Bulletin*	1T	*Testimonies for the Church*, vol. 1 (2T, etc., for vol. 2-9)
GH	*Good Health*		
GW	*Gospel Workers*		
H to L	*How to Live*	TM	*Testimonies to Ministers and Gospel Workers*
HR	*Health Reformer*		
HS	*Historical Sketches of S.D.A. Missions*	WM	*Welfare Ministry*
		YI	*Youth's Instructor*

JANUARY

1 YI, Jan. 5, 1881
2 Signs, Jan. 4, 1883
3 YI, Jan. 5, 1881
4 MB, 162
5 YI, June 30, 1898
6 PP, 352-353
7 R&H, Oct. 2, 1900
8 SC, 74
9 YI, Feb. 2, 1893
10 YI, Feb. 13, 1902
11 R&H, May 5, 1891
12 SC, 49
13 TM, 419
14 R&H, Oct. 23, 1888
15 HS, 130, 131
16 MH, 65, 66
17 2T, 139, 140
18 PK, 157
19 Letter 19e, 1892
20 YI, Aug. 18, 1886
21 R&H, Dec. 13, 1887
22 Signs, Dec. 12, 1906
23 R&H, Dec. 13, 1887
24 HS, 132, 133
25 Signs, Nov. 14, 1906
26 BE, Jan. 15, 1892
27 MH, 509
28 GC, 525
29 SC, 103
30 GW, 258
31 YI, July 7, 1892
32 R&H, April 1, 1890
33 5T, 161, 162
34 MH, 511
35 Signs, July 1, 1886
36 GC, 622
37 YI, Feb. 15, 1900
38 PP, 203
39 BE, Nov., 1887
40 BE, Nov., 1887
41 BE, Oct. 1, 1889
42 R&H, April 23, 1889
43 Signs, July 1, 1886
44 MYP, 330
45 5T, 266
46 Signs, July 11, 1906
47 YI, July 28, 1892
48 Signs, April 11, 1906
49 R&H, Aug. 22, 1912
50 R&H, Dec. 18, 1913
51 Signs, April 18, 1906

52 Letter 117, 1897
53 R&H, Feb. 6, 1900
54 Letter 107, 1898
55 Signs, March 21, 1906
56 Signs, March 21, 1906
57 Signs, April 25, 1906
58 Signs, March 28, 1906
59 R&H, Feb. 6, 1900
60 Letter 207, 1904
61 BE, Oct. 15, 1892
62 Letter 25, 1903
63 GC, 600
64 YI, July 28, 1892
65 Letter 76, 1901
66 R&H, Jan. 6, 1910
67 MS 19, 1900
68 1T, 397, 398
69 MS 12, 1898
70 SC, 108, 109
71 MS 102, 1901
72 MS 70, Undated
73 Ed, 52
74 Ed, 61
75 Signs, Sept. 26, 1906
76 PUR, May 22, 1902
77 R&H, Nov. 8, 1906
78 R&H, Dec. 23, 1902
79 SC, 107-109
80 R&H, Oct. 22, 1889
81 YI, May 5, 1898
82 PUR, May 22, 1902
83 PUR, May 22, 1902

FEBRUARY

1 BE, Feb. 27, 1899
2 BE, May 22, 1899
3 COL, 327
4 8T, 19-21
5 6T, 48-50
6 6T, 291
7 6T, 291
8 MB, 77
9 GCB, May 31, 1909
10 Signs, Dec 19, 1906
11 GC, v, vi
12 4T, 12, 13
13 4T, 147, 148
14 PK, 22
15 GC, vi, vii
16 GC, vi
17 MS 17, 1908
18 Letter 71, 1903

19 3T, 257
20 2T, 693, 694
21 AA, 52
22 AA, 119, 120
23 R&H, April 25, 1893
24 Signs, Oct. 10, 1906
25 GC, 599, 600
26 CPT, 171, 172
27 Signs, March 28, 1906
28 DA, 355
29 R&H, Oct. 1, 1908
30 R&H, Nov. 19, 1908
31 BE, May 22, 1899
32 DA, 826
33 R&H, March 22, 1898
34 MS 71, 1903
35 R&H, Nov. 19, 1908
36 R&H, June 26, 1894
37 5T, 426
38 MS 1, 1892
39 MH, 417
40 Letter 155, 1902
41 DA, 827
42 TM, 122
43 R&H May 10, 1892
44 Signs, Oct. 22, 1896
45 R&H, Aug. 24, 1897
46 R&H, Jan. 4, 1887
47 R&H, Oct. 23, 1900
48 YI, June 26, 1902
49 R&H, May 30, 1882
50 R&H, Jan. 4, 1887
51 Letter 185, 1905
52 R&H, Nov. 16, 1886
53 Letter 2, 1903
54 YI, April 9, 1903
55 GW, 372
56 3T, 536
57 R&H, Dec. 21, 1886
58 YI, June 22, 1893
59 2T, 305
60 MS 42, 1900
61 Letter 15, 1899
62 MYP, 125
63 PK, 386-388
64 YI, Nov. 21, 1883
65 3T, 335
66 3T, 536
67 NL, No. 24, pp. 1, 2
68 COL, 61
69 R&H, June 10, 1902
70 R&H, March 29, 1892

71 R&H, April 1, 1909
72 DA, 672
73 MS 107, 1903
74 R&H, June 10, 1902
75 Sp. T., Series B, No. 7, p. 64
76 R&H, July 21, 1896
77 AA, 49
78 AA, 38
79 Signs, Feb. 17, 1914
80 AA, 55
81 Letter 213, 1903
82 Watchman, May 22, 1906
83 R&H, April 1, 1909
84 CPT, 166, 167
85 R&H, July 16, 1895
86 EW, 278, 279
87 9T, 126

MARCH

1 PK, 600, 601
2 Ed, 263
3 Signs, Dec. 5, 1906
4 R&H, May 20, 1884
5 PP, 222
6 MS 11, 1900
7 R&H, April 29, 1890
8 YI, April 7, 1908
9 YI, Oct. 29, 1907
10 YI, May 28, 1884
11 Signs, May 25, 1904
12 GH, Nov., 1880
13 YI, Nov. 12, 1907
14 YI, Oct. 10, 1883
15 R&H, Feb. 22, 1906
16 CPT, 257
17 CPT, 85
18 CH, 20
19 CTBH, 75
20 CTBH, 130, 131
21 R&H, May 9, 1899
22 Signs, Oct. 10, 1906
23 YI, April, 1872
24 YI, Sept., 1873
25 8T, 208
26 Signs, Nov. 7, 1906
27 Letter 21, 1901
28 PK, 548
29 Signs, Sept. 28, 1882
30 PP, 217, 218
31 R&H, July 24, 1894

32 MH, 130, 131
33 CPT, 294, 295
34 4T, 452
35 Ed, 203, 204
36 YI, April 12, 1900
37 Signs, May 25, 1904
38 3T, 532
39 Signs, May 25, 1904
40 Ed, 206
41 PHJ, April, 1890
42 PHJ, May, 1890
43 Ed, 206
44 R&H, June 12, 1888
45 R&H, Nov. 9, 1886
46 4T, 624
47 MS 60, 1903
48 Letter 18b, 1891
49 Signs, Nov. 14, 1892
50 2T, 417
51 CE, 168
52 MYP, 285, 286
53 MYP, 76
54 3T, 507
55 2T, 410
56 4T, 652, 653
57 PP, 459, 460
58 3T, 324
59 MS 8, 1900
60 NL, No. 25, p. 3
61 MH, 444, 445
62 7T, 64
63 MS 53, 1911
64 YI, Aug. 14, 1906
65 1T, 509, 510
66 Ed, 167, 168
67 MS 16, 1895
68 Ed, 168
69 YI, Dec. 27, 1900
70 R&H, April 10, 1894
71 R&H, April 10, 1894
72 MB, 172, 173
73 R&H, April 29, 1890

APRIL

1 AA, 530
2 YI, Jan. 5, 1893
3 1T, 552
4 R&H, Feb. 21, 1888
5 R&H, Feb. 21, 1888
6 HS, 134
7 R&H, Feb. 21, 1888
8 R&H, Feb. 21, 1888

9 AA, 532, 533
10 R&H, June 10, 1884
11 Letter 98b, 1896
12 Letter 58, 1909
13 YI, June 8, 1893
14 AA, 532, 533
15 Signs, Feb. 17, 1904
16 MS 140, 1897
17 Signs, Feb. 17, 1904
18 COL, 50
19 Signs, Nov. 14, 1892
20 R&H, Sept. 15, 1891
21 Signs, Nov. 14, 1892
22 YI, Feb. 3, 1898
23 R&H, June 7, 1887
24 Letter 71, 1893
25 YI, Aug. 11, 1892
26 R&H, June 22, 1886
27 YI, May 12, 1898
28 CPT, 50-52
29 YI, Nov. 24, 1903
30 Signs, June 13, 1906
31 Signs, June 6, 1906
32 GH, Aug. 1882
33 Signs, Sept. 12, 1906
34 R&H, Jan. 28, 1904
35 COL, 146
36 R&H, Oct. 4, 1906
37 R&H, Feb. 22, 1906
38 Letter 59, 1896
39 Letter 40, 1901
40 R&H, May 17, 1898
41 CPT, 186, 187
42 Ed, 100
43 4T, 581
44 GCB, April 23, 1901
45 MS 36, 1899
46 Letter 75, 1898
47 COL, 336-339
48 YI, Jan. 1, 1903
49 CPT, 354
50 COL, 342, 343
51 YI, June 30, 1898
52 YI, June 8, 1893
53 6T, 452, 453
54 COL, 351
55 COL, 348-351
56 NL, No. 30, p. 2
57 R&H, Jan. 8, 1880
58 MS, 146, 1902
59 COL, 352-354
60 YI, Feb. 2, 1893

61 MYP, 417, 418
62 PHJ, June, 1890
63 YI, May 4, 1886
64 YI, Aug. 25, 1886
65 YI, Sept. 1, 1886
66 YI, Jan. 1, 1907
67 MYP, 418
68 AA, 511
69 HR, Nov., 1871
70 YI, May 6, 1897
71 3T, 366
72 HR, Nov., 1871
73 YI, Sept., 1873
74 R&H, Oct. 9, 1900
75 Signs, Feb. 17, 1904
76 R&H, June 6, 1899
77 MH, 355
78 MS 126, 1903

MAY

1 CH, 41, 42
2 CH, 50, 51
3 R&H, June 18, 1895
4 SR, 21
5 GH, March, 1883
6 3T, 138, 139
7 Ed, 20
8 MH, 417
9 MM, 221
10 MS, 49, 1897
11 Ed, 201
12 CH, 49
13 Ed, 198
14 MH, 272, 273
15 Ed, 198, 199
16 Letter 63, 1904
17 MH, 276
18 CTBH, 142
19 R&H, June 10, 1902
20 CTBH, 142, 143
21 MH, 276
22 R&H, June 10, 1902
23 2T, 528
24 3T, 77, 78
25 MH, 237, 238
26 Sp. T., Series B, No. 1, 28-30
27 Sp. T., Series B, No. 1, 29
28 YI, July 27, 1893
29 MH, 51
30 Diary, 1894, p. 37

31 MH, 295
32 CH, 114, 115
33 MH, 385
34 R&H, Feb. 21, 1888
35 YI, Feb. 3, 1898
36 R&H, Nov. 14, 1893
37 R&H, Nov. 7, 1893
38 CH, 622
39 R&H, June 20, 1912
40 PHJ, Aug., 1890
41 YI, April 7, 1898
42 CH, 59
43 MH, 112, 113
44 MH, 127
45 7T, 76, 77
46 7T, 85
47 R&H, Nov. 12, 1901
48 Ed, 21
49 MM, 296, 297
50 CH, 173
51 HR, May, 1872
52 2T, 531
53 CH, 174
54 1T, 701
55 MH, 274
56 CH, 173
57 1T, 702
58 HR, April, 1872
59 CH, 60
60 HR, April, 1871
61 CTBH, 91
62 HR, May, 1871
63 HR, April, 1871
64 CH, 196
65 CH, 54
66 MH, 237
67 H to L, chap. 4, p. 55
68 R&H, July 29, 1884
69 H to L, chap. 4, p. 60
70 MM, 227
71 PP, 412
72 DA, 183
73 1T, 532, 533
74 MS 3, 1879
75 Ed, 251
76 CH, 165
77 CTBH, 52
78 R&H, May 27, 1902
79 6T, 374, 375
80 YI, Aug. 25, 1886
81 HR, April, 1877
82 CH, 99

83 HR, Jan., 1877
84 Temperance, 139
85 GW, 244
86 CH, 186
87 YI, Sept. 7, 1893
88 Ed, 205
89 HR, Oct., 1871
90 YI, Jan. 28, 1897
91 CTBH, 82, 83
92 CPT, 290, 291
93 CTBH, 83
94 MH, 288, 289
95 2T, 531
96 Letter 19, 1897
97 CH, 118
98 HR, May, 1877
99 MH, 384
100 MH, 303, 304
101 Signs, Feb. 11, 1875
102 R&H, May 27, 1902
103 YI, July 9, 1903
104 3T, 136
105 3T, 69
106 2T, 347
107 Ch Ed, 125
108 HR, Sept., 1871
109 HR, Nov., 1871
110 R&H, July 29,1884
111 CH, 163
112 Med. Miss., Nov. and Dec., 1892
113 5T, 444
114 CTBH, 13, 14
115 R&H, April 9, 1901
116 CTBH, 13
117 HR, March, 1872
118 2T, 534
119 R&H, March 11, 1880
120 MH, 241
121 MH, 281
122 Ed, 197
123 CH, 28
124 3T, 13
125 1T, 306, 307
126 MH, 374
127 Signs, June 20, 1911
128 MH, 393
129 MS 61, 1900
130 Letter 320, 1906
131 Signs, Feb. 12, 1885
132 MH, 111
133 R&H, Oct. 16, 1883

134 4T, 579
135 YI, Dec. 29, 1898
136 Ed, 113
137 MH, 115, 116

JUNE

1 YI, June 26, 1902
2 R&H, Aug. 19, 1884
3 YI, Oct. 25, 1900
4 YI, Nov. 6, 1902
5 Letter 48, 1897
6 YI, Feb. 12, 1903
7 YI, Oct. 13, 1892
8 R&H, March 11, 1880
9 YI, Jan. 1, 1907
10 Letter 15, 1899
11 GH, Aug., 1882
12 3T, 377
13 PP, 600
14 PP, 641, 642
15 Letter 28, 1888
16 YI, Aug. 3, 1887
17 YI, Sept., 1873
18 R&H, Aug. 19, 1884
19 YI, April, 1872
20 MS 36, 1900
21 Letter 48, 1897
22 R&H, Oct. 16, 1883
23 Signs, April 15, 1886
24 Signs, June 13, 1900
25 Letter 23a, 1893
26 R&H, Nov. 19, 1908
27 CPT, 454
28 PP, 337
29 PHJ, April, 1890
30 PHJ, Sept., 1890
31 R&H, Aug. 30, 1881
32 MS 49, 1901
33 MS 132, 1902
34 YI, April 9, 1903
35 5T, 607
36 4T, 145
37 YI, Aug. 22, 1901
38 R&H, Aug. 26, 1884
39 HR, June, 1878
40 HR, June, 1878
41 YI, Dec. 5, 1901
42 CTBH, 97
43 4T, 621, 622
44 HR, Feb., 1877
45 R&H, Nov. 13, 1894
46 R&H, May 7, 1908

47 R&H, July 11, 1899
48 Signs, Oct. 22, 1896
49 MH, 254
50 Ed, 216
51 2T, 700
52 3T, 80
53 Letter 16, 1886
54 Ed, 114
55 MB, 123
56 Letter 18b, 1891
57 Signs, June 20, 1911
58 3T, 539
59 CPT, 114
60 MH, 388
61 1T, 465
62 YI, Dec. 27, 1900
63 MH, 254
64 R&H, July 25, 1871
65 GH, Aug., 1882
66 MS 121, 1902
67 R&H, March 11, 1880
68 Letter 8, 1888
69 Letter 130, 1898
70 R&H, Nov. 27, 1894
71 HR, June, 1871
72 Letter 28, 1897
73 R&H, July 25, 1871
74 Letter 37, 1891
75 Letter 16, 1886
76 MS 61, 1900
77 4T, 138
78 5T, 488
79 Signs, June 20, 1911
80 Ed, 113, 114
81 R&H, Oct. 16, 1883
82 R&H, Oct. 16, 1883
83 DA, 330
84 Signs, Jan. 13, 1904
85 DA, 330
86 GC, 526-530
87 DA, 794
88 Letter 33, 1895
89 Letter 57, 1897
90 R&H, April 29, 1890
91 Letter 13, 1904
92 R&H, Feb. 27, 1894
93 YI, Jan. 23, 1902

JULY

1 Signs, Nov. 22, 1877
2 MS 132, 1902
3 MS 108, 1903

4 GW, 119
5 Y1, Dec. 9, 1897
6 MH, 25, 26
7 MS 59, 1897
8 MH, 496
9 R&H, Oct. 2, 1900
10 Signs, Sept. 10, 1885
11 Signs, Sept. 10, 1885
12 Ed, 241, 242
13 MYP, 420
14 Ed, 240
15 R&H, Sept. 8, 1885
16 3T, 539, 540
17 R&H, Sept. 8, 1885
18 MS 41, 1903
19 6T, 342-345
20 DA, 639
21 4T, 62
22 Signs, Feb. 12, 1885
23 AUCR, Nov. 1, 1904
24 MS 1, 1867
25 R&H, Sept. 20, 1892
26 R&H, April 29, 1884
27 R&H, July 11, 1899
28 R&H, Sept. 20, 1892
29 6T, 174
30 MH, 388, 389
31 HR, Dec., 1877
32 R&H, Aug. 8, 1899
33 Signs, Dec. 6, 1877
34 YI, May 6, 1897
35 Signs, Feb. 22, 1892
36 1T, 388
37 CTBH, 65
38 R&H, July 29, 1902
39 FE, 18
40 MH, 394
41 FE, 58
42 MS 18, 1891
43 Signs, Sept. 1, 1898
44 Signs, Oct. 2, 1884
45 Signs, April 17, 1884
46 Signs, July 1, 1886
47 HR, Aug., 1877
48 6T, 344
49 MH, 352-355
50 MH, 354
51 R&H, Nov. 10, 1885
52 MH, 354, 355
53 MH, 362
54 MH, 392, 393
55 MYP, 342

⁵⁶ MH, 355
⁵⁷ Ed, 41
⁵⁸ 6T, 172
⁵⁹ 4T, 587
⁶⁰ MH, 360
⁶¹ YI, Feb. 4, 1897
⁶² YI, Aug. 14, 1906
⁶³ 1T, 514, 515
⁶⁴ R&H, Nov. 10, 1885
⁶⁵ DA, 326
⁶⁶ DA, 524, 525
⁶⁷ AA, 498-508
⁶⁸ PP, 649
⁶⁹ PP, 660
⁷⁰ Ed, 157
⁷¹ COL, 384, 385
⁷² R&H, July 25, 1871
⁷³ 1T, 565
⁷⁴ 1T, 501
⁷⁵ CPT, 325
⁷⁶ R&H, Jan. 29, 1884
⁷⁷ R&H, Aug. 19, 1884
⁷⁸ CPT, 535
⁷⁹ CPT, 335
⁸⁰ Ed, 207
⁸¹ Living by Principles, 1898, pp. 19, 20
⁸² 1T, 514
⁸³ Ed, 212
⁸⁴ CPT, 343
⁸⁵ 4T, 653
⁸⁶ 2T, 586-589
⁸⁷ MS 60, 1894
⁸⁸ MYP, 371
⁸⁹ MYP, 388, 389
⁹⁰ YI, May 4, 1893
⁹¹ CPT, 324
⁹² R&H, May 25, 1886
⁹³ CPT, 336, 337
⁹⁴ R&H, Nov. 27, 1894

AUGUST

¹ R&H, June 22, 1886
² R&H, March 1, 1906
³ Letter 48, 1897
⁴ COL, 326-331
⁵ R&H, Jan. 5, 1905
⁶ YI, Dec. 15, 1886
⁷ YI, Sept. 29, 1892
⁸ HS, 181, 182
⁹ Signs, Sept. 1, 1898
¹⁰ R&H, Dec. 17, 1903

¹¹ PK, 244-246
¹² Signs, Jan. 22, 1902
¹³ Sp. Test., Series A, No. 10, 3, 4
¹⁴ R&H, March 4, 1902
¹⁵ DA, 640
¹⁶ Letter 168, 1902
¹⁷ CPT, 466, 467
¹⁸ R&H, May 5, 1904
¹⁹ Ev, 544
²⁰ MH, 156, 157
²¹ R&H, April 7, 1904
²² R&H, April 24,1888
²³ COL, 229
²⁴ DA, 511, 512
²⁵ Letter 104, 1897
²⁶ CPT, 172
²⁷ 6T, 429
²⁸ MM, 312
²⁹ 7T, 112
³⁰ Ed, 179
³¹ 7T, 58
³² MH, 216
³³ WM, 116
³⁴ Med. Mis., Jan., 1891
³⁵ Redemption, No. 3, 46
³⁶ DA, 207
³⁷ 4T, 539
³⁸ 7T, 106
³⁹ COL, 376
⁴⁰ R&H, Nov. 12, 1895
⁴¹ R&H, Jan. 1895
⁴² Letter 113, 1901
⁴³ GW, 193
⁴⁴ WM, 91
⁴⁵ R&H, Nov. 21, 1907
⁴⁶ R&H, May 13, 1902
⁴⁷ 9T, 118
⁴⁸ GW, 198, 199
⁴⁹ 5T, 612, 613
⁵⁰ R&H, Aug. 24, 1897
⁵¹ R&H, April 29, 1884
⁵² Letter 30, 1887
⁵³ Ed, 48
⁵⁴ PK, 32, 33
⁵⁵ R&H, July 19, 1887
⁵⁶ COL, 385-389
⁵⁷ 5T, 133
⁵⁸ R&H, Nov. 21, 1907
⁵⁹ R&H, June 6, 1912
⁶⁰ R&H, Nov. 11, 1902
⁶¹ R&H, Feb. 4, 1904

⁶² R&H, June 27, 1893
⁶³ MH, 203
⁶⁴ MH, 202
⁶⁵ 3T, 512
⁶⁶ R&H, Nov. 12, 1895
⁶⁷ 6T, 385
⁶⁸ 6T, 275
⁶⁹ DA, 639, 640
⁷⁰ R&H, Nov. 21, 1878
⁷¹ R&H, Aug. 20, 1895
⁷² Letter 30, 1887
⁷³ Letter 30, 1887
⁷⁴ 2T, 25
⁷⁵ MS, 109, 1902
⁷⁶ 3T, 516, 517
⁷⁷ R&H, Jan. 15, 1895
⁷⁸ Signs, June 13, 1892
⁷⁹ MM, 243
⁸⁰ 4T, 227
⁸¹ WM, 169
⁸² WM, 172
⁸³ MH, 201
⁸⁴ WM, 181
⁸⁵ WM, 210
⁸⁶ WM, 168
⁸⁷ 6T, 269
⁸⁸ Med . Mis., June, 1891
⁸⁹ 2T, 29
⁹⁰ 4T, 56
⁹¹ R&H, Oct. 15, 1901
⁹² 5T, 395
⁹³ COL, 404
⁹⁴ 6T, 348
⁹⁵ 6T, 305
⁹⁶ 5T, 449

SEPTEMBER

¹ SL, 7-9
² LS, 237
³ 1T, 339, 340
⁴ 2T, 505
⁵ SL, 49
⁶ Letter 155, 1902
⁷ COL, 360
⁸ Signs, June 16, 1890
⁹ GC, 477, 478
¹⁰ SL, 11-14
¹¹ R&H, July 2, 1889
¹² SL, 12, 13
¹³ SL, 18, 19
¹⁴ SL, 39
¹⁵ GH, Nov., 1882

16 CDF, 59, 60
17 PP, 84, 85
18 SL, 29, 30
19 SL, 61
20 SL, 41
21 SL, 48
22 SL, 44
23 SL, 54
24 6T, 353
25 R&H, Feb. 28, 1888
26 R&H, April 14, 1885
27 R&H, July 26, 1906
28 Signs, Sept. 10, 1894
29 R&H, April 14, 1885
30 Signs, Feb. 17, 1904
31 Signs, Oct. 17, 1906
32 R&H, Dec. 3, 1889
33 Signs, Sept. 19, 1906
34 YI, Jan. 5, 1893
35 Letter 117, 1897
36 R&H, Oct. 23, 1888
37 Ed, 14
38 Ed, 127
39 5T, 439
40 HS, 123, 124
41 GCB, Jan. 28, 1893
42 MS, 91, 1907
43 YI, Feb. 2, 1893
44 R&H, May 5, 1891
45 AA, 600, 601
46 R&H, Aug. 26, 1884
47 YI, Nov. 23, 1893
48 YI, Nov. 3, 1886
49 MYP, 100, 101
50 CPT, 225, 226
51 YI, Nov. 3, 1886
52 YI, Aug. 31, 1893
53 7T, 264
54 9T, 37
55 YI, Dec. 15, 1886
56 BE, Feb. 1, 1892
57 DA, 313
58 MH, 36, 37
59 COL, 330, 331
60 MH, 131
61 COL, 310-312
62 Ed, 249
63 COL, 315
64 R&H, Aug. 24, 1897
65 Signs, Nov. 14, 1892
66 MS 99a, 1908
67 DA, 389

68 PP, 277, 278
69 DA, 660
70 Signs, Dec. 19, 1906
71 YI, Feb. 13, 1902
72 Letter 58, 1894
73 CPT, 51, 52

OCTOBER
1 R&H, Nov. 15, 1892
2 YI, July 10, 1906
3 R&H, Nov. 15, 1892
4 4T, 339, 340
5 Ed, 244
6 AA, 522
7 1T, 361, 362
8 AA, 69
9 9T, 238
10 Ed, 242, 243
11 PP, 252
12 Ed, 243
13 MS, 126, 1901
14 PP, 306, 307
15 EW, 70
16 MB, 157
17 Letter 94, 1893
18 Signs, April 4, 1906
19 Signs, March 28, 1906
20 FE, 194, 195
21 MS, 93, 1901
22 Signs, Sept. 1, 1898
23 R&H, Feb. 19, 1895
24 5T, 424
25 Letter 14, 1900
26 CPT, 111
27 Ed, 244
28 5T, 496-500
29 YI, Oct. 8, 1896
30 5T, 492-496
31 YI, Oct. 8, 1896
32 MS 57, 1897
33 R&H, April 14, 1885
34 2T, 583, 584
35 6T, 351
36 6T, 356
37 R&H, March 18, 1915
38 BE, Aug. 15, 1889
39 Letter 30, 1892
40 COL, 142
41 MS 1, 1891
42 Letter 31, 1892
43 DA, 23-25
44 R&H, May 30,1899

45 AUCR, Jan. 1, 1902
46 MS, 14, 1894
47 Signs, July 31, 1901
48 Letter 14, 1900
49 Signs, Nov. 17, 1898
50 BE, Sept. 1, 1889
51 BE, Sept. 1, 1889
52 MH, 425, 426
53 Signs, June 4, 1874
54 BTS, Nov., 1908
55 Signs, June 4, 1874
56 YI, Aug. 4, 1898
57 YI, Aug. 11, 1898
58 YI, March, 1872
59 MH, 71, 72
60 9T, 186
61 DA, 68-70
62 YI, Feb., 1873
63 YI, June 23, 1892
64 Ed, 172
65 1T, 179
66 7T, 67
67 GC, 512, 513
68 EW, 39
69 R&H, Feb. 15, 1906
70 AA, 152-154
71 R&H, April 16, 1895
72 YI, Feb. 14, 1901
73 MS 29, 1900
74 Letter 45, 1892
75 MS 21, 1900
76 MS 65, 1900
77 AA, 146-153
78 Letter 45, 1892
79 YI, Sept. 1, 1892
80 DA, 21
81 R&H, June 7, 1887
82 Letter 138, 1897
83 R&H May 13, 1902
84 EW, 38

NOVEMBER
1 7T, 190
2 GC, 510
3 EW, 46
4 HS, 197
5 R&H, Dec. 3, 1889
6 YI, Nov. 10, 1886
7 PK, 725
8 Signs, Nov. 22, 1905
9 Letter 32, 1906
10 7T, 237

11 MH, 142, 143
12 MH, 141
13 1T, 302
14 Letter 33, 1895
15 4T, 213, 214
16 Ev. 286, 287
17 YI, Aug. 3, 1887
18 R&H, Feb. 28, 1888
19 YI, Dec. 15, 1898
20 YI, Dec. 22, 1898
21 R&H, Sept. 8, 1874
22 YI, Aug. 22, 1901
23 MH, 90
24 YI, March 9, 1893
25 CTBH, 147, 148
26 6T, 354
27 Ed, 295
28 Signs, April 6, 1888
29 5T, 120
30 R&H, July 29, 1873
31 R&H, Feb. 7, 1893
32 R&H, Aug. 26, 1884
33 R&H, Oct. 16, 1883
34 NL vol. 1, No. 24
35 MS, 121, 1898
36 YI, June 2, 1898
37 MS 15,1908
38 DA, 679, 680
39 MS 15, 1908
40 AA, 596-598
41 SL, 68, 69
42 HS, 130
43 PK, 420, 421
44 Signs, Feb. 12, 1885
45 PK, 162-164
46 DA, 218, 219
47 Letter 3, 1878
48 MS 139, 1898
49 MS 126, 1897
50 R&H, April 13, 1905
51 AA, 76
52 Letter 110, 1897
53 R&H, May 4, 1905
54 YI, March 28, 1905
55 4T, 634
56 1T, 134

57 DA, 436, 437
58 PK, 30
59 AA, 75
60 3T, 548
61 R&H, Sept. 8, 1885
62 Ed, 114
63 Sp. Test., Series B, No. 4, pp. 19-23
64 HS, 221
65 HS, 220, 221
66 TM, 111
67 MH, 122
68 YI, Jan. 23, 1902
69 Letter 27, 1886

December

1 MS 99a, 1908
2 MS 3, 1906
3 MS 99a, 1908
4 Letter 155, 1902
5 PP, 62
6 MS 11, 1901
7 R&H, May 13, 1890
8 PP, 87
9 R&H, Aug. 8, 1907
10 8T, 252-254
11 GC, 636-640
12 R&H, Nov. 22, 1906
13 GC, 640-645
14 EW, 287
15 R&H, Nov. 24, 1904
16 GC, 665, 666
17 GC, 645, 646
18 Signs, Nov. 2, 1882
19 R&H, June 15, 1905
20 9T, 285
21 R&H, Nov. 26, 1903
22 MS 18, 1894
23 Signs, Feb. 8, 1892
24 GC, 674
25 Signs, Nov. 10, 1887
26 GC, 646
27 SC, 131, 132
28 DA, 632
29 GC, 645
30 Signs, July 1, 1886

31 R&H, Sept. 3, 1903
32 Signs, June 20, 1911
33 R&H, Jan. 5, 1905
34 GC, 674, 675
35 YI, Oct., 1852
36 Diary, March 24, 1859
37 EW, 17
38 8T, 288
39 YI, Oct., 1852
40 EW, 289
41 DA, 151
42 GC, 427
43 YI, Oct., 1852
44 GC, 675
45 PK, 730, 731
46 Letter 11, 1899
47 CTBH, 99
48 GC, 677
49 GC, 667
50 7T, 244
51 2T, 239
52 YI, Oct., 1852
53 Signs, April 18, 1906
54 Signs, April 25, 1906
55 GH, Aug., 1882
56 R&H, Jan. 3, 1907
57 Letter 242, 1908
58 MS 16, 1895
59 GC, 677, 678
60 R&H, April 5, 1906
61 R&H, Dec. 9, 1884
62 DA, 48
63 DA, 769, 770
64 PK, 732, 733
65 DA, 283
66 GC, 676, 677
67 R&H, Oct. 22, 1908
68 DA, 331
69 8T, 268
70 BE, Jan. 15, 1892
71 Ed, 303-306
72 Ed, 304, 305
73 Ed, 308
74 GC, 651, 652
75 2T, 261, 262
76 2T, 268